Knowledge and Communities

Resources for the Knowledge-Based Economy Series

KNOWLEDGE, GROUPWARE AND THE INTERNET
David E. Smith

KNOWLEDGE AND STRATEGY
Michael H. Zack

KNOWLEDGE AND SPECIAL LIBRARIES
James M. Matarazzo and Suzanne D. Connolly

RISE OF THE KNOWLEDGE WORKER
James W. Cortada

THE ECONOMIC IMPACT OF KNOWLEDGE
Dale Neef, G. Anthony Siesfeld, and Jacquelyn Cefola

THE KNOWLEDGE ECONOMY
Dale Neef

KNOWLEDGE IN ORGANIZATIONS
Laurence Prusak

KNOWLEDGE MANAGEMENT AND ORGANIZATIONAL DESIGN
Paul S. Myers

KNOWLEDGE MANAGEMENT TOOLS
Rudy L. Ruggles, III

THE STRATEGIC MANAGEMENT OF INTELLECTUAL CAPITAL
David A. Klein

KNOWLEDGE AND SOCIAL CAPITAL
Eric L. Lesser

STRATEGIC LEARNING IN A KNOWLEDGE ECONOMY
Rob Cross and Sam Israelit

Knowledge and Communities

Edited By
Eric L. Lesser
Michael A. Fontaine
Jason A. Slusher

An Imprint of Elsevier
Boston Oxford Auckland Johannesburg Melbourne New Delhi

Recognizing the importance of preserving what has been written, Butterworth–Heinemann prints its books on acid-free paper whenever possible.

 Butterworth–Heinemann supports the efforts of American Forests and the Global ReLeaf program in its campaign for the betterment of trees, forests, and our environment.

Library of Congress Cataloging-in-Publication Data

Knowledge and communities / edited by Eric L. Lesser, Michael A. Fontaine, Jason A. Slusher.
     p.   cm.—(Resources for the knowledge based economy series)
     Includes bibliographical references and index.
     ISBN 0-7506-7293-5 (paper: alk. paper)
     1. Organizational learning. 2. Knowledge management. 3. Community life. 4. Community. I. Lesser, Eric. II. Fontaine, Michael. III. Slusher, Jason. IV. Resources for the knowledge-based economy
     HD58.82.R47 2000
     307—dc21

                                                     00-039808

British Library Cataloguing-in-Publication Data
A catalogue record for this book is available from the British Library.

The publisher offers special discounts on bulk orders of this book.
For information, please contact:
Manager of Special Sales
Butterworth–Heinemann
225 Wildwood Avenue
Woburn, MA 01801-2041
Tel: 781-904-2500
Fax: 781-904-2620

For information on all Butterworth–Heinemann publications available, contact our World Wide Web home page at: http://www.bh.com

10 9 8 7 6 5 4 3 2

Printed in the United States of America

Contents

Preface

The subject of communities in the business environment has recently taken on heightened interest among some of the world's largest companies. Organizations such as BPAmoco, Royal Dutch Shell, IBM, Xerox, The World Bank, and British Telecom have all undertaken significant community development efforts in an attempt to leverage the collective knowledge of their employees. These organizations, and many others, have begun to recognize that knowledge critical to business success is often created and shared by informal groups of individuals with common work practices or interests. This includes both the firm's explicit knowledge (i.e., knowledge that is captured in a written or visual form) and the informal social networks that contain the more tacit forms of knowledge. These communities also serve as the repository for the organization's memory, preserving valuable insights that can be easily lost in an age of employee mobility and early retirement.

Many of these early community-building activities have illustrated a host of potential benefits, both to the organizations that sponsor them and the individuals who partake in them. In our work with members of the IBM Institute for Knowledge Management, we have seen community development efforts lead to increased revenues from new business development, greater efficiency from the reuse of knowledge assets, and greater levels of innovation. Further, community participation can also provide a number of benefits that are less tangible, though equally significant. These include developing a heightened sense of identity among disparate workers, improving one's access to experts within the organization, and decreasing the time associated with acclimating to a new job or position. While these benefits are somewhat more difficult to quantify, they play a critical role in the success of the knowledge-based firm.

It is also not surprising that many companies are undertaking community initiatives in hopes of better leveraging not only their own knowledge, but the knowledge of external parties, such as customers, suppliers, and alliance partners. Using online communities, organizations are hoping to foster critical interactions between and across organizational lines. While primarily virtual in nature, these communities have been able to encourage conversations that exchange valuable knowledge across the value chain and reinforce a sense of loyalty among business partners.

COMMUNITIES: PEOPLE, PLACES, AND THINGS

People

At their most basic level, communities consist of three components: people, places, and things. Not surprisingly, *people* are the primary ingredient in any community effort. A community is composed of people who interact on a regular basis around a common set of issues, interests, or needs. In these communities, individuals participate through sharing experiences, pooling resources, representing the interests of larger groups, and building relationships with other like-minded individuals. Community participation is often voluntary, with individuals opting to play different roles with varying levels of intensity and time commitment. Some individuals will serve as the nucleus, directing and shaping the community's direction and resource allocation. Others will operate on the periphery, tapping into the community knowledge and insight on an as-needed basis. To maintain the relationships between individuals, formal roles and responsibilities are sometimes developed to improve the community's effectiveness. For example, communities may retain a small staff to maintain membership lists, recruit outside speakers, and help in scheduling community meetings and activities. However, at the core, people who voluntarily contribute time, energy, and other scarce resources in the pursuit of common interests ultimately drive communities.

Places

To be effective, communities need *places* for their members to gather. In conventional community environments, the place is often a physical space where members meet and exchange ideas and insights. Whether it is a conference room where software developers hold an open breakfast every Tuesday, or a local restaurant where delivery workers meet to discuss the day's efforts, the physical place helps establish a common reference point where individuals interact with others engaged in similar practices. This place becomes a unique identifier that reinforces the group's sense of commonality.

Of course, in today's electronic world, meeting places do not necessarily have to be physical spaces. The development of the Internet has provided a virtual medium where individuals can effectively interact across boundaries of time and space. Many of the organizations we have studied have developed (or are in the process of developing) computer-based tools to support community efforts. These technologies allow individuals to connect with others to discuss similar work challenges, capture and share common tools and techniques, conduct real-time dialogues, solve problems, and introduce outside ideas and influences. Several organizations have used videoconferencing and other multimedia technologies to further enrich conversations within the community and closely simulate the face-to-face environment generated in physical meeting places. Also, while many organizations are choosing to buy the technologies needed to provide these places, others have chosen to rent these places from third-party application service providers (ASPs). Some of these providers even offer management and maintenance services to meet the community's collaboration requirements.

Things

Etienne Wenger, a leading expert on the subject of communities in organizations, writes about a critical activity performed within communities: the management of "boundary objects" or *things*. In the workplace, these objects are the rules, norms, procedures, tools, and other artifacts that communities use to accomplish their tasks. Individuals use these *things* as mechanisms for documenting and sharing what they know and how the work they perform should be accomplished. For example, a community of information technology project managers might use documents such as work plans, team member resumes, and directories of outside experts to capture and transfer the collective knowledge of the group. Similarly, service personnel might have a series of diagnostic tools and procedure manuals that are commonly used to solve customer problems. Through these *things*, communities provide a vehicle to share their common tools of the trade, and to the extent possible, codify the less articulated forms of community knowledge. Individuals within a community relate to these common objects and use them as vehicles for expanding the collective knowledge of the group.

Through the interaction of people, places, and things, communities help individuals develop a sense of identity within their organization. This is especially critical given the cultural changes in modern organizations, such as flextime workers, telecommuters, and work teams that interact across time and space. As more and more people "go virtual" and find themselves working with individuals who they typically do not see on a day-to-day basis, communities fill an important void. Not only do they help people make connections that are vital to learning new skills, they also help make sense of the larger environment and provide a mechanism for sharing critical knowledge across the organization.

ABOUT THIS BOOK

Over the past nine years, academicians, technologists, and management professionals have written a great deal on knowledge and communities. While some experts have focused on the theoretical associations of like-minded people—gathered around common interests or shared contexts—others have recently highlighted the real-world human potential that exists when communities are successfully developed and supported within organizations. As a result, the chapters in this book are organized into two primary sections: *Practical Applications* and *Theory Development*.

The first section, *Practical Applications*, is designed to provide a broad survey of recent work focusing on real-world examples of communities in the business world. In Chapter 1, Etienne Wenger describes how communities forge new connections and relationships through sharing common work practices, foster a sense of belonging, and deploy an organization's knowledge strategy. Keeping with this theme, Richard McDermott highlights how communities play a critical role in organizing, codifying, and transforming an organization's explicit and tacit knowledge. Next, William Judge, Gerald Fyxell, and Robert Dooley illustrate how communities can foster an environment that supports creativity and innovation. Importantly, they also highlight the actions managers can take to maintain these types of cultures.

The next two chapters in the *Practical Applications* section discuss how Xerox has applied the use of communities in different parts of the corporation. David Stamps uses Xerox's Integrated Customer Service project to demonstrate how groups of individuals with common sets of interests and expertise can be used to educate each other in a real-time setting. John Storck and Patricia Hill then describe the use of "strategic communities" within Xerox as a mechanism to facilitate knowledge sharing across information technology managers. The final article in this section goes beyond the organization's boundaries and discusses communities of customers. Arthur Armstrong and John Hagel stress that by providing customers the opportunity to interact with the organization and with each other, companies can foster deep relationships and brand loyalty. Further, these customer dialogues can help customize products and services to meet consumers' needs and interests. All told, this compilation of practical applications provides readers with numerous examples of how others have developed effective community-based approaches.

The second section, *Theory Development*, provides some of the underlying theoretical perspectives that support the practical applications in the earlier chapters. The first chapter in this section, written by John Seely Brown and Paul Duguid, describes the importance of communities as a vehicle for fostering organizational learning. In the next work, Eric Lesser and Laurence Prusak focus on how communities build the social capital necessary to share organizational knowledge. In another chapter, Jeanne Liedtka states that communities may help to circumvent the issues within a company that can lead to complacency and failure by allowing organizations to more easily adapt to environmental and market change. Robin Teigland uses a case study of a technology firm to illustrate how individual work performance is influenced by communities and highlights the importance of knowledge flows across organizational boundaries.

As part of this *Theory Development* section, Barry Wellman and a number of colleagues from the Center for Urban and Community Studies at the University of Toronto examine the use of computer-supported social networks (CSSN). Their chapter attempts to link the size, structure, and composition of virtual communities and workgroups to the types of communication that affect telework, domestic work, and the larger networked organization. In a related study, Vivian Franco, Hsiao-Yun Hu, Bruce Lewenstein, Roberta Piirto, Ross Underwood, and Noni Korf Vidal study the effects of electronic communication conflicts and determine that they can lead to negative as well as positive effects. In the concluding chapter, Catherine Marshall, Frank Shipman, and Raymond McCall consider the difficulty of knowledge retrieval given that communities are now storing their collective thoughts in large-scale electronic libraries. In short, the *Theory Development* chapters provide readers with cutting-edge research that serves as the basis for the chapters in the *Practical Application* section.

ACKNOWLEDGEMENTS

We have been fortunate to work with a number of individuals who have helped form and shape our views of communities in organizations. The IBM Institute for Knowledge Management has given us a forum where we have been able to work with organizations to better understand the use of communities in the business environment. Laurence Prusak, the Executive Director of the Institute, has been instrumental in providing support and encouragement for this effort. We have also been fortunate to work with a number of insightful colleagues during our research effort, including Kathleen Curley, Linda Carotenuto, and Matthew Simpson from Lotus Research, John Storck from Boston University, and Etienne Wenger. Our long discussions and working sessions have helped develop a clearer understanding of the topic and its associated challenges and opportunities.

PART ONE

Practical Applications

1

Communities of Practice: The Key to Knowledge Strategy*

Etienne Wenger

Communities of practice are everywhere. They exist within businesses and across business units and company boundaries. Even though they are informally constituted and reside within a specific area of practice, these self-organizing systems share the capacity to create and use organizational knowledge through informal learning and mutual engagement. Wenger believes that communities of practice are key to understanding the complex knowledge challenges faced by most organizations in today's knowledge economy. To that end, Wenger sets the boundaries of what constitutes a community of practice and how it resides within different types of organizations. In this chapter, Wenger proposes a framework that motivates firms to recognize the critical knowledge generated by communities of practice to engage and identify common work practices, foster belonging, and deploy a knowledge strategy through transformation. With his framework, Wenger highlights how communities forge new connections and relationships with the greater organization—where the community is legitimized as a place for sharing and creating knowledge.

What if the key to the complex knowledge challenges faced by most organizations today lies in age-old, utterly familiar, and largely informal social structures known today as communities of practice? How would we "manage" knowledge? What shape would a knowledge strategy take?

Executives have long understood the value of knowledge and learning, at least at some intuitive level. More recently, these concerns have come to the fore with talk of a new economy, knowledge-based organizations, and learning as the ultimate competitive advantage. But what to do about such elusive, dynamic processes as learning and knowledge has not been quite so obvious.

* Reprinted with permission from *Knowledge Directions: The Journal of the Institute for Knowledge Management*, 1 (Fall 1999): 48–63.

Although most of us appreciate that we have learned as much through informal processes as in classrooms, we are not sure how to combine informal and formal aspects of learning in our organizations. And even though most of us are painfully aware that we know much more than we can ever tell, that knowledge in practice is much more a living process than an object, we can't seem to refrain from treating it as a "thing" when we consider the need to "manage" it. Typical solutions have ranged from large training departments and corporate centers of excellence to complex information systems and collections of knowledge bases on Intranets. All with mixed results. Managers have focused on these formal efforts, not so much because they necessarily believed these were ideal or complete solutions, but because such approaches seemed tangible, justifiable, and amenable to such hallmarks of organizational success as formal design, implementation, and measurement.

Managers needed to move decisively, but missed a key element—a clear understanding of the kind of structure that could in practice take responsibility for learning and knowledge. They had clear structures for other purposes, and had replaced the silos and ivory towers of traditional functional organizations with business units—structures they found better suited for focusing on markets and product lines. More recently, they discovered teams as the ideal structures for locating the ownership of tasks and projects. But what about the ownership of knowledge? Where should it be located? What was going to be the new structure to take on this responsibility?

The answer to this very contemporary organizational question lies in an age-old structure. Since the beginning of history, human beings have formed communities that accumulate collective learning into social practices—communities of practice.[1] Tribes are an early example. More recent instances include the guilds of the Middle Ages that took on the stewardship of a trade, and scientific communities that collectively define what counts as valid knowledge in a specific area of investigation. Less obvious cases could be your local magician club, nurses in a ward, a street gang, or a group of software engineers meeting regularly in the cafeteria to share tips. Such communities do not take knowledge in their specialty to be an object; it is a living part of their practice even when they document it. Knowing is an act of participation.

Communities of practice may well represent the natural social structure for the ownership of knowledge, but they have been around for a long time, and they are everywhere. Organizations are already full of them. So what is new here? Why even pay attention? Well, what is new is the need for organizations to become more intentional and systematic about "managing" knowledge, and therefore the need to give these age-old structures a new, central role in running a business. A growing number of leading organizations in the private and public sectors (some of which are mentioned below) are pioneering this approach. Communities of practice represent the latest wave in an ongoing evolution of organizational structures, whose four primary types can be summarized in Figure 1.1.

Because of their informal nature, communities of practice have remained largely invisible within organizations and have not been part of the language of

TYPE OF ORGANIZATION	DOMINANT STRUCTURE	DISTINCTIVE ADVANTAGE	DISADVANTAGE
Functional	Functional division	Concentration of expertise under hierarchical control	Functional silos with internal focus on specialties rather than on market needs and opportunities
Muti-divisional	Business unit	Integrates functional expertise to focus on business lines and market segments	Divisional boundaries impede learning and knowledge transfer
Project-based	Project team	Market agility and individual customer focus	Short-term focus on tasks, much learning is lost or localized
Knowledge-based	Community of practice	Integrates the stewarding of key competencies into the very fabric of the organization	Competing priorities for people who belong to multiple structures at once (business unit, team, communities of practice)

FIGURE 1.1 Four Waves in Organizational Design

management until recently. Now they represent the new frontier for organizations, the promise of great opportunities for pioneers of the knowledge age. They must be acknowledged, supported and fully integrated into the operation of organizations; and all this without disrupting the informality, collegiality, self-organization, and internal leadership that are critical to their ability to steward an area of expertise effectively.[2]

A KNOWLEDGE STRATEGY

If communities of practice are the natural stewards of knowledge in an organization, what does a knowledge strategy look like that takes this as its foundation? What is its overall shape? A knowledge strategy based on communities of practice consists of seven basic steps grouped into four streams of activity:

1. Understand strategic knowledge needs: what knowledge is critical to success?
2. Engage practice domains (find communities): where will people form communities around practices they can engage in and identify with?
3. Develop communities: how to help key communities reach their full potential?

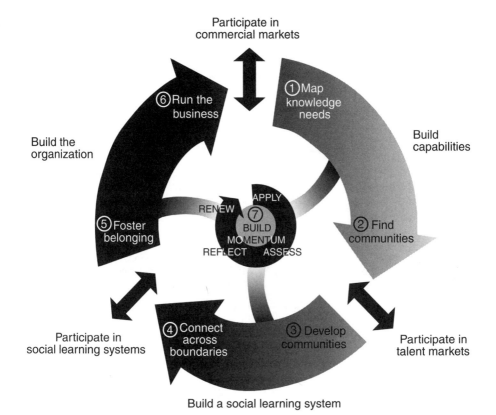

FIGURE 1.2 A Knowledge Strategy Based on Communities of Practice

Note that the strategy is not linear. Rather it is an ongoing, dynamic process of renewing the capabilities of the organization by cycling through these steps. The strategy does not simply start at step 1 and end at step 7. Steps can happen in parallel, and every step can be a point of entry into the whole process. You may start at step 1 mapping the knowledge needs of a business strategy and the practices required to realize this strategy. But you may also start at step 3 if some people want to connect better with their peers by forming communities, or at step 4 if some communities need to learn how to communicate across boundaries. You may even start with a need to foster belonging in order to solidify your organization and galvanize it around its mission. No matter where you start, eventually you will need to have the whole wheel rolling.

4. Work the boundaries: how to link communities into broader learning systems?
5. Foster belonging: how to engage people's identities and sense of meaning?
6. Run the business: how to integrate communities of practice into running the business of the organization?
7. Apply, assess, reflect, and renew: how to deploy a knowledge strategy through waves of organizational transformation?

The overall structure of this knowledge strategy is represented in Figure 1.2. The first six steps are paired in three curved arrows that represent three streams of activity, with the fourth in the center keeping the momentum of the whole process. The shading indicates both the tension between the steps in one arrow and the complementarity of the end of one arrow with the beginning of the next. The double arrows at the breaks indicate interactions with three kinds of broader socio-economic systems in which a knowledge organization participates:

- It participates in traditional economic markets where it offers its products and services and where it learns about needs and opportunities
- It also participates in talent markets because its ability to respond to its knowledge challenge depends on its ability to recruit, develop, and retain talent
- Last but not least, it participates in what I call "social learning systems," such as an industry, a region (e.g., Silicon Valley), or a consortium where learning requirements blur relations of competition and collaboration. I argue elsewhere that in a knowledge economy, participating in these broader social learning systems is as crucial to success as participation in economic markets.[3]

BUILD A STRATEGIC CAPABILITY FRAMEWORK

The work of developing the organizational capabilities needed for success has two aspects. On the one hand, it requires the analytical work of translating a strategy into a description of the knowledge required. On the other hand, a capability must be realized in the form of practices that people can engage in and develop by investing their personal interests. This requires a social understanding of how communities can form to take responsibility for these practices.

Step 1. Map Key Knowledge Needs

The first step is to establish the organization's knowledge needs as determined by such traditional factors as core competencies, effects on performance and reliance on innovation.

Core Competencies

Companies need to choose the competencies they will focus on as a source of distinctive advantage.[4] Such strategic competencies include the basic knowledge necessary to be a player in a given industry as well as the specialized knowledge necessary to be a leader in the organization's areas of strategic focus. Then companies must make sure that they build internal capabilities in these areas, lest their market position be usurped by a competitor. They will need to nurture communities of practice that grow and maintain these capabilities.

Effects on Performance

The ultimate purpose of developing capabilities is to enable performance. Establishing knowledge needs will require an understanding of how specific kinds of knowledge influence the performance indicators that the organization decides to monitor.[5] This involves an analysis of core business processes to determine the source, significance and cost of suboptimal performance, and to discover what knowledge is needed for improvement. For example, you can determine what kind of knowledge will increase your chances of fixing a problem on the phone with a customer, and avoid a costly trip to the customer site by a technician.

Reliance on Innovation

Developing a community of practice with this knowledge would benefit performance. Some strategies rely more on innovation than others for their success. If you focus on leading-edge technological innovation, for instance, then you need the kind of vibrant practices that will push the envelope in these areas. But there are other kinds of innovation. Some companies will concentrate on operational efficiency or distribution logistics to compete on price in a commodity market. Others will emphasize marketing inventiveness or customer-specific innovation based on an intimate knowledge of their clients. Once dependence on innovation needs have been clarified, you can work to create new knowledge where innovation matters.

Articulating these strategic knowledge needs provides a framework for developing communities of practice. It helps the organization set priorities, direct resources, and respond to opportunities. It also helps communities clarify their relationship with the organization, legitimize their work and participate more actively in shaping strategic directions. Even if they focus on an emerging area that is not the current strategic focus, having a language to connect knowledge and performance is a tool to articulate, the value they create.

Step 2. Find Communities

The second step is to translate the knowledge needs of the organization into a set of critical practices around which people can form communities. These domains of practice should be concrete enough to permit members to engage wholeheartedly and develop their expertise and their professional identifies. Without personal engagement and passion for the topic, communities of practice will not thrive. A core competence, for instance, is often defined too broadly and abstractly for any one to form a practice around it. If passenger safety is a core competence for an airline, it will translate into a multitude of actual practices in maintenance, in training for flight attendants, or in pre-flight check-ups.

The way to perform this translation is to find or recognize existing or potential communities in key areas. Shell and Chevron, for instance, have developed an interviewing process to accomplish this by following existing networks and exploring the potential benefits of forming communities of practice. In most organizations there are usually people who are already involved in thinking about areas of strategic significance and who are likely to have some connections with each other, however loose. At National Semiconductor, senior managers put together a list of strategic competencies to carve a market niche; they realized the list was not enough. To develop these competencies actively they needed to know what they looked like in practice. They launched a pilot effort to interview multiple practitioners whose work related to one of these competencies. These interviews uncovered the nature of the relevant domains of practice, the identity of key practitioners, the connections that did and did not exist and the issues they faced related to these domains. The very process of interviewing practitioners and potential leaders prompted many to take the initiative to form tighter communities with colleagues in other business units.

An exploratory process oriented to practice is necessary because the formal structure of the organization may not be a good point of departure. In fact, it is precisely where the formal organization leaves some white spaces—as any structure inevitably does—that the greatest potential often exists. Sometimes the translation between knowledge needs and practices is relatively easy because the relevant practices are well-established disciplines such as subspecies of geology for oil exploration or subsystems in automotive engineering. Sometimes, it is less obvious if the areas are new, in transition, or constantly in flux, as in software engineering, telecommunication, or management consulting. When it is not so clear what the domains of competence are, it is important to let communities of practice emerge in less predictable ways.

Some organizations combine a well-orchestrated process with a more chaotic one in order to focus organizational resources and attention on current strategic objectives, while preserving the innovative potential of pure self-organizing. Companies such as American Management Systems (AMS) or DaimlerChrysler have a small number of established strategic communities in which they invest explicitly, but at the same time welcome the initiative of people who wish to form their own. Often such emerging communities can graduate to official sponsorship if they reach a level of participation or strategic relevance that warrants such a step.

Understanding strategic knowledge needs and defining practice domains are closely interrelated tasks. The trick here is to develop domain definitions that respond to the needs of the organization while engaging the professional knowledge, ability, identities, and aspirations of the people who will take on the stewardship of these areas of expertise. This process must involve the participation of potential community members so that it can translate into a compelling interest and respond to actual needs. Unlike task-oriented teams, which can be pulled together and chartered with a predefined goal, communities of practice must grow organically as their learning unfolds. They are dynamic by definition. They will only work if people identify with the enterprise and the learning agenda that the community pursues. Only then will members keep coming together and investing themselves in pushing the community and its practice forward.

The process of framing strategic capabilities and identifying practice domains is both analytical and social—to understand what knowledge is important for organizational performance and success, but also to create a process by which these knowledge requirements can be enacted into practices by those who will need, create, and use the knowledge in their day-to-day activities.

BUILD A SOCIAL LEARNING SYSTEM

After strategic capabilities have been identified and properly framed in community terms they must be realized in a social learning system. For the purpose of this article, I will consider that such a system consists of two complementary aspects: a constellation of various communities of practice that must each develop in their own ways, and a configuration of boundary processes by which these communities interact and are integrated into a broader learning ecology.

Step 3. Develop Communities

Once enough convergence between organizational needs and members' interests has been achieved, the next step is for members to develop their community. This development process must combine three complementary aspects. First, members must come to a sense of joint enterprise—an understanding of what the community is about. This joint enterprise will evolve, of course, but must remain something that members negotiate among themselves and identify with. Second, members must have enough opportunities to interact with one another in joint activities to build relationships, trust, and personal identities. This ongoing mutual engagement makes the community real as an experience and weaves the social fabric necessary to support joint learning. And third, members must develop a shared repertoire of concepts, tools, language, stories, and sensitivities that will embody the distinctive knowledge of the community and become a unique resource for further learning. It is the combination of these three aspects—identification with a joint enterprise, renewed mutual engagement, and an evolving shared repertoire—that makes a community of practice an ideal structure in which to locate the ownership of knowledge.

A given community will begin at whatever stage of development it has reached. If it is just a loose network, members need to come together and find common ground. They may have a launch workshop where participants lay the groundwork for their incipient community, choose a coordinator and agree on a rhythm of activities—or they may simply hold a less visible series of informal meetings in which people progressively discover the value of learning together. In either case, they coalesce into a community. Another milestone in maturity is reached when a community is ready to take active ownership of its practice and to start developing it self-consciously: negotiating standards, finding gaps in its knowledge, and creating a learning agenda. If the community is already actively pursuing a learning agenda, it may need to deal with growth and find ways to include newcomers. It may also seek contacts with communities or experts outside the organization. Alternatively it may seek a more influential voice within the organization. It may even be going through a mid-life crisis and have to reconsider what it is about.

At any of these stages, communities may need some help from the organization. You may be the best engineer, but that does not mean that you understand all the subtleties of community development or that you know how to organize the best workshop. Most communities also need some technological infrastructure so members can stay in touch at a distance and build a shared repository for capturing the aspects of their practice that lend themselves to documentation. Many organizations have established "support teams" that provide consulting, educational, and technological resources to communities—coaching community leaders, helping organize community events or establishing websites. Companies such as Johnson & Johnson, IBM, and HP, for instance, have small groups of internal consultants who develop expertise in launching communities of practice. Shell has even commissioned a community-development toolkit that helps guide communities through successive life stages. There is much organizations can do to foster the development of communities of practice and to systematize the processes by which these communities contribute to their performance. Still, an organization's support should be more like the nurturing art of gardening than traditional management. Successful communities are driven by the passion, identification, and leadership of their members, and the environment can either favor or hinder their growth.

Step 4. Connect Across Boundaries

Communities of practice do not exist in isolation. Their effectiveness is not a matter of their internal development alone, but also a matter of how well they connect with other communities and constituencies inside and outside the organization.

Boundaries of practice are usually not formal. I remember sitting in a meeting of electronic engineers who had welcomed observers because they actually enjoyed the new attention their practice was receiving. But no matter how welcome I was, it was clear that there was a boundary of practice between us—nothing personal, nothing formalized, no membership card—but a clear boundary nonetheless. A few short minutes and quick sketches after someone had started to present a problem for which he needed help from the community, everyone understood the situation and knew what the difficulty was. They were all ready to work—but not me—I had not even begun to grasp what the situation was or what needed resolving. Such is the learning efficiency of a community. But this very efficiency is an inevitable source of boundary.

Boundaries usually have negative connotations. For many people, they connote limitations and exclusion. Indeed, communities of practice can become liabilities if their expertise becomes insular or their very success becomes a blinder (what Dorothy Leonard calls a "core rigidity").[6] Within a practice shared by a tight community, a lot of implicit assumptions can go unquestioned. When these background assumptions diverge, people from different communities often talk past each other even if they use similar terms. Miscommunication and misunderstandings are commonplace at boundaries—when there is communication at all. Different communities have different enterprises, and therefore different perceptions of what matters. They also have different ways of interacting and different repertoires. When researchers and marketing people, or doctors and administrators talk to each other, the difficulties they encounter stem from different practices and repertoires, but also from different identities that entail different ways of being in the world. To create a true bridge across practices, you not only need to translate or suspend judgment; you have to suspend who you are and open your identity. This is not easy.

Boundaries are not only a source of problems, however. Interacting across practices forces members to take a fresh look at their own assumptions. As a result, boundary processes can be the source of a deep kind of learning. While the core of a practice is a locus of expertise, radically new insights often arise at the boundary between communities. A discipline such as psychoneuroimmunology still bears witness in its name to its origin at the boundary between practices. Something very creative can take place in the meeting of perspectives at these boundaries when participants make a genuine effort to listen to each other or to solve a common problem. So, boundaries are learning assets in their own right.

Most organizations are not designed to encourage boundary interactions. People are often rewarded for focusing on their own area. Yet for both the difficulties they create and the opportunities they present, it is important to pay as much attention to the boundaries of communities of practice as to their core, and to make sure that there is enough activity at these boundaries to prevent fragmentation and renew learning.

Xerox is one company that has started to focus seriously on boundary processes, and for good reasons. It learned the lesson of boundaries of practice the hard way. Scientists at its advanced research center invented the modern PC but the company failed to capitalize on it. The distance between the practices of researchers and the practices of management was just too great. Much closer were the programmers at Apple, who knew a good design when they saw one. Among peers all it took was one visit. To avoid repeating this missed opportunity, Xerox now works hard to connect researchers with other people in the company and to find ways to understand each other's perspectives.[7]

The World Bank faces similar issues among its numerous communities of practice. Its development specialists must learn to coordinate efforts across disciplines so projects can address all aspects of poverty such as economy, basic services, or education. For example, the education and transportation communities of practice recently came together to solve a school bus problem, but this collaboration was serendipitous. It highlighted the need for communities to take some responsibility for how their practices interact with others so that practitioners in the field understand better how to conduct coordinated projects. This is all the more important because the Bank also wants to facilitate knowledge exchanges among its clients and with other organizations involved in development projects. In all these cases, facilitating boundary processes will be critical to the Bank's knowledge strategy.

Communities of practice truly become knowledge assets when their core and boundaries are active in complementary ways. Knowledge organizations must understand the processes by which these communities interact. Bridges across practices can take many forms:

- People whose multimembership allows them to act as "knowledge brokers" across boundaries (this is often the tacit role of first-line managers)
- Boundary objects that can accommodate multiple perspectives (e.g., a well-written contract or design proposal)
- Boundary activities, interactions, and even practices that force people of various communities to rub their experiences and perspectives
- Technology platforms that make communication across boundaries easier

We need to build organizational and technological infrastructures that do not dismiss or impede these processes, but rather recognize, support, and leverage them. Communities must connect with each other and with other groups to create broader learning systems both inside and across organizations. This requires building trust not only inside communities but also through sustained boundary interactions. There is a tension between a focus on communities of practice and a focus on boundaries. To the degree that communities of practice deepen their learning, they inevitably create boundaries. This is a natural outcome of joint learning. But to the degree that members get involved in a lot of interactions with other people in an effort to overcome these boundaries, they may lose their focus and the depth of their home expertise. I would argue that the learning potential of an organization lies in this balancing act between deep core practices and active boundary processes.

BUILD A KNOWLEDGE ORGANIZATION

When managers come to understand that communities of practice are self-organizing and cannot be controlled in traditional ways, some conclude that they must leave them alone. But ignoring them will only marginalize them. Trying to control communities of practice, or leaving them alone are in fact two sides of the same attitude. To build a knowledge organization, managers need to honor the self-organizing character of communities of practice, and at the same time engage them in negotiating how communities and organizations can relate and contribute to each other.

Again, there are two interacting aspects to the task. Knowledge organizations have to be what Charles Handy calls "collegiate," that is, based on an experience of belonging that promotes professional development and involves people's identities and sense of meaning in shaping the purpose of the organization.[8] This experience of belonging—traditionally a "soft" issue, is not separate from performance requirements—traditionally a "hard" issue. On the contrary, organizations will only fully realize the potential of communities of practice when they view them as an integral part of running the business, not something "extra" at the margin.

Step 5. Foster Belonging

Pharmaceutical companies need researchers to create the molecules that can lead to new drugs. But these chemists also build their professional identities in scientific communities where they publish and keep in good standing. Membership of this wider community may seem to distract them from their job, but in fact an organization will foster belonging by embracing the full identity of its members.

It may have been the case—and even this is debatable—that if all you wanted was for people to tighten a bolt on a wheel or place candies in a box all day, you could ask them to hang their identities and their sense of meaningfulness with their coats, to be retrieved on the way out at the end of the day: forget who you are and do as you are told. But if you want a knowledge organization based on creativity and involvement, then people's identities and sense of meaningfulness cannot be left at the door. We solve problems creatively when we immerse the intelligence of our whole being in the issue. Identity and meaningfulness are the wellspring of creativity.

Willingness and ability to share knowledge is a concern in many organizations. Here again, belonging is a key factor. Sharing what you know or exploring a new idea with a colleague is not something you do in the abstract. It is part of your identity as a member of a community where what you share has meaning and currency. If you are married and come home after a business trip, you will discuss what happened with your spouse, not because sharing is a good thing in and of itself, but because it is a natural part of how you belong to a couple. But focusing on sharing per se can create an artificial situation. I remember having dinner with a family where the mother carefully went around and asked each child to share what had happened in school that day. Her intentions were good, but it felt a bit stilted. It reminded me of a best-practice sharing session—the children carefully obliged, but I would have preferred something a bit less artificial. If you belong to a community of engineers, helping a colleague with a new design or discussing a new idea is part of your identity as member. It just brings out the engineer in you. Sharing itself is not the problem. It is belonging that is the real issue: sharing is a natural by-product of belonging.

Belonging happens at multiple levels at once, and through different processes. Small local communities are often embedded in larger, more global ones. Belonging to your local church is a way to belong to your religion. It gives you a practical way to make this belonging real by attending services or participating in activities, but it is also important that it be part of a broader religious community that you see yourself a part of. Similarly, belonging to a local community of doctors allows you to interact with colleagues, but it is important that this local community be aligned with a broader set of medical practices.

Our identities depend not only on the forms of engagement that we find in our local communities, but also on the images that we create of the world and of ourselves, and on the broader ramifications of our actions. To foster belonging, organizations must nurture people's imagination and provide them with opportunities to participate in large-scale enterprises. When World Bank president James Wolfensohn promotes the vision of a "knowledge bank" that shares knowledge to fight poverty, he is opening a way to belong.[9] He is nurturing people's imagination in order to expand the meaning of their actions and the scope of their identities. As a result, when they build their own community of practice, they can understand their participation in the context of this broader enterprise.

Step 6. Run the Business

When I argue that communities of practice promote belonging, I am not suggesting that they are something extra you do to make your employees feel good or develop personally. They are not like company picnics, baseball teams, parenting classes, or ropes courses. I have nothing against these activities, but the real opportunity presented by communities of practice lies in connecting professional identities directly with the actual functioning of the organization: this lets those who own the knowledge steward it, and integrates the stewarding of knowledge into the running of the business.

Organizations that want to take full advantage of this opportunity must be ready to support communities adequately—but light-handedly—and involve them intensely—but judiciously.

Support them adequately...

If communities of practice are key to running your business, they deserve adequate support, attention and investment, like any other key function. Establishing appropriate support structures not only enables these communities to deliver the value you would expect, it also demonstrates the organization's commitment. Ways to provide support devised by companies include:

- A sponsoring board of senior managers who give legitimacy to communities of practice and keep them in the loop
- Recognition of community participation in performance evaluations and promotions
- Tuning the organizational systems and removing obvious barriers if communities run up against counterproductive policies
- Budgets to cover such items as time, travel, and teleconferences, as well as occasional extra funding for learning projects that a community must undertake to push its knowledge

...But light-handedly

If your commitment to knowledge and learning is high you might be tempted to lavish your support on communities of practice or force everyone to participate. But it is better to be light-handed. For the most part, communities of practice have modest needs. Too much support easily becomes a distraction. If the support has strings attached, the community will spend too much time making sure it is accountable. (In other words, it will do just what you want, which is precisely the wrong response from a community whose value lies in taking charge of its own learning.) If lavish support comes without strings attached communities may become self-involved and insular. If participation is made compulsory, it may become perfunctory.

Many companies provide some dedicated financial support to free up time for community leaders and coordinators, but rarely for general participation. HP Consulting, for instance, decided against having a charge account for community of practice activities. They decided that these activities should provide enough learning value that consultants would choose to use their existing non-billable allowance to participate.

Involve them intensely ...

A great advantage of communities of practice is that their members are also in teams and business units. Community-of-practice people are not distinct from line people. The same people manage the knowledge and put it to use in their other responsibilities. So, the management of knowledge is as close as possible to the activities where it creates value.

Organizations should count on communities of practice to produce or gather the knowledge necessary to run the business and involve them in decisions that have to do with their domain of expertise. To be effective, communities must be well connected to other parts of the organization where something related to their area is taking place: relevant information, activities, or decisions that could use their expertise. What good is all the knowledge that a repair technician has accumulated about your product if it does not make it back into your engineering communities? So, link communities of practice closely to critical functions and initiatives, such as strategic planning, quality management, customer satisfaction, process improvement, and training.

...But judiciously

You might believe in the value of communities of practice so much that you are tempted to put them in charge of a product or service, but this temptation is probably best resisted. You want communities to be close to the business, but not conflated with it. You want them to remain a distinct structure focusing on knowledge. Leave the delivery of product and services to the teams and business units where community members also belong. Let communities of practice be a place of help for special problem solving, reflection, synthesis, exploration, and sharing. Don't distract them with direct line accountability lest they lose their focus on knowledge.

At DaimlerChrysler, engineering communities of practice, called "Tech Clubs," bring together specialists in a particular subsystem, such as brakes or seats. These Tech Clubs ensure that the company's expertise across all car platforms is world-class. They discuss issues, coordinate efforts, document engineering practices and lessons learned, maintain relationships with vendors, make recommendations to purchasing, and work closely with training and competitive teardown. But the Tech Clubs are Tech Clubs; they don't build cars, or even parts. This is something their members do in their car-platform teams where they apply their expertise to fulfilling line responsibilities.

BUILD AN ACTION-LEARNING MOMENTUM

Basing a knowledge strategy on communities of practice entails a transformation process that must gain momentum to encourage initiative. It often starts small and then grows. But even when it starts with some pilots, it is not a straight "pilot first then roll out" process by which an initial template is perfected and then replicated. Rather it is a learning process by which people discover new ways to participate in the organization.

Step 7. Apply, Assess, Reflect, and Renew—Build Momentum

Building a knowledge strategy with communities of practice is something you do "live." You focus initially on an area where building knowledge will have a significant impact on performance and where there is passion and energy. To understand the effects of community participation, you collect enough stories to create a picture of how the activities of communities of practice affect members and the organization. These stories fulfill several purposes. They allow you to reflect on the process and learn from your experience. They help convince management that communities of practice are a promising idea and deserve their support. And last but not least, they inspire others to examine their own needs and when appropriate to start their own communities of practice.

To learn from experience as the process spreads, a number of organizations have set up a community whose practice is community development. It includes community leaders, knowledge managers, and members of the support team. It collects stories and publicizes them. It creates connections between initiatives. It reflects on the whole process, accumulates insights about how to base a knowledge strategy on communities of practice and builds its own knowledge base. It educates the organization by promoting a common language to talk about these communities, the ways people participate in them, and the value they bring to individuals and the organization. This evolving repertoire of stories, language, and implementation frameworks raises the awareness of the organization and its ability to take action.

The spread and development of communities of practice must be understood as a learning process. It gains momentum with various combinations of top-down directives and encouragement and bottom-up initiative and responsiveness. In companies such as Shell, HP, and the World Bank, the process is vigorously promoted but quite open, and communities of practice are invited to take the initiative. (At the World Bank, the number of registered communities of practice grew very rapidly from about 30 to more than 100 after it was announced that the organization would respond to initiatives with support.) Even companies such as DaimlerChrysler, AMS, and Lucent, that have adopted a more directive approach have left room for emerging communities of practice to prosper and make a case for their value.

A knowledge strategy based on communities of practice is not a plan to be designed and implemented. It is more akin to a social movement that gains momentum as a new idea spreads, changing people's expectations and sense of possibilities. The purpose is to create a cycle of application, assessment, reflection, and renewal by which an organization learns through action how to identify and take responsibility for key areas of knowledge.

TRUE "KNOWLEDGE MANAGEMENT"

With such a knowledge strategy, you don't manage knowledge. Communities of practice do. You support them and involve them in the running of the organization. They own the knowledge; they steward it. This I would argue is true knowledge management. Knowledge managers who think that their role is to manage knowledge had better think twice. Knowledge is not an object that can be managed from the outside. It is an integral part of the life of communities—the people in the best position to take stewardship of it.

Should we get rid of knowledge managers then? Probably not, even if the name is misleading. Most organizations that have decided to adopt communities of practice as the centerpiece of their response to the knowledge challenge have found it useful to have people who shepherd the program. But the main task of knowledge managers then is to devise a knowledge strategy and guide the organization through the seven steps outlined here. Such an approach suggests new functions for knowledge managers:

- Help map strategic knowledge requirements into practice domains
- Support community development and coach community leaders
- Educate managers and advocate on behalf of communities
- Lead the support team and coordinate with the board of sponsors

- Understand the ways in which the environment helps and hinders the process and propose changes
- Connect communities within and outside the organization
- Specify technology platforms that support communities, their practices and boundary interactions among them
- Lead a community of practice on communities of practice
- Devise a process to assess the knowledge strategy and redirect its course as necessary

This new set of responsibilities is a long way from the technical emphasis of traditional knowledge management jobs. It requires what I call an "anthropological nose"—the refined ability to act out of a deep understanding of how human communities create complex systems of meanings and identities. These are the conditions that enable us to be knowledgeable.

The knowledge strategy I just described may come both as a relief and as a worry. On the one hand, it may be a relief that you don't have to "manage" knowledge yourself. Communities of practice will do it for you. And because it is their knowledge, they are best qualified for the task and they will even do it gladly, given the right circumstances and support. On the other hand, this news may come as a worry because you have to deal with communities that have a life of their own. You cannot regiment them easily. But if you really believe that your organization has to run on knowledge and learning, then the regimenting idea was not a good one anyway. If you are really going to dance, don't look for a puppet. Would you not rather delight in the responsive unpredictability of a skillful partner?

ENDNOTES

1. Jean Lave and Etienne Wenger, *Situated Learning: Legitimate Peripheral Participation* (New York, Cambridge University Press, 1991) and Etienne Wenger *Communities of Practice: Learning, Meaning, and Identity* (New York: Cambridge University Press, 1998).
2. Etienne Wenger and Williams Snyder, "Communities of Practice: The Organizational Frontier" in *Harvard Business Review*, January–February 2000, in press.
3. Etienne Wenger, "Communities of Practice and Social Learning Systems" in *Organization*, in press.
4. C. K. Prahalad and Gary Hamel, "The Core Competencies of the Corporation" in *Harvard Business Review* 68: pp. 79–91.
5. Williams Snyder, "Organizational Learning and Performance" (Ph.D. diss., University of Southern California, Los Angeles. 1996).
6. Dorothy Leonard, *Wellsprings of Knowledge: Building and Sustaining the Sources of Innovation* (Cambridge, MA: Harvard Business School Press, 1995).
7. John Seely Brown and Don Cohen, "Conversation with John Seely Brown" in *Knowledge Directions*. Vol. 1 (Spring 1999) pp. 28–35.

8. Charles Handy, *The Age of Unreason* (Cambridge, MA: Harvard Business School Press, 1990).

9. Richard McDermott, "How to Encourage Learning Across Teams" in *Knowledge Management Review*, Issue 8 (May June, 1999).

2

Why Information Technology Inspired but Cannot Deliver Knowledge Management*

Richard McDermott

Technology can provide organizations with vast electronic libraries that end up acting as storehouses of information. However, these repositories are often limited in their ability to enable organizations to truly share knowledge. In this chapter, McDermott argues that people learn by participating in communities. He proposes that communities are not only the places best suited to decide how, where, and why new knowledge should be created and utilized, but also the best places to organize, codify, and transform the company's knowledge. McDermott highlights four key community-building challenges—technical, social, managerial, and personal—all of which must be overcome if organizations seek to construct more fluid and flexible learning environments.

> "Knowledge is experience. Everything else is just information."—Albert Einstein

A few years ago British Petroleum placed a full-page ad in the *London Times* announcing that it learned a key technology for deep-sea oil exploration from its partnership with Shell Oil Company in the Gulf of Mexico and was beginning deep-sea exploration on its own, west of the Shetland Islands. British Petroleum's ability to leverage knowledge is key to its competitive strategy. Rather than conducting its own basic research, British Petroleum learns from its partners and quickly spreads that knowledge through the company. It does this not by building

* Copyright © 1999, by The Regents of the University of California. Reprinted from the *California Management Review*, Vol. 41, No. 4. By permission of the Regents.

a large electronic library of best practices, but by connecting people so they can think together.

Information technology has led many companies to imagine a new world of leveraged knowledge. E-mail and the Internet have made it possible for professionals to draw on the latest thinking of their peers no matter where they are located. A chemist in Minnesota can instantly tap all his company's research on a compound. A geologist can compare data on an oil field to similar fields across the globe to assess its commercial potential. An engineer can compare operational data on machine performance with data from a dozen other plants to find patterns of performance problems. As a result, many companies are rethinking how work gets done, linking people through electronic media so they can leverage each other's knowledge. A consulting company set up a best practices database with detailed descriptions of projects so consultants around the globe could draw from each other's experience. A computer company's systems design group created an electronic library of system configurations so designers could draw from a store of pre-developed components. These companies believe that if they could get people to simply document their insights and draw on each other's work, they could create a web of global knowledge that would enable their staff to work with greater effectiveness and efficiency.

While information technology has inspired this vision, it itself cannot bring the vision into being. Most companies soon find that leveraging knowledge is very hard to achieve. Several years ago Texaco's Information Technology group installed Lotus Notes, hoping it would lead to more collaboration. They soon discovered that they only used Notes for e-mail. Not until they found an urgent need to collaborate and changed the way they worked together, did they use Notes effectively. Studies show that information technology usually reinforces an organization's norms about documenting, sharing information, and using the ideas of others. People send most e-mail to those they work with daily. Computer mediated interaction is usually more polite than face-to-face, despite occasional flaming. Computer-aided decision making is no more democratic than face-to-face decision making. Virtual teams need to build a relationship, often through face-to-face meetings, *before* they can effectively collaborate electronically.[1] The difficulty in most knowledge management effort lies in changing organizational culture and people's work habits. It lies in getting people to take the time to articulate and share the really good stuff. If a group of people don't already share knowledge, don't already have plenty of contact, don't already understand what insights and information will be useful to each other, information technology is not likely to create it. However, most knowledge management efforts treat these cultural issues as secondary, implementation issues. They typically focus on information systems—identifying what information to capture, constructing taxonomies for organizing information, determining access, and so on. *The great trap in knowledge management is using information management tools and concepts to design knowledge management systems.*

Creating Information Junkyards

A good example of how information technology alone cannot increase the leverage of professional knowledge comes from a large consumer products company. As part of reorganization, the company decided to improve professional work. Professional staff were instructed to document their key work processes in an electronic database. It was a hated task. Most staff felt their work was too varied to capture in a set of procedures. But after much berating by senior managers about being "disciplined," they completed the task. Within a year the database was populated, but little used. Most people found it too general and generic to be useful. The help they needed to improve their work processes and share learning was not contained in it. The result was an expensive and useless information junkyard. Creating an information system without understanding what knowledge professionals needed, or the form and level of detail they needed, did little to leverage knowledge.

Knowledge is different from information and sharing it requires a different set of concepts and tools. Six characteristics of knowledge distinguish it from information:

- Knowing is a human act
- Knowledge is the residue of thinking
- Knowledge is created in the present moment
- Knowledge belongs to communities
- Knowledge circulates through communities in many ways
- New knowledge is created at the boundaries of old

Leveraging knowledge involves a unique combination of human and information systems.

KNOWING, THINKING, AND COMMUNITY

Knowing is a human act. Discussions of knowledge management often begin with definitions of data, information, and knowledge. I would like to take a different starting point: an inquiry into our own experience using, discovering, and sharing knowledge. By reflecting on our own individual experience, we can gain a deeper understanding of the nature of knowledge and how we and *others* use it.[2] As Maurice Merleau-Ponty observed, "We arrive at the universal, not by abandoning our individuality, but by turning it into a way of reaching out to others."[3]

Reflecting on our experience, the first thing that comes into view is that *we* know. Knowledge always involves a person who knows. My bookcase contains a lot of information on organizational change, but we would not say that it is knowledgeable about the subject. The same is true for my computer, even though it can store, sort, and organize information much more quickly than my bookcase. Thinking of our minds as a biochemical library is little different from treating it as a bookcase or computer. To know a topic or a discipline is not just to possess information about it. It is the very human ability to *use* that information.

The art of professional practice is to turn information into solutions. To know a city is to know its streets, not as a list of street names or a map, but as a set of sights and routes useful for different *purposes*. Driving through your hometown to avoid rush-hour traffic, find an interesting restaurant, bring relatives sightseeing, or go bargain hunting, you not only draw on a vast amount of information, you *use* the information in different ways. Your purpose determines the information you focus on and remember, the routes that come to mind. Professionals do the same thing. They face a stream of problems; when to run a product promotion, how to estimate the size of an oil field, how to reduce the weight and cost of a structure. To solve these problems, professionals *piece information together, reflect* on their experience, *generate* insights, and *use* those insights to *solve* problems.

Thinking is at the heart of professional practice. If we look at our own experience, *thinking* is key to making information useful. Thinking transforms information into insights and insights into solutions. When jamming, jazz musicians get a feel for where the music is going, adjust to their partners' moves, change direction, and readjust. They take in information, make sense of it, generate new musical ideas, and apply their insights to the ongoing musical conversation. Responding to each other, they draw on tunes, chords, progressions, and musical "feels" they have known before, even though at any moment they could not predict "what's next." Jamming is a kind of musical thinking.[4] Science, architecture, engineering, marketing, and other practical professions are not that different. Professionals do not just cut and paste "best practice" from the past to the current situation. They draw from their experience to *think about* a problem. An architect looking for a design that will work on a steeply sloping site, looks at the site "through the eyes" of one idea, discards it and sees it again "through the eyes" of a different idea, drawing on different information about the site in each thought experiment. In running these experiments, the architect is not just looking for pre-made solutions, but thinking about how those solutions might apply and letting ideas *seep* from one framework to the next, so a new, creative idea can emerge.[5] Professional practice is also a kind of improvisation within a territory, whether that's a keyboard, a science, or a computer application. As knowledgeable practitioners, we move around the territory, sometimes with accuracy and efficiency, sometimes with grace and inspiration. A group of systems designers for a computer company tried to leverage their knowledge by storing their system documentation in a common database. They soon discovered that they did not need each other's system documentation. They needed to understand the logic other system designers used—why *that* software, with *that* hardware and *that* type of service plan. They needed to know the path of thinking other system designers took through the field. *To know a field or a discipline is to be able to think within its territory.*

Knowledge is the residue of thinking. Knowledge comes from experience. However, it is not just raw experience. It comes from experience that we have reflected on, made sense of, tested against other's experience. It is experience that is *informed by* theory, facts, and understanding. It is experience we make sense of in relationship to a field or discipline. Knowledge is what we retain as a result of thinking through a problem, what we remember from the route of thinking we took through the field. While developing a report on a competitor, a researcher deepens her understanding of her research question, the competitor, and the information sources she used, particularly if she used a new question, source, or approach. *From the point of view of the person who knows, knowledge is a kind of sticky residue of insight about using information and experience to think.*

Knowledge is always *recreated* in the present moment. Most of us cannot articulate what we know. It is largely invisible and often comes to mind only when we need it to answer a question or solve a problem. This isn't because knowledge is hard to find in our memory. It is because knowledge resides in our body. To find it we don't search. We engage in an act of knowing.[6] Knowledge is what a lathe operator has in his hands about the feel of the work after turning hundreds of blocks of wood. Knowledge is the insight an engineer has in the back of her mind about which analytic tools work well together and when to use them. To use our knowledge we need to make sense of our experience again, here in the present. When I think through how to champion an organizational change, I draw from the constantly evolving landscape of what I know now about change, my evolving "mental models" of change. I put that insight together in a new sense, one created just here and now. Sometimes it includes new insights freshly made. Sometimes it forgets old ones. Learning from past experience, sharing insights, or even sharing "best practices" is always rooted in the present application, the thinking we are doing now. *Insights from the past are always mediated by the present, living act of knowing.*[7]

To share knowledge we need to *think about* the present. Sharing knowledge involves guiding someone through our thinking or using our insights to help them see their own situation better. To do this we need to know something about those who will use our insights, the problems they are trying to solve, the level of detail they need, maybe even the style of thinking they use. For example, novices frequently solve problems by following step-by-step procedures, but experts solve problems in an entirely different way. They typically develop a theory of potential causes based on their experience and test to see if the theory is correct, often testing the least complex or expensive theories, rather than the logically correct ones, first.[8] The knowledge useful to novices is very different from the knowledge useful to experienced practitioners. Sharing knowledge is *an act of knowing* who will use it and for what purpose. For peers, this often involves mutually discovering which insights from the past are relevant in the present. To document for a general audience, like writing a textbook, also involves imagining a user, the novice. It is our picture of the user—their needs and competencies—that determines the level of detail, tone and focus of the insights we share.

Playing "Give Me Your Best Line"

Years ago a geoscientist at Shell Oil Company who had an uncanny knack for finding oil, initiated an odd lunch-time game. Geoscientists explore prospective sites using seismic data, which give a two dimensional picture of the earth, like the side of a slice of cake. The more lines of seismic data, the more complete and three-dimensional the picture of the prospect. His game was to gather a group of geoscientists and guess at the structure of the prospect, using the fewest number of seismic lines, and therefore the least amount of information possible. Since a prospect's geology is key to finding oil, the game had serious practical consequences. This game caused people to think together about the prospect. With very little data, it was easy to pose different theories, challenge assumptions, and reformulate their ideas. The lack of data encouraged them to consider a wider variety of models of the geography than they would have with more complete data. As they collected more data about the prospect, they continued the game and discovered which theories had been correct. The game was a powerful exercise in leveraging knowledge. It enabled this group to share their thinking and reformulate their assumptions as they expanded their understanding.

Knowledge belongs to *communities*. The idea that knowledge is the stuff "between the ears of the individual" is a myth. We don't learn on our own. We are born into a world already *full* of knowledge, a world that already makes sense to other people—our parents, neighbors, church members, community, country. We learn by participating in these communities and come to embody the ideas, perspective, prejudices, language, and practices of that community.[9] The same is true for learning a craft or discipline. When we learn a discipline, whether at school or on the job, we learn more than facts, ideas, and techniques. We enter a territory already occupied by others and learn by participating with them in the language of that discipline and seeing the world through its distinctions. We learn a way of thinking. Marketing specialists learn market survey methods; but they also learn a marketing perspective. They learn to ask questions about product use, customer demographics, lifestyle, product life cycles, and so forth. This perspective is embedded in the discipline and handed down through generations of practitioners. It is part of the background knowledge and accumulated wisdom of the discipline. Architects from different schools approach problems in characteristically different ways. Each school's approach is embedded in the everyday practices of its faculty, shared as they see the logic of each other's thinking. *Knowledge flows through professional communities, from one generation to the next.* Even though we do most of our thinking alone, in our office or study, we are building on the thinking of others and to contribute to a discipline, we must put our ideas out into the "public"—just stewards for a moment. Even when we develop ideas that contradict the inherited wisdom of the profession, our "revolutionary" ideas are meaningful only in relation to the community's beliefs. They are still a form of participation in that discipline.[10]

Despite changes in membership and dominant paradigms, the discipline itself continues often with its basic assumptions and approaches relatively intact for generations.

Knowledge circulates through communities in many ways. We typically think of a community's knowledge as the stuff in textbooks, articles, written procedures, individual file cabinets, and people's minds. However, many other "objects" contain a community's knowledge: unwritten work routines, tools, work products, machinery, the layout of a workspace or tools on a tray, stories, specialized language, and common wisdom about cause-effect relationships.[11] These unwritten artifacts circulate through the community in many ways. Stories are told at conferences and chance hallway meetings. People see each other's thinking as they solve problems together, in peer reviews, or in notes in the margins of work products. People observe and discuss informal work routines in the everyday course of work. So where does a community's knowledge reside? From the practitioner's perspective, only a small percentage is written. Most is in these informal, undocumented practices and artifacts. All contacts within the community can be vehicles for sharing knowledge, even though most are not intended to be. As Wallace Stevens wrote, "Thought is an infection, some thoughts are an epidemic."

New knowledge is created at the boundaries of old. If you reflect on how you learn new things, you probably find that most of the time you learn by comparing the new idea, fact, or tool to ones you already know. The everyday practice of professional work involves thinking that draws from experience and current information. But new knowledge typically does not come from thinking within the ordinary bounds of a discipline or craft. It comes from thinking at the edge of current practice. New, disruptive technology is often developed by small companies at the edge of a marketplace.[13] Scientists are frequently most productive a few years after they have crossed over from one specialty to another. New ideas in science frequently emerge, not from paradigm shifts at the heart of the discipline, but when scientists run out of interesting research questions—and publication opportunities—at the heart of their discipline and either shift to subspecialties on the margin of the discipline or combine the perspectives of different disciplines, forming new specialties such as psychopharmachology.[14] *New ideas emerge in the conflict of perspective, the clash of disciplines, the murky waters at the edge of a science, the technology that doesn't quite work, on the boundaries of old knowledge.*

In summary, when we look at our own experience, knowledge is much more—and much more elusive—than most definitions allow. Knowing is a *human act*, whereas information is an *object* that can be filed, stored, and moved around. Knowledge is a product of thinking, created in the *present moment*, whereas information is fully made and can sit in storage. To share knowledge, we need to *think about the current situation*, whereas we can simply move information from one mailbox to another. *However, knowledge is more than you think*. Knowledge settles into our body. It is a kind of "under the fingernails"

> **Thinking with Information at the Center for Molecular Genetics**
>
> Researchers at the Center for Molecular Genetics in Heidelberg use photographs extensively in their work. They take pictures of radioactively marked DNA and RNA strands using X-ray film. Their challenge is to make sense of these pictures, interpreting what the markings on the film indicate about the structure of the material and its implications for their experiments. As they pull photos from the darkroom, other people in the lab gather around to discuss what they see. These discussions frequently refer to other research, both published and current. They see the film through the eyes of one set of research findings, then another. Through these informal gatherings, the researchers think aloud together, challenge each other, try dead ends, draw metaphors from other disciplines, and use visual models and metaphors to make sense of their data and reach conclusions. Their collective know-how and knowledge of the research literature are the living backdrop for these discussions. Sometimes they talk through a procedure, looking for the meaning of a result in its minute details. Other times they focus on research findings, letting their procedures fade into the background as they compare their results to others. In these discussions, they use their knowledge of the literature and their lab know-how to think about and solve the current research problem.[12]

wisdom, the background know-how from which we draw. Most of us find it hard or impossible to articulate what we know; whereas information can be written or built into machinery. We acquire knowledge by participating in a community—using the tools, ideas, techniques, and unwritten artifacts of that community; whereas we acquire information by reading, observing, or otherwise absorbing it. *Ironically, when we look at our experience, the heart of knowledge is not the great body of stuff we learn, not even what the individual thinks, but a community in discourse, sharing ideas.*

IMPLICATIONS FOR LEVERAGING KNOWLEDGE

What are the implications of these philosophical reflections on the movement to manage knowledge? Clearly, leveraging knowledge involves much more than it seems. It is not surprising that documenting procedures, linking people electronically, or creating websites is often not enough to get people to think together, share insights they didn't know they had, or generate new knowledge. Using our own experience as a starting point to design knowledge management systems leads to a different set of design questions. Rather than identifying information needs and tools, we identify the community that cares about a topic and then enhance their ability to think together, stay in touch with each other, share ideas with each other, and connect with other communities. *Ironically, to leverage knowledge we need to focus on the community that owns it and the people who use it, not the knowledge itself.*

To Leverage Knowledge, Develop Existing Communities

Develop natural knowledge communities without formalizing them. Most organizations are laced with communities in which people share knowledge, help each other, and form opinions and judgments. *Increasing an organization's ability to leverage knowledge typically involves finding, nurturing, and supporting the communities that already share knowledge about key topics.* Allied Signal supports learning communities by giving staff time to attend community meetings, funding community events, creating community bulletins, and developing a directory of employee skills. If too formalized, learning communities can become bureaucratic structures, keepers of the discipline's "official story" that act as approval hurdles for operations groups. The key to nurturing communities is to tap their natural energy to share knowledge, build on the processes and systems they already use, and enhance the role of natural leaders.

Focus on Knowledge Important to Both the Business and the People

Learning communities are organized around important topics. Developing communities takes considerable effort. The best way to insure that the effort is well spent is to identify topics where leveraging knowledge will provide value to the business as well as community members. People naturally seek help, share insights, and build knowledge in areas they care about. At Chaparral Steel, blue-collar employees meet with customers, solve problems, create new alloys, and continually redesign the steel-making process. They share insights with each other as they search for innovative, cost-competitive solutions to customer needs. Sharing knowledge helps staff solve problems directly related to their day-to-day work.[15] *Natural learning communities focus on topics that people feel passionate about.* In Shell's Deepwater Division, most learning communities are formed around disciplines, like geology, or topics that present new challenges to the business or their field. They are topics people need to think about to do their work. Most are topics people have studied, find intrinsically interesting, and have become skillful at moving around in. As one geologist said, "With so many

---

Implications for Leveraging Knowledge

1. To leverage knowledge, develop communities.
2. Focus on knowledge important to both the business and the people.
3. Create forums for thinking as well as systems for sharing information.
4. Let the community decide what to share and how to share it.
5. Create a community support structure.
6. Use the community's terms for organizing knowledge.
7. Integrate sharing knowledge into the natural flow of work.
8. Treat culture change as a community issue.

meetings that aren't immediately relevant to your work, it's nice to go to one where we talk about rocks."

Create Forums for Thinking and Sharing Information

The ways to share knowledge should be as multidimensional as knowledge itself. Most corporate knowledge sharing efforts revolve around tools, typically electronic ones. The company finds a tool, or develops one, and then finds groups to use it. This may be good information, but since *knowing involves thinking about a field full of information, a knowledge management* system should include both systems for sharing information and forums for thinking. To paraphrase Henry Adams, facts without thinking are dead, and thinking without facts is pure fantasy.[16] The field of information can include statistics, maps, procedures, analyses, lessons learned, and other information with a long shelf life, but it can also include interpretations, half-formed judgements, ideas, and other perishable insights that are highly dependent on the context in which they were formed. The forums, whether face-to-face, telephone, electronic, or written, need to spark collaborative thinking not just make static presentations of ideas. In Shell's Deepwater Division, most learning communities hold regular collaborative problem-solving meetings facilitated by a community coordinator. These sessions have two purposes. First, by solving real day-to-day problems, community members help each other and build trust. Second, by solving problems in a public forum, they create a common understanding of tools, approaches, and solutions. One learning community in Shell, composed mostly of geologists, asks people to bring in paper maps and analyses. During the meetings, people literally huddle around the documents to discuss problems and ideas. The community coordinator encourages community members to make their assumptions visible. The combination of information and thinking leads to a rich discussion. While they discuss the issues, someone types notes on a laptop, so key points are captured. This community's process for leveraging knowledge includes thinking and information, human contact and IT. In the course of problem-solving discussions such as these, most communities discover areas where they need to create common standards or guidelines, commission a small group to develop them, and incorporate their recommendations. Most have a website where they post meeting notes and guidelines. Some have even more elaborate community libraries.

Let the Community Decide What to Share and How to Share It

Knowledge needs to have an "owner" who cares. It is tempting to create organization-wide systems for sharing knowledge so everyone can access it. This can be useful if all members of the organization truly need to work with that body of knowledge, but the further away you get from community's actual needs, the less useful the information. Communities vary greatly in the kind of knowledge they need to share. In Shell's Deepwater Division, operations groups need common standards to reduce redundancy and insure technology transfer between oil platforms. Their learning communities focus on developing, maintaining, and sharing standards. Geologists, on the other hand, need to help each other approach technical problems from different directions to find new solutions. They need to understand the logic behind each other's interpretations. Another community found they were each collecting exactly the same information from external sources, literally replicating each other's work. They needed a common library and someone responsible for document management. Since information is meaningful only to the community that uses it, the community itself needs to determine the balance of how much they need to think together, collect and organize common information, or generate standards. Since knowledge includes both information and thinking, only the community can keep that information up-to-date, rich, alive, available to community members at just the right time, and useful. Only community members can understand what parts of it are important. When communities determine what they need to share and what forum will best enable them to share it, they can more readily own both the knowledge and the forums for sharing it.

Create a Community Support Structure

Communities are held together by people who care about the community. In most natural communities, an individual or small group takes on the job of holding the community together, keeping people informed of what others are doing and creating opportunities for people to get together to share ideas. In intentional communities, this role is also critical to the community's survival, but it typically needs to be designed. Community coordinators are usually a well-respected member of the community. Their primary role is to keep the community alive, connecting members with each other, helping the community focus on important issues, and bringing in new ideas when the community starts to lose energy. In Allen's study, project engineers used information from technical consultants and suppliers more readily when it was funneled through an internal gatekeeper than when the consultants met with them directly.[17]

Use information technology to support communities. Most companies use information technology to support individual work, leaving it to each individual to sort through the information that comes their way, decide what is important, clean, and organize it. However, if communities own knowledge, then the community can organize, maintain, and distribute it to members. This is another key role of community coordinators or core group members. They use their knowledge of the discipline to judge what is important, groundbreaking, and useful and to enrich information by summarizing, combining, contrasting, and integrating it. When IBM introduced its web-based Intellectual Competencies system, anyone could contribute to the knowledge base. However, like many other

---

Many Forums for Discussing Petrophysics

A division of a Shell Oil Company recently organized its professional engineers into permanent cross-functional teams. Team members are located together and some engineering disciplines have only one member on the team. Once organized into this new structure, a group of petrophysicists realized how much they needed other members of their discipline to get advice and think through issues. In the past they just walked down the hall to get help, they now needed to go several floors away to find a peer.

So they decided to create a process for sharing knowledge with each other that crosses the boundaries of the operations teams. Some parts of this system are organic, some informal, some explicit, and some formal. For consulting each other on interpretations of data, they hold informal, agenda-less weekly meetings where anyone can get input on any topic. These are different from most agenda-driven meetings in that they emphasize open dialogue for exploring issues, with no pressure to come to resolution. To share knowledge that is more explicit, they have formal presentations on new technology. To ensure their data is consistent and widely available, they opened a common electronic data library that lets them compare data from many different sites. To ensure that informal help is available at any time, they established a senior coordinator who facilitates interaction among members of the discipline as well as provides his own insights and answers. Each of these forums is useful for sharing a different kind of knowledge, from fuzzy know-how to concrete data. Having all of them available ensures that each is used for sharing the knowledge most appropriate to it.

---

companies, IBM soon discovered that their staff did not want to hunt through redundant entries. Now a core group from each community organizes and evaluates entries, weeding out redundancies and highlighting particularly useful or groundbreaking work. Frequently, technical professionals see this as a "glorified librarian" role and many communities also have librarians or junior technical staff to do the more routine parts of organizing and distributing information.

Use the Community's Terms for Organizing Knowledge

Organize information naturally. Since knowledge is the sense we make of information, then the way information is organized is also a sense-making device. A good taxonomy should be intuitive for those who use it. To be "intuitive" it needs to tell the story of the key distinctions of the field, reflecting the natural way discipline members think about the field. Like the architecture of a building, a taxonomy enables people to move about within a bank of information, find familiar landmarks, use standard ways to get to key information, create their own "cowpaths," and browse for related items. This is a common way to spark insight. Of course, this means that if you have multiple communities in an organization, they are likely to have different taxonomies, not only in the key categories through which information is organized, but also in the way that information is presented. A group of geologists, who often work with maps, asked that their website for organizing information be a kind of visual picture.

They think in pictures. However, a group of engineers in the same organization wanted their website to be organized like a spreadsheet. They think in tables. *The key to making information easy to find is to organize it according to a scheme that tells a story about the discipline in the language of the discipline.*

How standard should company taxonomies be? Only as wide as the community of real users. There is a great temptation to make all systems for organizing knowledge the same. Certainly formatting information so it can easily be transferred—having the same metadata so it can be searched, indexed, and used in different contexts—can be very useful. However, beyond that the systems for organizing information should be the community's. If a community of people sharing knowledge spans several disciplines, then such things as terms and structures should be common among those communities.

Integrate Learning Communities into the Natural Flow of Work

Community members need to connect in many ways. Because communities create knowledge in the present moment, they need frequent enough contact to find commonality in the problems they face, see the value of each other's ideas, build trust, and create a common etiquette or set of norms on how to interact. When people work together or sit close enough to interact daily, they naturally build this connection. It simply emerges from their regular contact. When developing intentional learning communities, it is tempting to focus on their "official tasks"; developing standards, organizing information, or solving cross-cutting technical problems. However, it is also important for them to have enough open time for "technical schmoozing," sharing immediate work problems or successes, helping each other, just as they would if they were informally networking down the hall. This informal connection is most useful if it can happen in the spontaneous flow of people's work as they encounter problems or develop ideas. So community members need many opportunities to talk one-on-one or in small groups on the telephone, through e-mail, face-to-face, or through an Internet site. In Shell's Deepwater Division, community coordinators "walk the halls," finding out what people are working on, where they are having problems, and making connections to other community members. This informal connecting ensures that issues don't wait until community meetings to get discussed and keeps other channels of communication open.

Treat Culture Change as a Community Issue

Communities spread cultural change. Failures in implementing knowledge management systems are often blamed on the organization's culture. It is argued that people were unwilling to share their ideas or take the time to document their insights. However, organizational culture is hard to change. It rarely yields to efforts to change it directly by manipulation of rewards, policies, or organizational structure. Often it changes more by contagion than decree. People ask trusted peers for advice, teach newcomers, listen to discussions between experts, and form judgments in conversations. In the course of that connection with community members, they adopt new practices. Despite massive efforts by public health organizations to educate physicians, most physicians abandon old drugs and adapt new ones only after a colleague has personally recommended it. They rely on the *judgement* of their peers—as well as the information they get from them—to decide. New medical practices spread through the medical community like infectious diseases, through individual physician contact. Learning communities thrive in a culture that supports sharing knowledge. However, they are also vehicles for creating a culture of sharing. While it is important to align measurement, policies, and rewards to support sharing knowledge,[18] the key driver of a change toward sharing knowledge is likely to be within communities.[19]

CONCLUSION

Today, the "knowledge revolution" is upon us, but the heart of this revolution is not the electronic links common in every office. Ironically, while the knowledge revolution is inspired by new information systems, it takes human systems to realize it. This is not because people are reluctant to use information technology. It is because knowledge involves thinking with information. If all we do is increase the circulation of information, we have only addressed one of the components of knowledge. To leverage knowledge we need to enhance both thinking and information. The most natural way to do this is to build communities that cross teams, disciplines, time, space, and business units.

There are four key challenges in building these communities. The *technical challenge* is to design human and information systems that not only make information available, but help community members think together. The *social challenge* is to develop communities that share knowledge and still maintain enough diversity of thought to encourage thinking rather than sophisticated copying. The *management challenge* is to create an environment that truly values sharing knowledge. The *personal challenge* is to be open to the ideas of others, willing to share ideas, and maintain a thirst for new knowledge.

By combining human and information systems, organizations can build a capacity for learning broader than the learning of any of the individuals within it.

NOTES

1. M. Lynne and Robert Benjamin Marcus, "The Magic Bullet Theory in IT-Enabled Transformation," *Sloan Management Review*, 38/2 (Winter 1997): 55–68; Matt Alvesson, "Organizaions as Rhetoric: Knowledge-Intensive Firms and the Struggle with Ambiguity," *Journal of Management Studies*, 30/6 (November 1993): 997–1020; Ronald Rice, August Grant, Joseph Schmitz, and Jack Torbin, "Individual and

Network Influences on the Adoption and Perceived Outcome of Electronic Messaging," *Social Networks*. 12 (1990): 27–55; Jolene Galegher, Robert E. Kraut, and Carmen Egido, *Technology for Intellectual Teamwork: Perspective on Research and Design* (Hillsdale, NJ: Lawrence Erlbaum Associates, 1990); Guiseppe Mantovani, "Is Computer Mediated Communication Intrinsically Apt to Enhance Democracy in Organizaions?" *Human Relations*, 47/1 (1994): 45–62.

2. This is the starting point philosophical inquiry. See Husserl and Merleau-Ponty on the importance of founding scientific theory on philosophical inquiry. Edmund Husserl, *The Crisis of European Sciences and Transcendental Phenomenology* (Evanston, IL: Northwestern University Press, 1970); Maurice Merleau-Ponty, *The Phenomenology of Perception* (London: Routledge & Kegan Paul, 1962).

3. Maurice Merleau-Ponty, *Sense and Non-Sense* (Evanston, IL: Northwestern University Press, 1964).

4. David Sudnow, *Ways of the Hand: The Organization of Improvised Conduct* (Cambridge, MA: Harvard University Press, 1978).

5. Donald Schon, *The Reflective Practitioner* (New York, NY: Basic Books, 1983).

6. Merleau-Ponty (1962), op. cit.

7. Ibid.; Schon, op. cit.; Peter Senge *The Fifth Discipline* (New York, NY: Doubleday, 1990); Maurice Merleau-Ponty, *The Visible and the Invisible* (Evanston, IL: Northwestern University Press, 1969).

8. Udo Konradt, "Strategies of Failure Diagnosis in Computer-Controlled Manufacturing Systems," *International Journal of Human Computer Studies*, 43 (1995): 503–521.

9. Thomas Kuhn, *The Structure of Scientific Revolutions* (Chicago, IL: University of Chicago Press, 1962); Etienne Wenger, *Communities of Practice* (Cambridge: Cambridge University Press, 1998).

10. Michel Foucault, *The Order of Things* (New York, NY: Vintage Press, 1970).

11. Michel Foucault, *The Birth of the Clinic* (New York, NY: Vintage Press, 1975).

12. Klaus Amann and Karin Knorr-Cetina, "Thinking through Talk: An Ethnographic Study of a Molecular Biology Laboratory," *Knowledge and Society: Studies in the Sociology of Science Past and Present*, 8 (1989): 3–36.

13. Joseph Bower and Clayton Christensen, "Disruptive Technologies: Catching the Wave," *Harvard Business Review*, 73/1 (January/February 1995): 43–53.

14. M. F. Mulkay, "Three Models of Scientific Development," Kolner Zeitshrift (1974); Dorothy Leonard-Barton, *Wellsprings of Knowledge: Building and Sustaining the Sources of Innovation* (Boston, MA: Harvard Business School Press, 1995).

15. Leonard-Barton, op. cit.

16. Henry Adams, *The Education of Henry Adams* (London: Penguin, 1995).

17. Tom Allen, *Managing the Flow of Technology* (Cambridge, MA: MIT Press, 1997).

18. Q. Wang and A. Majchrzak, "Breaking the Functional Mindset in Process Organizations," *Harvard Business Review*, 74/5 (September/October 1996): 92–99.

19. Etienne Wenger, op. cit.

3

The New Task of R&D Management: Creating Goal-Directed Communities for Innovation*

William Q. Judge, Gerald E. Fryxell, and Robert S. Dooley

In this chapter, Judge, Fryxell, and Dooley report research findings on a study of innovation and R&D communities within the biotech industry. The study examines two important questions:

1. What kind of workplace cultures are conducive to creativity and innovation in an R&D unit?
2. How can managers create and maintain an innovative workplace culture?

The answers to these questions are inextricably linked to the entrepreneurial and family-like atmosphere of successful R&D groups. Specifically, techology-cycle time (TCT) was found to be shorter in highly innovative units that were focused on a "sense of community" rather than a "bureaucratic hierarchy." Also, communication, learning, and knowledge flowed easily in *goal-directed communities* where management developed strategic objectives and context, but gave great freedom and autonomy to the R&D units. Other findings pointed to four management practices that affected goal-directed communities:

- *Balanced Autonomy*—where operational and strategic autonomy encouraged entrepreneurial spirit and promoted a sense of individual, self-directed accomplishment.

Author's Note: We gratefully acknowledge the financial support of the National Science Foundation as well as the cooperation of Chi Research, Inc.

- *Personalized Recognition*—where intrinsic rewards in the form of recognition by one's peers or managers far-outpaced extrinsic or financial incentives.
- *Integrated Sociotechnical System*—where group cohesiveness and a sense of sharing were greatly affected by social fit. An effort to recruit individuals with similar sociotechnical interests presented a strong effect on the existing social environment.
- *Continuity of Slack*—where a cushion of resources enabled an organization to change gears or adapt to changes in the workplace or marketplace with little internal pressure.

As global competition intensifies and shortened product life cycles become the norm, U.S. corporations need to enhance their innovation capabilities.[1] Despite the increasing pressures for firms to be more innovative, R&D budgets are being tightened; and higher patent costs are forcing American firms to "learn new tricks" to being innovative with fewer resources.[2]

Further complicating the situation is the fact that there are few prescriptions for managing technological innovation. Fryxell[3] and Bahrami[4] have suggested that the management of innovation involves a dialectical process of synthesis between multiple dilemmas (e.g., freedom and control, flexibility and focus, differentiation and integration, incrementalism and discontinuity). This management situation is even more challenging for "radical" innovations that involve totally new products and services.[5]

While some theorists have begun to describe the complexities of organizational creativity and the innovation process,[6] there is still much that needs to be learned.[7] Due to the ambiguous, unique, and inherently uncertain process of industrial innovation, research and development units must be managed quite differently from other work units where the work is more routine.[8] As a result, most of our understanding of the management of industrial innovation comes from anecdotes,[9] with very few systematic studies linking management practices to innovativeness outcomes for the entire R&D unit.

The one area of agreement for researchers into the innovation management process is that the organizational culture within the R&D unit is a key driver of innovation. Creativity is a subtle and delicate process that does not respond well to the heavy hand of traditional bureaucratic controls or market mechanisms. For example, Burns and Stalker argued for organic (versus mechanistic) cultures.[10] Also emphasizing culture, Peters and Waterman argue that to facilitate innovation, work environments must be simultaneously loose and tight.[11] Similarly, Burgelman and Sayles argue that innovation is largely dependent on the development and maintenance of the appropriate context within which it occurs.[12]

Unfortunately, there is not much agreement as to what *kind* of workplace culture is necessary and even less about how management can create the appropriate workplace culture even once it is identified. This study examines these two fundamental questions. First, what kind of workplace cultures are conducive to creativity and innovation in an R&D unit? Second, how can managers create and maintain an innovative workplace culture?

METHODOLOGY

We conducted multiple interviews at eight new publicly-held biotechnology firms located in the United States. Descriptive statistics are provided for each firm in Table 3.1. The biotechnology firms chosen for this study were randomly selected from the *Genetic Engineering and Biotechnology Related Firms Directory*.[13] Two researchers first conducted a semi-structured interview with the R&D manager. This was followed by interviews with a research scientist and a laboratory technician, which served to verify what the R&D manager said as well as identify any important evidence that may have been omitted. This dual interview approach limits the bias that can be introduced by a single interviewer as well as improves the subsequent analysis of the transcripts.[14]

Patent citation analysis addresses the problem of measuring the quality and quantity of research output.[15] It assumes that the greater the quality, influence, or importance of a particular patent publication, the more frequently it will be cited in the scientific literature. Patent citation analysis is increasingly being used as a technology innovation indicator. For example, *Business Week* recently employed Chi Research to do a patent citation analysis to determine the innovativeness of global innovators.[16] Furthermore, patent citation analytical techniques have been found to be valid and reliable technique for measuring technological innovativeness.[17]

The citation analysis measure that we used in this study is called "technology cycle time" (TCT). TCT is defined as the median age of all patents cited in a company's new patents. Specifically, the shorter the cycle time, the faster the company is developing new technology and the more innovative the research unit is. In other words, TCT is a measure of how fast a firm is able to "reinvent" itself. Previous research has demonstrated that those firms with faster technology cycle times are also more innovative and more efficient at generating new knowledge than firms with slower technology cycle times.[18]

TABLE 3.1 Descriptions of the Biotechnology Firms in This Study (as of 1992)[a]

Firm	Employees	Year Founded	R&D Expenses/Sales[b]
Biocare	111	1982	16%
Transtech	41	1986	19%
Newkit	85	1984	60%
Cyclone	11	1985	18%
Genetwist	336	1982	78%
Teamtech	300	1975	19%
Spiral	91	1987	322%
Agrigene	35	1985	266%

a. To preserve anonymity, we created fictitious names for each organization.

b. Because of fluctuating sales levels, this ratio was averaged for 1990, 1991, and 1992.

TABLE 3.2 Level of Innovativeness of the Biotechnology Firms

Firm	Level of Innovativeness[a]	Innovativeness Group
Spiral	3.8	High
Genetwist	5.2	High
Biocare	6.0	High
Teamtech	7.3	High
Transtech	10.2	Low
Cyclone	10.5	Low
Newkit	10.5	Low
Agrigene	16.0	Low

a. Technology Cycle Time (1987–91).

To avoid bias in the data collection process, data analysis did not commence until after all eight sets of interviews were completed. Parallel with these efforts, a third researcher grouped the eight firms into two levels of innovativeness based on their technology cycle times over the past five years. To make this grouping, we used the median value of TCT to distinguish between the two groups of firms (see Table 3.2). Then all three researchers examined the interview transcripts to determine how the organizational cultures differed between the two sets of firms and to elicit differences in management practices between the highly innovative and the less innovative R&D units.

WORKPLACE CULTURE AND INNOVATIVENESS IN R&D UNITS

Based on comparisons of the cultures of the two sets of firms, we found significant differences between the highly innovative and the less innovative R&D units in the biotechnology industry. For the firms in our study, the ability of management to create a sense of community in the workplace was the key differentiating factor. Highly innovative units behaved as focused communities, while less innovative units behaved more like traditional bureaucratic departments.

One of the pioneering writers on community in the workplace is Peck, who defines it as: "A group of individuals who have learned how to communicate honestly with each other, whose relationships go deeper than their masks of composure, and who have developed some significant commitment to make others' conditions our own."[19] Borei describes community in the workplace as a situation where the organization "seemed to be more in focus and possessed a new ability to deal with tasks efficiently and productively. There is a noticeable lack of suspicion of hidden agendas and a genuine desire to reach consensus on solutions to problems."[20] Maynard and Mehrtens describe community in the workplace as a situation where "barriers between people are brought down."[21] Gozdz notes that when community is present, "Work becomes a safe place and creativity emerges. The group as a whole makes decisions co-creatively, learns as an entity, and innovates as a whole."[22]

Employees in the highly innovative units used a wide variety of words that captured the spirit of community. Perhaps the most common phrase used was a "family feeling." For example, a scientist at Genetwist (a highly innovative unit) stated that "the family type atmosphere here is the best way to describe what it is like to work here." Similarly, the R&D manager at Biocare (another innovative unit) noted, "We're very close knit back here. We socialize a lot. We go out together after work frequently. We have a lot of the same interests outside of work. So, over a period of time, it's just sort of like an extended family."

Along with this family feeling is a sense of trust and caring. One technician stated, "It's the feeling you have about the other people here. We really care about each other." As the R&D manager of Teamtech described it, "I think overall it is the message that we care about you coming here and we want you to feel at home." These words were not just pretty rhetoric, but were echoed by a technician at Teamtech, who stated, "I like coming to work; we really care about each other here—it's not just a job."

In the spirit of being a learning organization, workplace communities contemplate and self examine.[23] As one manager from a community-based unit stated, "We talk as much about how we do work around here as what we work on. The key is to constantly learn from previous experiences and continuously improve our workplace relationships." Another scientist from that same unit declared, "This organization is different from any other that I have been a member. Discussion is maximized and hierarchy is minimized." Information flows easily and decision making gets accelerated and improved. Indeed, this learning approach has been found to be crucial to the process of innovation in other studies.[24]

The workplace community also captures the synthesis between individualism and collectivism that is so crucial to effective research and development.[25] While there are personalized rewards and recognition as well as the freedom for individuals to get the work done, these individuals also work well within teams and have an allegiance to the overall organization.

However, "community" is not created for its own sake—it occurs within an overarching set of goals prescribed by top management. As Quinn observed, successful industrial innovation can be likened to "chaos within guidelines."[26] In our study, the most innovative units were *goal-directed* communities where management developed the strategic objectives and context, but gave great freedom to the researchers within that context.[27] Goal-directed communities in the workplace offer some new insights into what Wilkins and Ouchi call "clan control."[28] Similar to clan-like organizations, they have a heavy emphasis on socialization and common values which bond the organizational members together. However, workplace communities do not rely on control as much as on empowering the workers to do their best within a set of collective objectives. As a result, the role of the manager is quite different in goal-directed communities than in traditional hierarchies. Rather than being a commander, the manager's primary role is community builder—which Bourgeois and Brodwin labeled the "crescive" approach.[29]

MANAGERIAL PRACTICES AND INNOVATIVENESS

In our study, we found four managerial practices that had a major influence on whether or not there was a goal-directed community in the R&D unit:

- balanced autonomy,
- personalized recognition systems,
- integrated sociotechnical systems, and
- continuity of slack.

Balanced Autonomy

The concept of autonomy is central to the problem confronting managers of R&D units.[30] Autonomy refers to having control over the means as well as the ends of one's own work.[31] Bailyn differentiates between two spheres of autonomy: strategic autonomy—the freedom to set one's own agenda; and operational autonomy—the freedom to attack a problem, once it has been set by the organization, in ways determined by oneself.[32] Strategic and operational autonomy issues often lead to conflict between researchers and management.[33]

In our study, the relationship between autonomy and the level of innovation was fairly clear. Operational autonomy encouraged the entrepreneurial spirit and promoted a sense of individual accomplishment upon project completion, while strategic autonomy aligned individual researcher interests with organizational interests. Based on our data, those firms that were the most innovative emphasized the importance of operational autonomy for the researchers, but retained strategic autonomy for top management.

For example, the manager at one of the most innovative units, Biocare, focused his researchers on a specific set of goals, but gave them a lot of latitude to determine how to reach those goals. He explained, "The culture here is one of excitement in what we are doing and the fact that the researchers are controlling a lot of their own work." He went on to add, "Top management and I are constantly specifying the ultimate goals to be attained, but we are careful to allow our scientists creative ways of achieving those goals."

However, some managers gave their researchers too much autonomy by not specifying the end result being sought. In Bailyn's terms, these managers gave strategic autonomy to their workers. When, this happened, we found that the unit was unbalanced and, consequently, less innovative. For example, the manager of Cyclone, a less innovative unit, boasted, "What we give people here is a tremendous amount of freedom to determine their destiny." At this particular firm, top management specified that a particular new technology had to be investigated, but the product-market focus was unspecified and researchers were given complete freedom to investigate any new market. As a result, researchers lacked guidelines and focus to their research. Notably, this firm was not very innovative compared to the other firms.

In contrast, other units granted too little operational autonomy to their researchers. This also created a sense of imbalance. For example, the manager at Agrigene informed us, "We provide very specific road maps [for our scientists]. Every month we write out a monthly status report, and all our goals and our approaches for tackling these goals are listed in these reports. Then we compare our performance against these goals and against prior promises and progress."

Another example of too little operational autonomy was observed at Transtech. Here, top management was overly specific about the timing and the product-market goals. A scientist commented, "Most of what we do here is development work. However, I think that everyone would like to do a bit of path-breaking research." In a later interview, a technician at this same unit stated, "The work gets tedious after a while. What motivates me is just having any kind of a challenge. Things get pretty routine around here sometimes." Clearly, this is not a research unit "on fire" with creativity.

Woodman, Sawyer, and Griffin argued that organizations must permit their members to experiment and take risks in order to be innovative.[34] They demonstrated that too much management control stifles innovation and creativity. Relatedly, we also found that too little control by top management causes a disconnection between business goals and the scientific enterprise. A balance between operational and strategic autonomy promotes innovation by encouraging researchers to be creative in organizationally beneficial ways.

Personalized Recognition

Recognition is the acknowledgment of individual contributions to the organization.[35] While recognition can take many forms, a common distinction is usually made between intrinsic rewards and extrinsic rewards. Intrinsic rewards are those that elicit internal feelings of accomplishment by the recipient, while extrinsic rewards are externally determined and delivered.[36] Common examples of intrinsic rewards are finding meaning in one's work, being recognized by one's peers, and receiving acknowledgment from superiors. Examples of extrinsic rewards are salary increases, bonuses, and stock options.

We found that the less innovative units placed almost exclusive emphasis on relatively impersonal, extrinsic rewards. For example, the manager at Cyclone believed that the best way to motivate and reward his scientists was exclusively through economic incentives. He flatly stated, "People know how they are contributing. We reward our people through bonuses, stock options, and promotions." Similarly, when the manager of Transtech was asked how he motivated his researchers, he stated, "I think the one thing that most motivates people is that all of our employees receive stock options.... It's an incentive for them to do whatever they can to get the stock to rise and they get the benefit of it." Interestingly, the scientist interviewed at this same unit told us:

> "I can tell you that the only investment that I have asked for was I want a title change; I want to be the manager of these drug products. I mean I got a really good review and nice raise recently. But I told (the R&D manager), you can keep the money, what I want is the title. He said he thought that was unlikely, but he is checking into it.... Stock options are nice, but they don't make me work any harder or better."

While this response exemplifies the "carrot" or positive sanctions approach to extrinsic rewards, other units took the "stick" or negative sanctions approach. For example, at Agrigene, the manager declared, "In order to quantify if someone has been outstanding, or just ho-hum, or whatever, we have a basic set of goals for each researcher. That researcher better damn well achieve those goals or else he or she might be fired." When that same manager was asked whether she ever provided recognition or affirmation of good work, she admitted, "I would say that we have been defective in that area. I haven't been able to give these folks enough of my attention to do that."

In comparison, the more innovative units relied heavily on highly personalized intrinsic rewards to recognize individual and group successes. Demonstrating this, the manager from Biocare stated, "The salary and stock options provide the basic incentives to do a good job, but you have to offer more personalized rewards than just money." Another manager of an innovative unit declared, "Part of my job is to figure out what motivates my workers and then to creatively and flexibly develop an individualized reward system." In fact, all four managers of the most innovative units personalized their recognition systems by tailoring nonmonetary rewards to the unique needs of the recipients.

When researchers are motivated more by intrinsic desires than extrinsic rewards, there is greater room for creative thought and action.[37] A recent review of the research literature shows that exclusive reliance on extrinsic rewards provides temporary compliance, ruptures work relationships, inhibits organizational learning, discourages risk taking, and undermines interest in the work itself.[38] In other words, extrinsic rewards can actually misdirect worker energy while intrinsic rewards can unleash worker energy in a creative endeavor.[39]

Integrated Sociotechnical System

All work groups can be thought of as a sociotechnical system that integrates individuals and groups (i.e., the sociological subsystem) with the skills and knowledge to convert inputs into outputs (i.e., the technical subsystem).[40] In high-technology industries, such as biotechnology, where the leading technologies are constantly being improved and displaced, effective technical subsystems are clearly essential.[41] However, we found that when the R&D manager focused exclusively on bioscience (the technical subsystem), the unit was *less* innovative than units where the R&D manager placed equal attention to group cohesiveness (the sociological subsystem).

Group cohesiveness is the sense of sharing or togetherness in the organization.[42] To foster cohesiveness, managers of highly innovative R&D units put a great deal of effort into recruitment to ensure that individuals fit into the unit's existing social environment. For example, the manager of Genetwist stated, "We put a priority on the ability to work with others.... We can't afford prima donnas.... They are not worth the extra brilliance." The manager of Spiral considered "fit" the most important qualification of recruitment by stating, "The whole key is how they fit. How do they relate to people? Can they get along?" The importance of fit was reemphasized by a scientist at Spiral who stated, "We've been careful taking into consideration not only people's technical qualifications but how they will socially fit into the group that we currently have."

R&D units that were less innovative placed less emphasis on social "fit" in the recruitment process and more emphasis on individual abilities and motivations. The manager of Cyclone stated, "Your have to find those who are doers, and who are hands-on people, and who have an agenda and have a certain sense of urgency about what they are doing. That is what I look for when hiring for this unit." Similarly, the manager of Agrigene focused exclusively on highly individualistic skills in the recruitment process. She stated, "I have a little chart on what I identified as the critical skills required for this job. What I am looking for is broad knowledge, creativity, and tenacity, because I don't want someone coming in and saying, 'Well, I can't do this so I'd like to drop it.'"

In addition to the selection process, the socialization process also affected the group's level of integration.[43] Based on our study, the goal formation process appeared to be the primary differentiator by which the employees were socialized. Specifically, the less innovative units had explicit, aggressive goals with firm deadlines. One manager stated, "We do tend to have very stretched goals for everyone here. So we expect a lot of our people—far more than perhaps normal. The company needs you to do everything." Another manager from Cyclone noted, "Our scientists have a lot of time lines to meet. They are under tremendous pressure." These overly ambitious goals and tight deadlines appeared to reduce the ability of the members in the unit to interact and cohere. As one scientist from a less innovative unit stated, "We jump from one thing to another to handle what is top priority. Each one of us works fairly independently. It's pretty much an independent operation."

Highly innovative units stressed the importance of reasonable goals and de-emphasized deadlines. The manager of Teamtech stated, "We have learned from the past that it is best to try to minimize the number of major projects each person is assigned to. If they have too broad a range often they get lost. They can never do anything except step from the top of each pile to the next." The reduced time pressure in the highly innovative units was perhaps best expressed by the manager of Biocare, who stated, "They [top management] don't come to me and say: '[the manager's name], we've got to have this product in six months.'"

Continuity of Slack

Bourgeois defined organizational slack as: "The cushion of actual or potential resources which allows an organization to adapt successfully to internal pressures for change in policy as well as to initiate changes in strategy with respect to the external environment"[44] Numerous studies have demonstrated that organizational slack is positively related to technological innovation.[45] However, there is little, if any, understanding about the longitudinal effects of slack on innovation.[46]

Although all eight firms in our study had adequate levels of slack to pursue technological innovation at the time the data were collected, we failed to find any association between slack and innovation as previous correlational research suggested.[47] Instead, we found that the less innovative firms had experienced significant disruptions, or discontinuities, of slack in their past or expected disruptions in the future. For example, after reviewing the history of Cyclone, we learned that it had experienced a significant cash flow problem in 1989 which caused it to reduce employment from 29 to 5 employees at one point. Although it had a successful recent stock offering that brought in $50 million, the manager stated, "We know what it's like to almost be out of business and while I'm elated that we are now flush with cash, I want to invest it just as carefully as when cash was tight."

Similarly, we learned that Newkit was originally managed by scientists and that this approach almost led to financial ruin. Consequently, according to the R&D manager, top management was replaced with "business types who quickly drove out some key scientists." While the firm currently appears to have a better balance between science and business leadership, as well as a solid cushion of resources, the trauma of discontinuous slack from the past seemed to affect their approach toward industrial research today.

The two other less innovative firms, Transtech and Agrigene, were worried about disruptions in slack in the future. Most of Transtech's work was for the Department of Defense and all of its contracts were winding down with no concrete work for the future in sight. Agrigene had a major contract with a multinational agricultural firm, but due to uncertain market potential, future resources were in question. A scientist at Agrigene perhaps summed it up best when she stated, "It sure would be nice to worry more about my experiments and worry less about our business prospects."

In contrast, the relatively innovative units not only had continuous flows of slack over the organization's entire (but admittedly short) history, but they also seemed relatively confident about having enough slack for the future. For these firms, organizational slack had varied since their founding, but the cushion never disappeared. Consequently, it appears that not only is slack important for technological innovations, but it must also be provided continuously over the organization's life cycle, including future expectations.

R&D "COMMUNITIES" VERSUS R&D DEPARTMENTS

The four managerial practices described above interact to generate an organization sub-culture that can best be described a "goal-directed community" that is key to the innovation process. While the managers in our study used a wide variety of terms to describe their work situation, this construct best characterizes the culture of the most innovative units. This study offers four actionable levers of change for R&D managers to consider:

- The better the balance between the operational autonomy of the researchers with the strategic autonomy of the managers, the more innovative the R&D unit.
- The more emphasis placed on personalized intrinsic rewards, the more innovative the R&D unit.
- The more integrated the sociotechnical system, the more innovative the R&D unit.
- The more continuous the slack resources, the more innovative the R&D unit.

In addition, this study provides a "north star" for management to focus its time and attention:

- The greater the level of goal-directed community achieved in the R&D unit, the more innovative it is.

Nevertheless, there is the question of how generalizable these results are to larger, more established organizations with separate research units. At first glance, it does not appear to be very generalizable for several reasons. First, biotechnology is very unique compared to other technologies. Second, the small size of biotechnology units allows them to operate in a less bureaucratic fashion. Third, unlike older organizations, the relative newness of these firms enables them to be unencumbered by established organizational tradition and history.

However, recent research suggests that the key issue is not the size of the firm or the particular technology involved, but the sub-culture created within the R&D unit. For example, Damanpour, in his meta-analysis of innovation management research, concluded that large innovative organizations are creating the required flexibility and autonomy needed for innovation by imitating the management practices of smaller, more innovative firms.[48] In addition, Pearson, after studying numerous firms in the textile industry, argued that the critical factor is not size, but culture.[49] Furthermore, recent research by Hamel and Prahalad suggests that the only sustainable competitive advantage comes from productive and innovative cultures.[50] If Hamel and Prahalad are correct, it is not an overstatement to argue that the creation of goal-directed communities is worthy of experimentation in all firms that seek to become more innovative in their product and service offerings. In sum, the strategic imperative of innovation is too great to ignore the "best practices" of highly innovative industries such as biotechnology. Therefore, the results of our study are highly generalizable to larger firms to the extent that goal-directed communities can be created within their R&D unit.

Most observers are not optimistic about the ability of large firms to adapt and change. As Mintzberg points out, most large, mature organizations are run like "machine bureaucracies," which results in the death of creativity and innovativeness.[51] Furthermore, in a recent study of innovation in 15 large and mature firms, Dougherty and Hardy found that innovation occurs rarely in these firms—and when it does, it is in spite of the obstacles created by the organizational systems and culture.[52] Quinn criticizes large, mature firms for failing to leverage their intellectual capital and encourages them to find new ways of organizing and managing.[53]

Looking to the future, Maynard and Mehrtens contend that community-based organizations will be the ones that survive and prosper in the twenty-first century.[54] Notably Nirenberg[55] as well as the Center for Creative Leadership[56] offer broad and detailed arguments on how to transform teams and work units into workplace communities. Kiernan offers a somewhat more concise roadmap to create community in the workplace.[57] Clearly, this new workplace culture has attracted an increasing number of proponents.

Nonetheless, more research is needed to better identify and develop goal-directed communities. The next logical step in this line of research would be to design a research instrument with survey items that explore and identify the various dimensions of a goal-directed community. Key items would include such measures as goal clarity, organizational trust, conflict resolution capability, group cohesiveness, ease of interdepartmental communication, level of organizational commitment, and organizational caring. Properly administered, these measures would allow the researcher to test the generalizability of these results against various measures of research productivity.

The central task of R&D management is to blend powerful leadership with an empowered workforce, clear goals with an open and participative culture, and a focus on the task at hand as well as the process of working together. Perhaps Erich Fromm stated it best when he argued that

> true freedom is not the absence of structure—letting the employees go off and do whatever they want—but rather a clear structure that enables people to work within established boundaries in an autonomous and creative way.[58]

NOTES

1. M. E. Porter, *The Competitive Advantage of Nations* (New York, NY: Free Press, 1990).

2. *Business Week*, "American Inventors Are Reinventing Themselves," January 18, 1993, pp. 78–82.

3. G. E. Fryxell, "Managing the Culture of Innovation: The Synthesis of Multiple Dialectics," in L. R. Gomez-Mejia and M. W. Lawless, eds., *Organizational Issues in High Technology Management* (Greenwich, CT: JAI Press, 1990).

4. H. Bahrami, "The Emerging Flexible Organization: Perspectives from Silicon Valley," *California Management Review*, 34/4 (1992): 33–52.

5. R. A. Burgelman and L. R. Sayles, *Inside Corporate Innovation: Strategy, Structure, and Managerial Skills* (New York, NY: Free Press, 1986).

6. R. W. Woodman, J. E. Sawyer, and R. W. Griffin, "Toward a Theory of Organizational Creativity," *Academy of Management Review*, 18 (1993): 293–321.

7. C. A. Lengnick-Hall, "Innovation and Competitive Advantage: What We Know and What We Need to Know," *Journal of Management*, 18 (1992): 399–429.

8. T. Burns and G. M. Stalker, *The Management of Innovation* (London: Tavistock Publications, 1961); J. M. Beyer, "The Twin Dilemmas of Commitment and Coherence Posed by High Technology," in L. R. Gomez-Mejia and M. Lawless, eds., *Organizational Issues in High Technology Management* (Greenwich, CT: JAI Press, 1990), pp. 19–36.

9. See, for example, D. C. Pelz and F. Andrews, *Scientists in Organizations* (Ann Arbor, MI: University of Michigan Press, 1976); T. J. Peters and R. H. Waterman, *In Search of Excellence: Lessons from America's Best-Run Companies* (New York: Harper & Row, 1982); G. Pinchot, *Intrapreneuring: Why You Don't Have to Leave the Corporation to Become an Entrepreneur* (New York: Harper & Row, 1985).

10. Burns and Stalker, op. cit.

11. Peters and Waterman, op. cit.

12. Burgelman and Sayles, op. cit.

13. Sitting & Noyes, *Genetic Engineering and Biotechnology Related Firms* (Kingston, NJ: Sittig & Noyes, 1992).

14. G. P. Huber and D. J. Power, "Retrospective Reports of Strategic-Level Managers: Guidelines for Increasing Their Accuracy," *Strategic Management Journal*, 6 (1985): 171–180.

15. M. B. Albert, D. Avery, F. Narin, and P. McAllister, "Direct Validation of Citation Counts as Indicators of Industrially Important Patents," *Research Policy*, 20 (1991): 251–259.

16. "Global Innovation: Who's in the Lead?" *Business Week*, April 3, 1992, pp. 68–73.

17. Albert et al., op. cit.: F. Narin, E. Noma, and R. Perry, "Patents as Indicators of Corporate Technological Strength," *Research Policy*, 16 (1987): 143–155; F. Narin and R. P. Rozek, "Bibliometric Analysis of U.S. Pharmaceutical Industry Research Performance," *Research Policy*, 17 (1988): 139–154.

18. See, for example, P. Bierly and A. Chakrabarti, "Determinants of Technology Cycle Time in the U.S. Pharmaceutical Industry," *R&D Management*, 26/2 (1996): 115–126.

19. M. S. Peck, *The Different Drum* (New York, NY: Simon & Schuster, 1987), p. 59.

20. J. M. Borei, "Chaos to Community: One Company's Journey Toward Transformation," *World Business Academy Perspectives*, 6/2 (1992): 77.

21. H. B. Maynard and S. E. Mehrtens, *The Fourth Wave: Business in the 21st Century* (San Francisco, CA: Berrett-Koehler, 1993), p. 13.

22. K. Gozdz, "Building Community as a Leadership Discipline," in M. Ray and A. Rinzler, eds., *The New Paradigm in Business* (New York, NY: Jeremy Tarcher, 1993), p. 112.

23. P. Senge, "The Leader's New Work: Building Learning Organizations. *Sloan Management Review*," 32/1 (1990): 7–23.

24. A. Van de Ven and D. Polley, "Learning while Innovating," *Organization Science*, 3 (1992): 92–116.

25. Fryxell, op. cit.; G. E. Fryxell and W. Q. Judge, "Individualism and Teamwork: Synthesizing the Dialectic in the Management of R&D in Biotechnology," *Journal of High Technology Management Research*, 6 (1995): 33–54.

26. J. B. Quinn, "Managing Innovation: Controlled Chaos," *Harvard Business Review*, 63/3 (1985): 73–84.

27. Burgelman and Sayles, op. cit.

28. A. Wilkens and W. G. Ouchi, "Efficient Cultures: Exploring the Relationship between Culture and Organizational Control," *Administrative Science Quarterly*, 28 (1983): 468–481.

29. L. J. Bourgeois and D. R. Brodwin, "Strategic Implementation: Five Approaches to an Elusive Phenomenon," *Strategic Management Journal*, 5 (1984): 241–264.

30. T. M. Amabile, "A Model of Creativity and Innovation in Organizations," in B. M. Staw and L. L. Cummings, eds., *Research in Organizational Behavior*, 10 (Greenwich, CT: JAI Press, 1988), pp. 123–168.

31. M. A. Von Glinow, *The New Professionals* (Cambridge, MA: Ballinger Publishing, 1988).

32. L. Bailyn, "Autonomy in the Industrial R&D Lab," *Human Resource Management*, 24/2 (1985): 129–146.

33. J. A. Raelin, *The Clash of Cultures* (Boston, MA: Harvard Business School Press, 1986).

34. Woodman et al., op. cit.

35. D. J. Koys and T. A. DeCotiis, "Inductive Measures of Psychological Climate," *Human Relations*, 44 (1991): 265–285.

36. L. Dyer and D. F. Parker, "Classifying Outcomes in Work Motivation Research: An Examination of the Intrinsic-Extrinsic Dichotomy," *Journal of Applied Psychology*, 60 (1975): 455–458.

37. Woodman et al., op. cit.

38. A. S. Kohn, "Why Incentive Plans Cannot Work," *Harvard Business Review*, 71/5 (1993): 54–63.

39. T. S. Pittman, J. Emery, and A. K. Boggiano, "Intrinsic and Extrinsic Motivational Orientations: Rewarding Induced Changes in Preference for Complexity," *Journal of Personality and Social Psychology* (March 1982), pp. 23–38.

40. F. E. Emery and E. L. Trist, *Towards a Social Ecology* (New York, NY: Plenum Press, 1973).

41. C. Pava, "Redesigning Sociotechnical Systems Design: Concepts and Methods for the 1990s," *Journal of Applied Behavioral Science*, 22/3 (1986): 201–222.

42. Koys and DeCotiis, op. cit.

43. Raelin, op. cit.

44. L. J. Bourgeois, "On the Measurement of Organizational Slack," *Academy of Management Journal*, 26 (1981): 30.

45. P. Bromiley, "Testing a Causal Model or Corporate Risk Taking and Performance," *Academy of Management Journal*, 34 (1991): 27–59; F. Damanpur, "The Adoption of Technological, Administrative, and Ancillary Innovations: Impact of Organizational Factors," *Journal of Management*, 13 (1987): 675–688; V. J. Singh, "Performance, Slack, and Risk Taking in Organizational Decision Making," *Academy of Management Journal*, 29 (1986): 562–585.

46. Bromiley, op. cit.

47. Damanpour, op. cit.; Singh, op. cit.

48. F. Damanpour, "Organizational Size and Innovation," *Organization Studies*, 13 (1992): 375–402.

49. G. J. Pearson, "Promoting Entrepreneurship in Large Companies," *Long Range Planning*, 22 (1989): 87–97.

50. G. Hamel and C. K. Prahalad, *Competing for the Future* (Boston, MA: Harvard Business School Press, 1994).

51. H. Mintzberg, *Mintzberg on Management* (New York, NY: Free Press, 1989).

52. D. Dougherty and C. Hardy, "Sustained Product Innovation in Large, Mature Organization: Overcoming Innovative to Organization Problems," *Academy of Management Journal*, 39 (1996): 1120–1153.

53. J. B. Quinn, *The Intelligent Enterprise* (New York, NY: Free Press, 1992).

54. Maynard and Mehrtens, op. cit.

55. J. Nirenberg, *The Living Organization: Transforming Teams into Workplace Communities* (New York, NY: Irwin, 1993).

56. S. Gryskiewicz and D. Hills, eds., *Readings in Innovation* (Greensboro, NC: Center for Creative Leadership, 1992).

57. M. J. Kiernan, "The New Strategic Architecture: Learning to Compete in the Twenty-First Century," *Academy of Management Executive*, 7/1 (1993): 7–21.

58. E. Fromm, *Escape from Freedom* (New York, NY: Rinehart, 1941).

4

Communities of Practice: Learning Is Social. Training Is Irrelevant?*

David Stamps
Associate Editor of TRAINING *Magazine*
DStamps@lakewoodpub.com

Informal communities of practice greatly impact the way organizations design and implement training. For many years, organizations have attempted to formalize and standardize the way instruction was delivered to employees, with little comprehension of how the work was actually performed. In this chapter, David Stamps uses Xerox's Integrated Customer Service project as an example of how individuals with common sets of interests and expertise can be used to facilitate peer-driven learning. Citing Wenger and Lave's work on learning, meaning, and identity, Stamps draws from Xerox's project to consider how a common way of thinking and learning results from the community's understanding of its own work activities and the larger organizational mission. At the center of this thinking lies the premise that work and learning are social activities, where learning occurs by doing and a shared sense of what it takes to get the job done. Although such thinking often requires a paradigm shift among managers and training departments, significant increases in productivity and innovation are among the benefits achieved by developing and executing a lifelong "learning" rather than "training" strategy.

As the end of a century draws near, the air is sure to thicken with prophecies about the future, including the future of work. The "knowledge worker" will be a favorite topic of management soothsaying; so will "the learning organization."

But for a clear vision of how learning *should* happen in a business setting, you need only talk to Dede Miller, a customer service representative for Xerox

---

* Reprinted with permission from the February 1997 issue of *TRAINING* magazine. Copyright 1997. Bill Communications, Inc., Minneapolis, MN. All rights reserved.

Corp. For two years she was treated to a tantalizing glimpse of the future. Today she finds herself wishing she could go back to it.

To know her story is to understand just how wide a gap still separates learning theory and common training practice—and how hard it will be to apply new approaches to workplace training, even those that make incontestable sense.

In 1994 Xerox began plotting an experiment in operations at its Louisville, TX, customer service center. The object was to see if three separate customer service departments could be integrated into a single unit. From the customers' standpoint, the change was eminently desirable; Xerox's customers had long complained about being shunted from one department to another when they called seeking assistance.

Despite the obvious benefit of reducing customer discontent, consolidation presented some tough questions: Would the advantages of an integrated service department offset the costs involved? People would need to be relocated: databases would have to be reconfigured to provide access to customer information residing in separate service departments.

And some in the company wondered if employees were up to the challenge of learning new jobs within the time constraints of the two-year consolidation experiment. Could account administrators, for instance, learn to do the job of the service reps who scheduled repairs? Could service reps learn the subtle tricks of the sales staff, whose job it was to sell supplies such as paper and toner?

Indeed, learning hurdles appeared to pose the most daunting challenge to Xerox's Integrated Customer Service (ICS) experiment. Back in Leesburg, VA, the corporate training department had painstakingly crafted separate curricula— each involving weeks or months of classroom indoctrination—for each aspect of the various customer service jobs. To combine these curricula and teach new ICS staffers all they'd need to know to perform in an integrated setting would take no fewer than 52 weeks of classroom training for each person. Or so the training professionals calculated.

Researchers at the Institute for Research on Learning proffered a different idea, however. IRL, based in Menlo Park, CA, traffics in a rich mixture of consulting, research, and something akin to corporate espionage. The preferred modus operandi of IRL researchers is to show up one day at a company and then hang around until they fade into the scenery—at which point they pull out their notebooks. Using the ethnographic techniques of anthropologists, IRL agents endeavor to discern how work *really* gets done in a given setting. As a research organization, IRL uses this information to refine its theories about workplace learning. As a consultancy, it advises clients how they can design learning that reflects the true nature of how employees do their jobs.

Jack and Marilyn Whalen, the IRL researchers contracted by Xerox to advise it on the ICS project, suggested that training need not take a full year; that it could, in fact, be dramatically shortened. How? By moving the service reps out of their isolated cubicles and bringing them together in shared work spaces, where a group of six or seven ICS staffers would be in constant contact with one another. In this communal environment, the workers would teach each other how to do their respective jobs; sales reps would share what they knew about selling, service reps what they knew about service and so on. And one other thing...the ICS workers would take customer calls from day one, putting into practice what they learned as soon as they learned it.

The response to this proposal from the corporate training unit back in Leesburg was a long, anguished wail that could be heard all the way to Texas. But Cheryl Thomas, the manager tapped to head up the ICS project, decided to seek a second opinion—actually, 30 second opinions. She asked the employees who'd been selected to be the ICS guinea pigs what they thought of the idea. To the question of whether or not workers could teach each other, the answer she heard was, "Why not? It's what we do already."

What Thomas heard from the trenches, in fact, did little to elevate her estimation of the training department's role in the learning process at Xerox. She was astonished to learn just how removed from the sphere of real work was the prolonged methodology for developing training classes, a process that unfolded along these lines: first came a flyover visit to determine training requirements. Those requirements were handed off to designers back in Leesburg, who designed a curriculum. Months later, training-delivery specialists parachuted onto the scene armed with a detailed script.

But these scripts were next to useless, according to the workers. They complained to Thomas that they heard way too much about tasks they never or seldom performed, and way too little about some of the most crucial aspects of the job. Moreover, there was never an opportunity to practice what they were taught until three or four weeks of classroom training ground to a blessed halt. By the time workers were actually back on the job, they'd forgotten most of what they'd been told. To learn billing and credit procedures, for instance, trainees endured 11 weeks of nonstop classroom lectures before taking their first customer call.

Worst of all, none of the talking heads had ever set foot in a customer service setting. "They tell us how work gets done based on what someone else has told them," the workers told Thomas. "When we finally get back to the job, coworkers have to explain to us how things really get done."

This common phenomenon has been discussed for years in training circles, but always with the problem attributed to "change resistance" by bullheaded workers and supervisors. As far as Thomas was concerned, the workers' complaints signaled a defect in the training, not in the trainees or their peers.

Over the initial objections of the training department (some trainers assigned to the ICS project later became staunch advocates of the new approach), IRL's recommendations were put into place. Not only did the ICS workers prove themselves adept at teaching their jobs to each other, by their own accounts they were exhilarated by the challenge of doing something new and different. "It was the best sort of team-building I'd ever seen," says Rick Hawkins, who came to the ICS project from account administration. "It forced us to rely on each other daily." In learning new skills for the ICS pilot, Hawkins estimates he spent no more than eight hours away from the job, listening to coworkers in an informal classroom setting; the rest he picked up while on the work floor.

Dede Miller describes the experience as nonstop learning. "We shared information with each other all the time. Even when we weren't asking for help, we were learning because we could hear other people in our work group on the phone with customers, and we'd pick up tips about how they handled certain kinds of calls."

Today Miller sits alone in a cubicle surrounded by other workers, each in their separate space, each doing exactly the same job. Though the ICS pilot proved that workers can learn by doing and by teaching each other, the business case for ICS was less compelling. At a time when money was tight at Xerox, the expense involved in integrating service departments was not insignificant. Following the retirement of Curt Stiles, the operations vice president who had been one of ICS's most ardent champions, a decision was made not to extend the project beyond its original two-year pilot phase, which ended last July. (Xerox has, however, taken steps to instill the project's learning precepts into other parts of the company—including, of all places, the corporate training department. More on that later.)

"None of us wanted to go back to our old jobs," sighs Miller. "For the first time ever we were able to solve all of a customer's problems without having to pass them off to someone else. That made us and the customer both very happy."

Which makes it all the more frustrating now when Miller has to transfer a customer to another department. "I know I could solve their problem if I could just get access to the information I had back in ICS," she says. "I wish people could have understood why we were so passionate about making it a success and sticking with it. I guess we were just too far ahead of the curve on this one."

In fairness to Xerox, the document company has been no slouch when it comes to experimenting with new ideas about workplace learning. Its own Palo Alto Research Center (PARC) has been a breeding ground for some of the very concepts that the folks at IRL and a handful of other innovative consulting firms are trying to apply. Still, Miller is right about being ahead of the curve; these emergent ideas run so contrary to traditional approaches to worker training that even forward-looking companies like Xerox can expect to encounter slow going when they attempt to put them into practice.

At the core of the new thinking is the notion that work and learning are social activities (see box page 58). As people work together, they not only learn from doing, they develop a shared sense of what has to happen to get the job done. They develop a common way of thinking and talking about their work. Eventually they come to share a sort of mutual identity—a single understanding of who they are and what their relationship to the larger organization is. It is in these groups where some of the most valuable and most innovative work-related learning occurs.

A few years ago a formal-sounding name was coined to describe such groups: "communities of practice." But these naturally occurring communities are anything but formal; they are so informal as to often be nearly invisible. If you want to find out how work really gets done in a company, say adherents of the communities-of-practice persuasion, don't look at the organizational chart; look for the hidden associations among workers.

Though communities of practice exist by the thousands—perhaps millions—in businesses large and small, our work culture does little to encourage them. In the name of privacy and productivity, workers are isolated in cubicles and encouraged to communicate via e-mail (the word interactive has come to mean one person watching a computer screen). In the name of consistency, companies pen elaborate instructions for every possible process and procedure.

But follow the corporate anthropologists down onto the work floor or into the office labyrinth, and what you'll find are workers craning their necks like giant birds to peer over a cube wall and carry on a conversation with their neighbor. And if you listen in on the conversation... well, yes, they might be talking about the game-winning goal that Mario Lemieux scored against the Blackhawks last night, but it might also be that they are trying to figure out how to circumvent the official processes and procedures in a way that will allow them to solve an unusual problem that's cropped up with an important customer.

Learning and innovation happen on the job every day. That much we know. The question is, can the ideas bubbling up around communities of practice be used to map a strategy for moving away from the artificial "training curricula" we have today to "learning curricula" that reflect the way work—and learning— really happens?

Lest all of this be dismissed as some malevolent attack by outsiders on the training profession, it should be noted that the profession's own most revered gurus have for years given voice to ideas and criticisms virtually identical to many of the points the communities-of-practice newcomers are trying to make:

From Malcolm Knowles came the lesson that much of the expertise one seeks to develop in a group of adult learners usually resides in some or all of the group members themselves.

From Thomas Gilbert came the admonition that the way to find out what's worth teaching is to study master performers, and that the only way to discover the behavior that *really* distinguish master performers from ordinary ones is to observe the masters directly while they work. (No, he didn't call this anthropology.)

From Bob Mager came the demand that training be lean and elegant, focused relentlessly on the skills people genuinely need to acquire in order to perform the job, and not on extraneous material that some trainer or manager believes would be "good for them."

As for the nagging reminder that the way people actually acquire skills is by practicing them, not by being lectured at... ever hear that one at a training conference?

But such bedrock training and performance theories have always been honored more in the breach than in the observance. As the ICS project at Xerox

Practice, Learning, Meaning, Identity

The term communities of practice *was first coined by Etienne Wenger and Jean Lave in their 1991 book* Situated Learning *(Cambridge University Press). The theory and philosophy shaping this view of social learning have since been fleshed out and will appear in a new book by Wenger,* Communities of Practice: Learning, Meaning and Identity. *The book, excerpted below, will be published later this year by Cambridge University Press.*

Being alive as human beings means that we are constantly engaged in the pursuit of enterprises of all kinds, from ensuring our physical survival to seeking the most lofty pleasures. As we define these enterprises and engage in their pursuit together, we interact with each other and with the world, and we tune our relations with each other and with the world accordingly. In other words, we learn.

Over time, this collective learning results in practices that reflect both the pursuit of our enterprises and the attendant social relations. These practices are thus the property of a kind of community created over time by the sustained pursuit of a shared enterprise.

It makes sense, therefore, to call these kinds of communities "communities of practice."

...Communities of practice are an integral part of our daily lives. They are so informal and so pervasive that they rarely come into explicit focus, but for the same reasons, they are also quite familiar. While the term may be new, the experience is not. Most communities of practice do not have a name or issue membership cards. Yet, if we care to consider our own life from that perspective for a moment, we can all construct a fairly good picture of the communities of practice we belong to now, those we belonged to in the past, those we would like to belong to in the future. We also have a pretty good idea of who belongs to our communities of practice and why, even though membership is rarely made explicit on a roster or a checklist of qualifying criteria. Furthermore, we can probably distinguish between a few communities of practice of which we are core members, and a number of others in which we have a more peripheral kind of membership.

...What is shared by a community of practice—what makes it a community—is its practice. The concept of practice connotes doing, but not just doing in and of itself. It is doing in a historical and social context that gives structure and meaning to what we do. When I talk about practice, I am talking about social practice.

Such a concept of practice includes both the explicit and the tacit. It includes what is said and what is left unsaid; what is represented and what is assumed. It includes the language, the tools, the documents, the images, the symbols, the well-defined roles, the specified criteria, the codified procedures, the regulations, and the contracts that various practices make explicit for a variety of purposes. But it also includes all the implicit relations, the tacit conventions, the subtle cues, the untold rules of thumb, the recognizable intuitions, the specific perceptions, the well-tuned sensitivities, the embodied understandings, the underlying assumptions, the shared worldviews, which may never be articulated, though they are unmistakable signs of membership in communities of practice and are crucial to the success of their enterprises.

Of course, the tacit is what we take for granted and it tends to fade into the background. If it is not forgotten, it tends to be relegated to the individual subconscious, to what we all know instinctively, to what comes naturally. But the tacit is no more individual and natural than what we make explicit to each other. Common sense is only commonsensical because it is sense held in common. Communities of practice are the prime context in which we can work out common sense through mutual engagement. Therefore the concept of practice highlights the social and negotiated character of both the explicit and the tacit in our lives.

...Learning is the engine of practice, and practice is the history of that learning. As a consequence, communities of practice have life cycles that reflect such a process. They come together, they develop, they evolve, they disperse, according to the timing, the logic, the rhythms, and the social energy of their learning. As a result, unlike more formal types of organizational structures, it is not so clear where they begin and end. They do not have launching and dismissal dates. In this sense, a community of practice is a different kind of entity than, say, a task force or a team. While a task force or a team starts with an assignment and ends with it, a community of practice may not congeal for a while after an assignment has started, and it may continue in unofficial ways far beyond the original assignment. Based on joint learning rather than reified tasks that begin and end, a community of practice takes a while to come into being, and it can linger long after an official group is disbanded.

Asserting that it is learning that gives rise to communities of practice is saying that learning is a source of social structure. But the kind of structure that this refers to is not an object in itself, which can be separated from the process that gives rise to it. Rather it is an emergent structure.

...Indeed, practice is ultimately produced by its members through the negotiation of meaning. The negotiation of meaning is an open process, with the constant potential for including new elements. It is also a recovery process, with the constant potential for continuing, rediscovering, or reproducing the old in the new.—**Etienne Wenger**

illustrated, these ideas routinely fail to translate into practice within actual corporate training departments.

Discussion around communities of practice will undoubtedly get muddied once trainers and management consultants weigh into the debate. For now, however, it's worth keeping in mind that the core principles of this nascent perspective are profoundly simple, and they reflect something many of us know in our bones to be true:

- Learning is social.
- Learning happens on the job.

Though classroom instruction may sometimes be necessary, we should be leery of any training that fails to keep learning as close to practice as possible.

If the principles underlying the communities-of-practice thinking are simple, what can or should be done with them is another matter altogether. Even if the only thing you want to do is to observe the communities in place within your company, you first have to identify them, and that can be a challenge in its own right. Communities of practice may exist within departments, but they are just as likely to cross departmental boundaries. Don't be terribly disappointed if, when you find them, they don't coincide with the self-directed work teams you rolled out with great fanfare a couple of years ago.

Bosses can be surprisingly blind to communities of practice flourishing under their noses, observes Peter Hillen, a partner with Congruity Corp., a consulting firm in Los Altos, CA. "A manager will say something like 'I see you spending a lot of time with the guys in the sales department. I hope that's not taking time away from your work.'"

"What the manager doesn't realize," says Hillen, "is that the guys in the sales department are helping him *do* his work."

Some companies confuse communities of practice with competencies and go looking for them in hopes of cataloging skill sets and maybe even enshrining those skills into some sort of corporate knowledge base. It is true enough that knowledge is the coin of the realm within communities of practice; moreover, one has to be able to give as well as take knowledge in order to remain a member in good standing. But the knowledge that gets passed around in these communities is not limited to the sort of explicit information that can be cataloged or computerized or bullet-pointed in a training curriculum. Quite often it takes the form of implicit, or tacit, knowledge.

In a December 1993 article in the *Journal of Management Inquiry*, researchers Scott Cook and Dvora Yanow described how tacit knowledge is employed at three small workshops in the Boston area to produce some of the finest flutes in the world. Since the physical dimensions and tolerances of the flutes have never been explicitly spelled out, craftsmen rely on imprecise statements like "It doesn't look right," or "It doesn't feel right."

"Yet the extremely precise standards of the instruments, on which the flute's ultimate style and quality depend, have been maintained through these sorts of individual and mutual judgments of hand and eye," the authors noted.

If that sounds too removed from the work world that most of us know, there are examples closer to home. IRL's researchers have observed workers at Xerox who reportedly can tell by its feel in their fingers which type of toner will work best with certain types of paper . . . but only by its feel. Congruity's Hillen claims to know of a company in Silicon Valley where a $6 million piece of equipment used to make semiconductors works less well when certain members of the manufacturing team are absent, though neither the company nor the team members can identify the exact reason why.

Of course, the $6 million question surrounding communities of practice turns on whether or not these informal groups can be created—or, to use a favorite management term, implemented.

Virtually everyone who has studied them agrees that communities of practice cannot be created out of the blue by management fiat; they form of their own accord, whether management tries to encourage them or hinder them.

That consensus of expert opinion has not deterred some companies from attempting to decree them into existence, however. Etienne Wenger, a senior research scientist at IRL, is not sure what to make of the occasional e-mail he receives informing him that the sender has "just implemented communities of practice." Apparently Wenger is supposed to be pleased by the news, since it was he who coined the term communities of practice in a 1991 book *Situated Learning* (Cambridge University press), co-authored with Jean Lave.

So far, Wenger has managed to maintain an air of forbearance. "They haven't implemented anything," he says. "Communities of practice are already there; they've existed as long as humans have been working together."

A community of practice is not a magic solution that companies should try to create at all costs, says Wenger. In fact, communities of practice can occasionally be the cause of problems instead of solutions. Outside work life, support groups such as Alcoholics Anonymous are an example of a community of practice. But strictly speaking, a street gang also meets the criteria, observes Wenger.

To concentrate on communities as the end product leads you in the wrong direction, says Wenger. "Communities are a way of thinking about how work gets done, a language to talk about something we've always known—that people learn on the job and they learn from working together. The idea is to take that understanding and develop learning that reflects the practices in those communities."

That said, it's probably just a matter of time before we see two-day seminars on building communities of practice, in which participants are sent home with three-ring binders and detailed blueprints. "These sorts of grass-roots movements have a history of getting co-opted," concedes Wenger.

For now, the notion that communities of practice can be willed into existence finds its principal adherents in the buzz surrounding the Internet and corporate intranets, where collaborative groupware supposedly will enable knowledge workers to "hotlink" their bright ideas from cubicle to cubicle.

"One of the great myths of the Information Age is the idea that technology will create collaboration," says Brook Manville, the former chief information officer at McKinsey & Co. who now directs that firm's research in the field of knowledge management. "For years the IT people have rolled out technology thinking that communities will cluster around it," observes Manville.

It doesn't happen that way. Common work issues and a desire to learn from one another are the drivers behind these communities, not technology.

To put it another way, "No one has yet invented a technology that replaces a pitcher of beer," says Congruity's Hillen. Hillen has nothing against technology; his firm works with Silicon Valley companies such as National Semiconductor to help them identify and foster the growth of some naturally occurring communities of practice. "The Web and the Internet can facilitate collaboration, but they don't create it," says Hillen. "You need people together in a room where they can see each other before you get the kind of rapport that leads to real collaboration."

An unproven (and perhaps unprovable) conjecture circulating through the communities-of-practice fraternity these days speaks to that very notion: that face-to-face contact is a condition for true collaboration. The theory purports to explain why, at a time when so much fevered activity centers around distance learning, videoconferencing and the Internet, the number of business miles traveled each year continues to rise. "The speculation is that once people have had an opportunity to interact—so to speak—from a distance, it's only a matter of time before they want to meet in person," says Susan Stucky, IRL's associate director. "I just wish there was a way to prove the idea," she adds.

While it's generally agreed that communities of practice cannot be commanded by management dictum or jump-started by technology, it is very easy to destroy them by meddling—even when the meddling is a well-intentioned effort to nurture them.

One of the worst things management can do, says Hillen, is to "reward" an informal work group by giving it a formal job to do. "Open management's eyes to the fact that a certain group of workers has developed collaborative links to others in a company, and the response is likely to be 'Hey, here's a resource we didn't know we had,'" says Hillen. "The community of practice needs to do the work it thinks it needs to do, not the work some guy in a suit tells it to do."

A few companies have found that the best way to foster embryonic communities is to stand back and let them grow. One of the best-documented cases of hands-off management occurred at National Semiconductor a couple of years ago, when word drifted up to management that product groups across the company were seeking out the advice of a certain informal group of design engineers who had gained a reputation for doing superior reviews of new chip designs. Management was astute enough not to try to force the group to write up its rules or to create a computerized library of chip designs that others could copy. The only way to spread this specialized knowledge throughout the company was to let other engineers interact with it, to become members of the community if they could.

RL's Wenger likes to point out that all communities of practice are local. That doesn't mean there aren't communities whose members are geographically dispersed; it means that every community of practice takes a parochial view of the organization. That's why communities can be the source of problems as well as solutions. Their local viewpoint may keep them from understanding the needs of others in the company. "No practice has the full picture," says Wenger, "not even the practice of management."

Communities are not isolated; they must interact with others. And it is in their interactions across community boundaries where troubles often flare up. The worst problems occur when some external force (read management) tries to force communication across boundaries.

McKinsey's Manville describes a classic, and not uncommon, scenario: A company observes that one of its plants seems to outperform others. To ensure that a newly built plant replicates this same efficiency, a team of industrial engineers is deployed to codify every process to the nth degree. The problem is, the industrial engineers may not be fluent in the language of the workers who actually make the plant such a model of success.

The codified processes then get handed off to instructional designers whose job it is to build a training curriculum around them. Now you've compounded the translation problems because trainers speak a language that is altogether different from that of either the workers or the engineers. In the end, management is left wondering why the new plant doesn't match the productivity of the one it was supposed to replicate.

"The smart thing would be to send workers from the first plant to train the new workers," says Manville. "Knowledge transfer will be much smoother between workers who speak a common language." On top of that, you might even be sowing the seeds of a future community; workers at the new plant now know someone they can call up and talk to when questions arise.

One needs only to look at Xerox's ICS project to see another example of communication that failed to transcend community boundaries. After hearing from Xerox's customer service employees about the perceived shortcomings of the corporate training department, Cheryl Thomas tried to make it as clear as possible to Xerox trainers that the old approach to instructional design would have to change.

At first, trainers resisted. "That's not how we work," they told her. Eventually they agreed to create a curriculum that interleaved classroom training with on-the-job practice. But this first effort was an utter failure. The trainers took notes and made observations and returned to their Leesburg laboratory. When they unveiled the new curriculum, it was still top-heavy with classroom instruction, even though the lectures were now punctuated with on-the-job practice sessions. The employees complained to Thomas that nothing had changed; it was the same old approach, with only slight modifications, as far as they could see.

"We had to throw away the first attempt and start all over again," says Thomas. This time, she told the instructional designers they wouldn't be going back to the lab; they were going to camp out on the job with the ICS staff. They were going to observe how the work got done. And they would develop the curriculum pieces—small pieces—for those discrete parts of the learning that, the workers felt, couldn't take place solely on the job and would need some sort of formal discussion.

That proved a bigger paradigm shift than some of the training designers could make, and those designers were taken off the project. "We were lucky," says Thomas. "Of the six designers, three got the message. In fact, they ended up saying, 'You know, I always felt that it made more sense to do it this way.'"

"It's not that we, as trainers, haven't always known that it makes sense to do it this way," says Carol Ivory, a program manager in Xerox's training department. "We know that people don't learn everything they need to know in the classroom." But managers want something that is neat and clean and easy to schedule, so that's how training gets designed—around set chunks of classroom time. Tell the average manager at Xerox that workers will be cutting into their work time to train each other and you'll get a lot of resistance, says Ivory.

That's not to say there wasn't some resistance from trainers to that very same idea, especially from classroom presenters, who felt most threatened by the new approach, Ivory concedes. "As trainers, we think we need to control every aspect of the trainee's activity. It was enlightening to see the ICS workers take off on their own and come up with some very creative ways of teaching each other."

Though the ICS project was not extended beyond its initial pilot, one unexpected development grew out of it. Shortly after the project ended, management asked Thomas to spearhead an effort to push some of the ICS approaches to instructional design into the corporate training department. The goal would be to revamp the design process to involve workers and managers more directly, and to create training products that used more on-the-job practice and less classroom time.

"I'd never seen training anywhere on my career path," says Thomas. "All I knew about instructional design was what I'd seen come out of it, and I didn't like it." Did management realize what they were asking? Thomas wondered. Did they realize how big a change this would entail? Three months later, Xerox came to Thomas with a strategy document and promises of management support. "If you can recognize and leverage the idea of naturally existing communities of practice, training gets better because you're not fighting human nature," says Ralph Volpe, manager of Xerox's Education and Learning Unit in Rochester, NY. "Learning becomes more efficient and less expensive, and people like it better when you involve them in the development."

Or, as Thomas puts it: "You only need to have seen the difference between the way employees operated in the ICS project compared with how they did their jobs before to recognize that this is the direction we need to be headed."

Back in Louisville, TX, Dede Miller takes consolation from the news that the company is headed in the direction of the sort of nonstop learning she so enjoyed in the ICS experiment. Miller herself seems to be headed in the opposite direction. Beginning last month she was scheduled to be enrolled in the credit and billing curriculum for customer account administration. That, you may recall, is the 11-week marathon classroom event.

Though pleased to be gaining new skills, Miller can't disguise how little she relishes the prospect of 11 weeks in a classroom. "I like the show-me-how approach," she says, "Let me get my hands on the PC and let me learn. Three months in a classroom isn't my personal learning style."

Is it anyone's?

 5

Knowledge Diffusion through "Strategic Communities"*

John Storck
*Assistant Professor in the Information Systems Department,
Boston University School of Management*

Patricia A. Hill
*Manager in the Technology Strategy and Infrastructure
Group, Xerox Corporation*

Even though "strategic communities" are formed to meet short term operational needs, they provide long term value to their organizations through learning, innovation, and knowledge transfer. While similar to communities of practice, strategic communities differ in two respects: they are created by management to address broad strategic objectives, and they are focused around achieving specific goals. In this regard, authors Storck and Hill give us an insider's view of Xerox's Transition Alliance—a strategic community of fifty IT professionals responsible for maintaining 70,000 workstations, 1,200 servers, and the systems vital for Xerox's competitive success. Notwithstanding, Storck and Hill suggest that strategic communities provide a number of organizational benefits:

- Higher quality knowledge creation
- Fewer surprises and revisions in plans
- Greater capacity to deal with unstructured problems
- More effective knowledge sharing among business units and corporate staff units
- Improved likelihood of implementing joint goal
- More effective individual development and learning

Strategic communities provide a means for Xerox to exploit the tacit knowledge of its IT professionals while encouraging, rather than mandating, membership. Storck and Hill chronicle how the Transition Alliance created

---

* Reprinted by permission from *Sloan Management Review* (Winter 2000): 63–74.

significant organizational relationships that were formed through a shared communication repertoire.

Several years ago, Chase Manhattan Bank embarked on an ambitious plan to develop a common back-office processing system for its overseas branches.[1] The bank established at headquarters a cross-functional team of information systems, finance, and operations professionals to develop the design and lay out the implementation approach. Later, the bank added branch operations managers to meet "local" requirements. These managers retained their reporting relationships within their country organization structure, yet headquarters staff managed and evaluated their work on the project team. Conflicts were inevitable. After months of frequently fractious meetings, the headquarters staff prevailed, and a small group of branch managers reluctantly agreed to support implementing the new system on a pilot basis. Because the team concentrated on reconciling differences rather than on understanding similarities, the project was extended over several years. Ultimately, the bank achieved its objective of operating on a common infrastructure, but at high political, human, and competitive costs.

When facing a similar need, a large Korean *chaebol* took a different approach.[2] To achieve its objective of global expansion, during the past decade the company focused on building production and marketing capabilities in many diverse geographies. Developing management control and reporting systems was lower priority and was principally the responsibility of local staff in each country. Under pressure to improve the timeliness and accuracy of financial reporting, the small corporate staff asked the functional managers in each country to make additional investments in the infrastructure of their management control systems. General guidelines were communicated at occasional meetings in Korea. Although the local managers discussed the generic applicability of these guidelines, they did not have a formal mechanism to identify substantive changes and elaborate on requirements. Local managers exercised substantial latitude in system specifications and implementation approach. Thus, although the reporting systems improved, concerns remained about the reliability and consistency of information across countries.

These two efforts are examples of infrastructure transitions, complex undertakings that require the cooperation of broad swaths of organizational resources. Not only is the economic justification for such efforts frequently unclear, but the legacy infrastructure also must remain operational during the transition. In managing these transitions, most global organizations establish teams drawn from headquarters staff and line business units, as did Chase and the Korean firm. Typically, such teams operate in a matrix structure. The way they function follows one of two patterns. In what we term a "thick" matrix (e.g., Chase), team leaders from headquarters interpret corporate strategy and ensure compliance through governance processes. In a "thin" matrix (e.g., the chaebol), team members from line business units interpret corporate strategy and determine the extent to which their units should comply.

Xerox Corporation, in making the transition from a proprietary information technology (IT) infrastructure to an industry standard, took a third approach: the purposeful development of a *strategic community* consisting of a large group of IT professionals working at corporate headquarters and in the business units (see "More about the Transition Alliance"). We believe that this structure is a new, important organizational phenomenon, of great use in a world of increasingly dispersed human resources where firms need to wisely leverage their intellectual capital. For Xerox, this approach produced a variety of benefits. First, the strategic community provided a means for IT professionals to manage their complex infrastructure more effectively. They were better able to provide high-quality, validated solutions to issues; to handle unstructured problems; and to deal with the never-ending new developments in hardware and software. Second, the group operated as an efficient mechanism for knowledge sharing, which filters into the business units. In either of the more traditional matrix structures, knowledge sharing may occur, but that knowledge frequently remains unused. Finally, motivation for learning and developing at an individual level seemed greater in this community structure than in other organizational forms, which has important implications for the longer-term performance of these individuals at Xerox (see Table 5.1).

We use the label "community" because it captures the sense of responsible, independent action that characterized this group, which, at the same time, continued to function within the standard boundaries of a large organization. Similarly, we believe that establishment of the community was "strategic," because its members' activities centered on a broad goal—more effective management of the global IT infrastructure—that was integral to overall business strategy. Moreover, we suggest that, in many important respects, this group differed from a

---

More about the Transition Alliance

When fully mobilized, the Xerox Transition Alliance team comprised about fifty IT management professionals. Collectively, they were responsible for managing about 70,000 desktop workstations, nearly 1,200 servers, and various networking hardware—all considered vital to the firm's competitive success. Because Xerox had expanded its manufacturing, sales, and service operations into five continents, these IT managers supported diversified and highly dispersed user communities encompassing accountants and salespeople, service engineers and production managers, product managers, and people engaged in basic research.

The Transition Alliance's relationship to the formal organizational structure of Xerox was never well defined. However, Alliance members knew that senior management (including many senior information officers responsible for monitoring and allocating corporate IT investments) supported their activities. In fact, the Transition Alliance "lived" (and generally thrived) as a relatively informal entity in a fairly structured environment of defined roles and processes. Consequently, Transition Alliance participants regularly reviewed the Alliance's internal processes and responsibilities toward stakeholders to ensure their effectiveness.

TABLE 5.1 Forms of Governance and Leadership Roles

	Form of Governance		
Leadership Role	Thick Matrix	Thin Matrix	Strategic Community
Corporate headquarters	Designing and mandating strategy.	Providing guidance.	Defining strategy, providing sponsorship, and facilitating the community.
Business unit manager	Ensuring compliance with corporate mandates.	Interpreting corporate advisories and making decisions.	Sharing knowledge among business units and providing feedback to corporate headquarters.

task-oriented team. The strategic community established its internal work processes, and its organizational structure was fluid. Although membership was managed and defined principally by organizational function, individuals chose whether to be highly active. Motivation to participate actively was based mostly on needs: to improve organizational performance, to learn, and to sustain professional identity.

We describe the Xerox experience, arguing that the existing community was a more effective infrastructure management strategy than either the thick or the thin matrix. Because community members engaged in the same professional practice, one might think of them as a *community of practice*. However, communities of practice are usually considered to be voluntary groups that emerge from common work practices,[3] whereas Xerox top management quite deliberately established the Alliance. By contrasting the Xerox initiative with traditional community-of-practice views, we can begin to form an understanding of how other firms might replicate Xerox's success. We also illustrate how strategic communities create value for the sponsoring organizations, and we conclude by identifying principles that drove the success of the Xerox group. Our conclusions are based on participating in community activities during the past several years, as well as directly observing the group in conjunction with a research study.

BUILDING THE ALLIANCE COMMUNITY

At the end of 1994, Xerox was a successful, large multinational corporation with an aging IT infrastructure based on technology that Xerox had developed internally and sold to others with limited success. Although the firm's technology was superior to other products on the market, Xerox managers also recognized that continuing down the proprietary path would limit the firm's ability to develop new products with broader market appeal. Xerox also needed an IT infrastructure that could support corporate-wide strategic initiatives, including mobile sales and service applications and increased electronic communications with suppliers and customers. The resulting strategy was to establish a consistent, industry-standard office environment in all Xerox locations with improved corporate-wide ability to exploit new technology promptly.

To support the new IT strategy, Xerox hired a program manager, whose IT career spanned 15 years and several industries. She had consulted for large U.S. and European companies, focusing on strategic client/server infrastructure and systems development projects. Her listening and motivational skills were considered critical to the success of the largest infrastructure transition in the corporation's history. Her challenge: To persuade 38,000 people worldwide to retire their beloved workstations, many of which had been in service since the early 1980s.

Initial ideas about how to organize to accomplish the transition ranged from what might be perceived as one-to-one confrontations with each business-unit manager to a traditional, thick-matrix governance structure, in which the corporate staff sets goals to ensure compliance through regular progress reporting. To identify the requirements for success and the major barriers to a worldwide transition, the corporate information-management planning group sponsored a roundtable discussion of representatives from the organizational units. Senior information systems (IS) managers from nearly all business units sent someone responsible for retiring the proprietary infrastructure. During the initial 2-day meeting, managers from the corporate unit discussed their objectives and reviewed the status of their program initiatives. In addition, the group engaged in facilitated brainstorming sessions. Attendees unanimously agreed to meet again in 2 months, and thereafter agreed to convene at 6-week intervals.

The thirty to forty people who attended the first few meetings represented the stakeholders in the new IT strategy—the corporate information-management function, the business units, and the outsourcing firm responsible for day-to-day operations and maintenance. Each meeting began with a clear agenda, and knowledgeable participants were present to answer questions and engage in dialogue. Action items were noted, classified, and assigned: "A" items were important to the whole group, whereas "B" items affected a subset of the business units. Each action item had a "question owner," who would ensure follow-up by an "action owner." The question owner reported the item's status at subsequent meetings until they resolved the problem. A dedicated scribe recorded key messages, decisions, and things learned at each meeting. A collective, post-meeting quality check was a key source of feedback used to improve subsequent meetings. During the quality check, each participant stated high and low points of the meeting (including assessments of food and facilities) to identify ways to obtain greater value from the gatherings.

Early on, each business unit agreed to meet the corporation's high expectations for the transition. The annual process of setting goals and objectives for the entire organization specified that the legacy infrastructure had to be retired in 3 years to allow Xerox to focus on the support and growth of a standards-based architecture. Retiring the legacy system was a key plank in the overall IT strategy (called IM2000), and top managers had committed the corporation to this goal. As a result, the infrastructure management program received exceptional visibility at senior levels. At each meeting, the group tracked the number of workstations and servers retired on a month-by-month basis. Visibly demonstrating each business unit's progress heightened the motivation of team members to maintain a high level of performance.

During seven meetings held in the first year, topics ranged from infrastructure deployment plans to progress reviews about developing transition tools. At each meeting, the group reviewed previously identified action items. The participants started to publish a group-sponsored, company-wide newsletter for end users—an important communication device that solidified the group's identity. A year later, Xerox's CIO reviewed progress and provided feedback about the group's effectiveness. The group, which began calling itself the "Transition Alliance," defined its mission as follows:

"The IM2000 Transition Alliance advocates the requirements and concerns of end users throughout the development and deployment of the IM2000 infrastructure. The team will identify, communicate, and leverage best practices, enabling Xerox to sustain a more productive, profitable, and competitive environment."

This signaled a shift in focus from simply transition to a broader and more complex scope. The Alliance was not only replacing the legacy infrastructure, but was also trying to improve and expand functionality. For example, following rapid adoption of the Internet via the World Wide Web, the firm revisited its earlier technology decisions regarding an industry-standard infrastructure. The Alliance had to develop methods for distributing upgraded versions of operating systems and other software components via a redesigned global communications network.

Even with broadened goals, the group's perceived effectiveness did not decline. In mid-1997, the CEO of Xerox formally recognized the contribution of the Transition Alliance, identifying it as one of the top-performing teams for achieving the initial infrastructure transition on time and within budget. Xerox Business Services included material about the infrastructure transition in documentation that garnered the business unit a Malcolm Baldrige National Quality Award.[4]

As the Alliance efforts expanded, Xerox managers started to consider whether they could share with other business areas what had been learned about the formation and functioning of this group. On the basis of surveys and interviews of Alliance members, we make three key observations that we discuss in greater detail.

- The attitudes and behavior of Alliance members differed from those of a traditional cross-functional, cross-divisional team. The Alliance's distinctions, which closely resembled the attitudes and behaviors of members of a community of practice, enhanced the value of the group to the organization.

- The Alliance represented a strategic knowledge management capability for Xerox and provided a means of more broadly exploiting tacit knowledge than would have been possible in a matrix structure. Members explored potential solutions to issues, learned from each other, transferred knowledge into business units (and from business units to headquarters staff), and willingly applied what they learned. Thus, this approach was a good way to develop and maintain effective infrastructure management practices.

- Although the Alliance was established to operate only in one domain—that is, the management of IT infrastructure—its management processes, encouragement of individual learning, and appreciation of a community culture represent lasting value for Xerox.

NEW ORGANIZATIONAL FORM

Superficially, the Xerox Transition Alliance seems similar to the teams that Chase and the Korean chaebol set up to manage their infrastructure transitions. In all three cases, people joined the group from headquarters (selected for their specialized knowledge) and business units (selected for job function). The cohesive Xerox group effectively resolved issues and managed implementation of agreed-on solutions. We suggest that a group like the Alliance differs from a traditional team along a number of dimensions; moreover, its characteristics are similar to those of a community of practice. After forming the Alliance, corporate intervention was minimal, taking the form of sponsorship rather than integration with management processes. This explains our initial motivation for using the term "community" in referring to the Alliance. Yet, recognizing that top management deliberately established it to help achieve corporate goals, the Alliance was more than a group that meets occasionally to discuss common issues relating to a single functional or professional area. That is, the Alliance was not what most people think of as a community of practice, because it had a defined relationship to formal organizational objectives. Therefore, we add the adjective "strategic" to our term. Although the word "community" is frequently used rather loosely in reference to informal organizations, Wenger has outlined three defining "dimensions of practice" that can inform our thinking about why the Alliance was such a successful corporate initiative.[5] Next, we discuss these dimensions of practice and why the Alliance's organizational structure differed from that of a typical task-oriented team or a community of practice.

Mutual Engagement

Both task-oriented teams and communities of practice are characterized partly by the nature of their members' relationships, which begin after people are assigned to a team or become team members by virtue of their organizational function. In a community of practice, relationships are defined not only by the way people engage with each other, but also by their interaction on a "playing field of practice." While the shape of the field is independent of how people engage when playing on it, the field establishes an initial set of boundaries on their relationships.

Xerox encouraged rather than mandated membership in the Alliance. Many members characterized their involvement as stemming from their *own* initiative— supported, rather than directed, by their manager. Attendance at meetings and electronic distribution of materials was loosely controlled by the facilitators. To participate, sponsorship by a current Alliance member and an internal accounting transfer of a nominal meeting fee were required. Interestingly, when the fee was imposed after about 2 years of operation, there was no decrease in meeting attendance. Through normal turnover, members from business units and head-quarters rotated. A central core of about twenty members attended 80 percent of the meetings. Depending on the agenda for the meeting, people outside of the core were invited. Some of these attended three or four meetings in a row; others just participated in one meeting. Clearly, with forty-five to fifty active members, the Alliance was much larger than the average team, yet the Alliance did not include an even larger community of about 250 systems professionals who were engaged in infrastructure management issues.

The core members were essential to maintenance of the Alliance. The core was more open than a typical team structure, allowing time for new members to become full participants. One senior manager, who had taken over for an original Alliance member, recognized that it took time to engage with the other members of the group. He remarked: "The opportunity to do networking will be important to me once I get settled into my job and understand what is on my plate." Thus, relationships within the Alliance also had a temporal quality. In this respect, the contrast between the Alliance and a task-oriented team is subtle. Superficially, one important differentiating factor appears to be life span. How-ever, even though most teams in organizations cease to exist after accomplishing their goal, this is certainly not always the case. For example, just as the life span of the Alliance was initially indeterminate, self-managing teams in a production setting and top-management decision-making teams may be relatively permanent features of the organizational landscape. Expecting that relationships would persist, core Alliance members were motivated to invest time in getting to know new members, which in turn led to developing mutual trust. This durable Alli-ance, as an organizational entity, provided the playing field of practice for its members.

Alliance members who participated in our survey believed that almost two-thirds of the group's value was derived from face-to-face networking at the regular meetings. One Alliance member who had an especially expensive and arduous journey attended every other meeting and participated by audiocon-ference when he could not attend in person. The importance of maintaining personal relationships in this way also distinguishes the Alliance from other high-performing teams, for which research indicates that physical proximity is not critical.[6] Although face-to-face meetings are not a requisite means of interaction for a community of practice, most communities do work this way.

Authority relationships in a typical task-oriented team are organizationally determined. Although the Alliance resembled a large, self-managed team in some respects, there were two clear differentiating characteristics. First, the members of the Alliance did not select the facilitators. This was, of course, consistent with the original objective of establishing the Alliance: namely, that it was a corporate initiative guided by the headquarters-based unit responsible for infrastructure strategy and management (i.e., the Technology and Strategy Infrastructure Group; see Figure 5.1 for information on key organizational relationships). Second, Alliance members clearly distinguished between the facilitators and what we term "knowledge leaders." Facilitators promoted and advanced the discussion. Knowledge leaders transferred their experience—what they had learned on their own or in other group settings—and shared their insights with the group as a whole. Knowledge leaders emerged on an issue-by-issue basis. Our analysis of e-mail files showed little consistency in whom the Alliance members gravitated toward when looking for answers. They tended to ask those Alliance members who had demonstrated knowledge of an issue in the past. They also acknowledged a small group of people as "knowing who knows." This subgroup often was able to point a questioner to someone with an answer.

These knowledge leaders were not leaders because of their organizational status or the size of their functional group. They assumed the role of knowledge leader on the basis of their ability to communicate knowledge of a particular

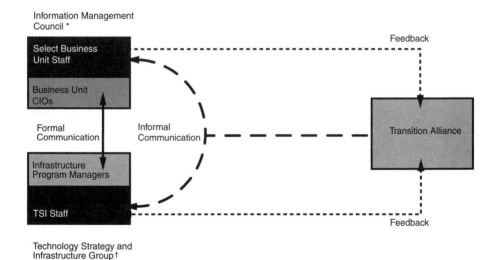

FIGURE 5.1 The Transition Alliance's Key Organizational Relationships

* The IMC monitors and allocates information technology investments for the organization.

† The TSIG is a corporate headquarters unit that designs and manages infrastructure programs.

field. This role also exists in a self-managed team. However, within the Alliance, the action-item process separated the knowledge leadership role from the facilitation role. The clear demarcation of responsibility helped Alliance members benefit from both the leadership skills of the facilitators and the knowledge available in the group.

Shared Communication Repertoire

Other important distinguishing characteristics of the Alliance as an organizational form relate to communication patterns and work processes. Most teams must satisfy well-defined requirements to communicate information to other parts of the organization. For example, teams may be required to submit regular status reports or to conduct briefing sessions for other units. Communication patterns both within the Alliance and from the Alliance to other parts of the Xerox organization were ad hoc and diffuse (see Figure 5.1). There was no formal requirement that the Alliance report on its activities. In fact, the first attempt to develop a formal process for informing senior managers of issues that the Alliance considered important was not successful. In lieu of standardized reporting processes, Alliance members used many approaches to inform colleagues of plans and issues, ranging from memos prepared after each meeting to hallway conversations. This resulted in an anomalous situation in which the formal organization that established the Alliance recognizes its value and provides support for its activities, but simultaneously did not incorporate the Alliance within its formal reporting structure and normal organizational communications patterns.

Within the Alliance, the communication repertoire was built upon the leadership training programs required for all Xerox employees. There was, as one Alliance member put it, "a vocabulary that everybody shares. The leadership programs teach people to listen." This person suggested that as a result of these programs, the Alliance was able "to distill consensus out of what appears to be a chaotic discussion."

Work processes developed within the Alliance supplement the common corporate vocabulary. As described earlier, handling action items, creating meeting agendas, and developing other processes were evidence of the self-directed nature of the group and, moreover, provided a context for communication. These characteristics are similar to those Brown identified when describing a community of practice: It has "a shape and membership that emerges in the process of activity, as opposed to being created to carry out a task."[7]

In summary, the Alliance exercised substantial group discretion not only in the scope of Alliance issues, but also in how the group defined its own operating environment—one in which the formal organization did not explicitly impose either work flow or controls. The level and frequency of engagement with each other built trust, which in turn reinforced the openness necessary to share fully. Unlike in the thick matrix of Chase, interaction was not required; Alliance members on the periphery gained even if they did not interact. When the knowledge flow was unidirectional, the Alliance was analogous to the environment of Honda's "brainstorming camps."[8] In such a setting, social interaction provides the contextual grease that allows practitioners of the same craft to smoothly engage their intellectual gears.

Joint Enterprise

The work of the Alliance was determined in part by the organization and in part by its members. During the first 2 years, however, the balance shifted toward what the members judged to be value-adding tasks and issues. In this shift, we see similarities in the way a community of practice negotiates the focus of its activities, and we see differences from the characteristics of a task-oriented team.

Most teams are predominantly oriented toward achieving a specific goal and, as noted above, most teams are dissolved after achieving their goal. Initially, the Alliance was also oriented toward a concrete goal—replacing the old, proprietary infrastructure—but as that was being achieved, the goal was supplanted and substantially expanded. The nature of work in the Alliance changed from a focus on current issues to a prospective focus, dealing more with infrastructure management practice. At first, one important new objective—global rollout of a new operating system—was similar in purpose and scope to the original goal. The members quickly expanded this objective to encompass other technologies outside of the operating system domain, such as a new e-mail service, remote access capability, and Web application features.

Thus, the work orientation of the Alliance became centered on the general practice of technology management as well as on the accomplishment of specific tasks. This became a key superordinate goal around which a shared vision and unified identity developed. Hackman uses the term "spiral" to describe how groups move up (or down) the performance curve from events that define their identity.[9] In the case of the Alliance, the performance implications of the upward spiral from the defining event—achieving its original goal—were primarily visible through the broader role that the Alliance played in infrastructure management issues. For a task-oriented team, the performance implications are usually measured only in operational output.

Alliance members determined their tasks and activities; they were not governed by a formal corporate structure. Previously hidden issues became explicit, perhaps because one-to-one discussions (business unit to corporate) were replaced by a forum in which people felt less constrained and more willing to express doubts, generate new ideas, and critique old ones. As one Alliance member put it: "Working with corporate staff used to be a series of ups and downs (mostly downs). The way we work has now changed. Instead of one-on-one discussions, our work is more of a joint effort that boosts everyone's performance." In seeking explanations for this change, we found that improved performance was an outcome of the nature of learning and knowledge processing within the Alliance and among its stakeholders.

NEW KNOWLEDGE MANAGEMENT CAPABILITY

We suggest that the Alliance represented a distinctive and informal, yet corporate-sanctioned, organizational entity. Nevertheless, one obvious question is: "So what?" To build on the description of the strategic community as a noteworthy organizational phenomenon, we identify the ways that it creates value. Specifically, we believe that the Alliance represented a new knowledge management capability for Xerox. This capability is replicable, provided that a firm consider the contextual characteristics of mutual engagement, shared communication repertoire, and joint enterprise. We characterize this capability as a way to manage knowledge because many of the outcomes of the Alliance revolved around learning. There is equally important evidence of more specific ways of adding value, as we discuss next. (For a summary of added values, see Table 5.2).

Over time, learning became an objective equal in importance to the information sharing engaged in by the Alliance members. In a sense, this was another superordinate goal of the group. One member said: "I gather information about programs and the methodologies that are being used to deploy development modules." At the end of a meeting, another member said publicly: "I am pleasantly shocked at the amount of information I obtained and how much I learned, even though not all of it is immediately applicable to my current job."

The lack of emphasis on positional authority elicited behaviors in Alliance members that were conducive to deep, relevant learning. However, one behavior that is particularly hard to teach is reflection. To overcome this, at the end of each day of the Alliance's customary 2-day meeting a small group of Alliance members discussed what they had learned that day. They distributed a one-page summary to Alliance members and to others in the larger infrastructure management community. At the meeting's end, leaders supplemented this loosely structured reflective process by polling Alliance members about what they learned during the company's usual end-of-meeting quality-check queries. Reflection is the mechanism that transforms tacit knowledge into explicit knowledge, not only for the attendees, but also for the larger Xerox community of interest.[10] The result is learning—individually and organizationally.

In practice, the openness of the forum and the different objectives of group members led to more opportunistic learning than occurs in a task-oriented team. Such learning becomes applicable beyond the immediate task, which in turn spurs innovation. When deploying new technology in a complex infrastructure environment, getting the technology "in the door" takes an extraordinary effort. The Alliance was consistently successful at uncovering operational implications—

TABLE 5.2 Strategic Community: Adding Value to the Organization

Nature of Added Value	Attributes That Create Value
Higher quality knowledge creation	• Diversity in membership and less emphasis on hierarchical status reduce the probability of group-think. • Limited requirement for formal reporting allows people to engage in riskier brainstorming. • Reflection process that occurs at the end of a meeting consolidates learning.
Fewer surprises and revisions in plans	• Broad participation diffuses knowledge across business units. • Openness of interaction format results in effective conflict resolution.
Greater capacity to deal with unstructured problems	• Work occurs under a set of superordinate goals rather than task goals. • Self-modification of the community role is acceptable to the sponsoring organization. • Knowledge leaders are allowed to emerge on the basis of issues rather than by assignment to a team or roles within a team.
More effective knowledge sharing among business units and corporate staff units	• Voluntary participation implies higher motivation that in turn leads to faster, deeper internalization of learning. • Indeterminate life span and long-term relationships increase trust.
Improved likelihood of implementing joint goal	• The community yields greater external validity because the community exists outside of the formal organizational structure. • The community has more influence than a single individual, particularly given the organizational level of the community members.
More effective individual development and learning	• Learning as part of a group is more effective than learning alone. • The opportunity to learn by engaging in practice is embodied in processes that the community developed.

those not identified or those of greater impact than the designers originally believed.

Moreover, the diverse makeup of this large group inherently meant there was less opportunity for group-think behavior to develop. In fact, the creative potential of the Alliance's heterogeneous membership was frequently evident. For example, representatives from corporate headquarters, the business units, and the design group disagreed with a supposedly carefully designed approach to software upgrades. Although at first defensive, after discussion the designers acknowledged that the requested modifications to the original plan would substantially improve the upgrade process. Collaborative, frank interaction at the Alliance meetings helped to validate knowledge beyond the initial output of the design team.

We also examined how learning became diffused throughout the organization. Typical of many teams, the Alliance was composed of people from different organizational units and disciplines. However, we believe that Alliance membership was more conducive to relatively honest opinion sharing. As described previously, people were encouraged to participate on a "need to know" basis, which resulted in deeper internalization of learning and better leveraging of skills. Furthermore, Alliance members, themselves, selectively facilitated effective diffusion of learning across organizational boundaries.

The application of learning differs in strategic communities and task-oriented teams. Most teams represent only a small organizational component, and they tend to be inwardly focused; typically, they are oriented toward completing a task. Wider dispersion of lessons learned greatly depends on a team's reputation, which may be organizationally limited. In contrast, implementation tactics and management practices that received the Alliance's "stamp of approval" carried considerable authority within Xerox. Alliance participants recognized that the sooner the Alliance was involved in an issue, the better the chance of avoiding a "replan." As a result, organizational units demonstrated greater willingness to modify plans when challenged. The authority and influence of the Alliance seemed to extend beyond its boundaries and reduced additional review and decision making in the business units, which were blindsided less frequently.

Almost all participants that we surveyed valued their membership in the Alliance and shared a sense of pride in belonging to this community. Sharing hundreds of years of collective knowledge fostered an environment that facilitated learning transfer and solved complex deployment and transition problems. Nonaka and Takeuchi use the term "community of interaction" to define the context in which knowledge creation occurs.[11] In the Alliance's strategic community, knowledge creation focused on what the members of the group practiced, namely, development and management of technology infrastructure. The members shared what they knew and learned through interaction.

PRINCIPLES OF EFFECTIVE STRATEGIC COMMUNITIES

Early in the life of the Alliance, some business-unit members expressed skepticism in the form of a "*we* vs. *they*" attitude. For example, one business-unit manager described the Alliance's objective as "rollout of their [i.e., headquarters'] programs into my space." Gradually, the Alliance developed, refined, and adopted processes such as agenda building and action-item management. These processes did not work perfectly, but they provided members with visible evidence of the commonality of their interests. In effect, interaction through adherence to these group norms stimulated and sustained the sense of community. Unlike emergent communities of practice, the Alliance did not form spontaneously or fortuitously around issues of common interest. Nonetheless, the processes and attitudes necessary to achieve the high performance and mutual learning characteristic of a strategic community had to develop over time despite initial corporate sponsorship. At the end of our study, members of the CIO's leadership team were making regular presentations at Alliance meetings, and business units were allocating budget monies to ensure that their managers could continue to participate.

Although a strategic community may focus on relatively short-term operational needs, it provides lasting value through learning, innovation, and knowledge transfer. The Alliance demonstrated that cultivating a strategic community is an organizational capability that maximizes the effective application of intellectual assets. Firms that want to compete in the knowledge economy must exploit the potential of strategic communities and sponsor their development.

How can other companies replicate this Xerox experience? Quinn suggests that effective organizations must structure their enterprises around intellect.[12] He uses the term "intellectual web" to describe phenomena similar to those that we observed in the Alliance. A company can create an intellectual web if the following key factors are present: regular interaction, mutual interest, recognition of the intrinsic value of learning, and incentives for sharing. Other research reinforces the importance of these factors.[13]

We have identified six key principles that were critical to the success of the Transition Alliance at Xerox (see Table 5.3).

1. Design an Interaction Format That Promotes Openness and Allows for Serendipity

In the Alliance, the facilitators managed a flexible agenda built around a few standard meeting components. Within this format, the role of the facilitators was clearly distinguished from the role of the group's knowledge leaders. In addition, the format provided significant time for social interaction during the meetings. Although electronic interaction (e.g., an e-mail distribution list) was useful in maintaining community-mindedness, we observed that technology alone was insufficient for effective community development. In fact, the Alliance members—all of whom were completely comfortable with a variety of interaction technologies—strongly believed in the value of face-to-face meetings. They told us that this was the primary means of shaping the deeper knowledge of colleagues and mutual trust that are precursors to effective group work with digital technologies.

2. Build Upon a Common Organizational Culture

Every Xerox employee must participate in the company's "Leadership through Quality" training program. A primary objective of this program is to develop sensitivity to the group dynamics issues that may limit productivity. Employees learn interaction and facilitation skills, but, more importantly, they

TABLE 5.3 Key Principles Supporting Strategic Communities

Community Characteristic	Actions
Interaction format	• Organize regular face-to-face meetings. • Stimulate candid dialogue. • Structure for serendipity.
Organizational culture	• Leverage common training, experience, and vocabulary. • Facilitate working around constraints.
Mutual interest	• Build commitment by demonstrating visible progress toward a common goal. • Promote continuous improvement of the community's processes.
Individual and collective learning	• Recognize and reward teaching others and learning from others. • Leverage knowledge and experience of respected peers. • Provide an environment in which reflection about learning occurs.
Knowledge sharing	• Embed knowledge sharing into work practices. • Reinforce its value with immediate feedback.
Community processes and norms	• Permit establishment of a "zone of safety" that builds trust and community identity. • Minimize linkage to the formal control structure. • Motivate the community to establish its own governance processes.

internalize the use of a common vocabulary that reinforces a strong sense of organizational culture. Appropriate application of acronyms such as TTM (time to market), XMM (Xerox management model), and XBA (Xerox business architecture) provides a common ground for effective communication and development of mutual understanding.[14] The result is a climate of social activism, in which the potential for counter-productive interaction is mitigated by following well-established organizational norms and processes. In this environment, the natural tenacity and determination of Alliance leaders produced successful outcomes from group work. Just as the leader of a jazz ensemble improvises around a theme familiar to everyone in the group, the leaders of the Alliance exercised these traits to develop and maintain effective infrastructure management practices.

3. Demonstrate the Existence of Mutual Interests After Initial Success at Resolving Issues and Achieving Corporate Goals

Group facilitators do this consciously by using and refining the processes that the community develops. In effect, these processes stimulate the emergence of "mutual influence systems" that mask differences in hierarchical status among the members.[15] These processes also balance local (i.e., at the individual and business-unit level) and global (i.e., at the corporate level) value. Combining flat structure and mutual influence processes results in high commitment to achieving goals, even in an organization strongly oriented toward control structures. Alliance members acknowledged their mutual interests and were willing to reconcile differences, recognizing that working together reduces uncertainty. After initial success, the community members grew confident that the group could get the work done. Broadly accepting that they have mutual interests and that everyone values sharing experiences led to learning.

4. Leverage Those Aspects of the Organizational Culture That Respect the Value of Collective Learning

Xerox not only values learning, but also appreciates the value of collective learning. Thus, Alliance members benefited from learning on an individual basis in a natural environment, in addition to learning from direct interaction with practicing colleagues. Rather than relying solely on a centralized "push" of information, a strategic community forms and shares knowledge by "pulling" individual members into an environment in which they learn from each other. Broadly based participation and engagement emerged as the dominant learning modes for Alliance members.

5. Embed Knowledge-Sharing Practices into the Work Processes of the Group

Xerox introduced this policy early in the life of the Alliance by asking business-unit managers to regularly present talks on their initiatives. Later, Alliance leaders introduced an agenda-building process—a means of polling members about their knowledge requirements. During the end-of-meeting quality check, they began to ask members what they had learned, which highlighted and reinforced valuable knowledge. In addition, a small group convened after each meeting to reflect on and record the key messages for the larger community. By incorporating knowledge sharing in group work, reflecting on acquired learning became a natural behavioral characteristic of its members.

6. Establish an Environment in Which Knowledge Sharing Is Based on Processes and Cultural Norms Defined by the Community Rather than Other Parts of the Organization

This is not an idealized view. In the Xerox case, the organization granted the community unusual autonomy to operate outside the formal control structure. This included, for example, the freedom not to report to the organization on the activities of the community. Here, the facilitator's role was to encourage openness and commitment to the group rather than to the organization. Over time, the community established a "zone of safety" for candidness. The facilitators also actively and regularly solicited feedback from the group to ensure that its work evolved in synchrony with its sponsoring organization.

CONCLUSION

We believe that developing strategic communities is of substantial value, and we offer some principles to guide achieving this. Although this article focuses on effectively managing technology infrastructure, we suggest that the principles outlined apply more broadly to the effective creation and use of organizational knowledge. By definition, infrastructure affects everyone, therefore effectively managing and using it can only be achieved by a broad transfer of knowledge. Strategic communities are an important way to attain this goal.

REFERENCES

Professors John Henderson of Boston University and Lee Sproull of New York University helped us characterize the nature and importance of a strategic community of practice.

1. This anecdote is based on the experience of the first author as a former officer of the bank.
2. This anecdote is based on discussions with a former employee of the Korean company.
3. See, for example:
   J. S. Brown and P. Duguid, "Organizational Learning and Communities-of-Practice: Toward a Unified View of Working, Learning and Innovation," *Organization Science*, volume 2, February 1991, pp. 40–57.
4. The Malcolm Baldrige National Quality Improvement Act of 1987 established an annual U.S. National Quality Award, which promotes performance excellence, improved competitiveness, and information sharing about successful performance strategies.
5. E. Wenger, *Communities of Practice: Learning, Meaning and Identity* (Cambridge, United Kingdom: Cambridge University Press, 1998).
6. For examples of groups performing work by using e-mail and other communication technologies, see:
   L. Sproull and S. Kiesler, *Connections: New Ways of Working in the Networked Organization* (Cambridge, Massachusetts: MIT Press, 1991).
7. Brown and Duguid (1991), p. 49.
8. I. Nonaka and H. Takeuchi, *The Knowledge Creating Company* (New York: Oxford University Press, 1995), p. 63.
9. J. R. Hackman, ed., *Groups That Work (and Those That Don't)* (San Francisco: Jossey-Bass, 1990).
10. J. A. Raelin, "A Model of Work-Based Learning," *Organization Science*, volume 8, November–December 1997, pp. 563–578.

11. Nonaka and Takeuchi (1995), p. 59.

12. J. B. Quinn, *Intelligent Enterprise: A Knowledge and Service Based Paradigm for Industry* (New York: Free Press, 1992).

13. For a review of the factors that promoted success in a variety of organizations, see: T. H. Davenport, D. W. DeLong, and M. C. Beers, "Successful Knowledge Management Projects," *Sloan Management Review*, volume 39, Winter 1998, pp. 43–57.

14. We appreciate the cooperation of Mary Anne Shew of Xerox for making available a working paper, in which she discussed the impact of these programs.

15. R. E. Walton, "From Control to Commitment in the Workplace," *Harvard Business Review*, volume 63, March–April 1985, pp. 4–12.

6

The Real Value of Online Communities*

Arthur Armstrong and John Hagel III

In this chapter, authors Armstrong and Hagel indicate that the Internet presents a social and economic opportunity for businesses to capitalize on electronic communities. While online commercial enterprises have done little more than advertise their wares or provide information about their services, they rarely encourage customer-to-company and customer-and-customer communication. However, by providing customers with the opportunity to interact with each other as well as with the company, organizations can foster deeper buyer relationships by customizing products and services to meet consumers' demands and interests. As a model for accomplishing this new customer-driven process, Armstrong and Hagel focus their attention on the following four types of electronic communities:

- *Communities of Transaction* facilitate the buying and selling of goods and services and provide information about these transactions. Participants are encouraged to interact to make informed purchase decisions.
- *Communities of Interest* bring together participants who interact extensively about specific topics of interest. Participants not only carry out transactions with one another, but their interactions are generally focused on a specific topic area.
- *Communities of Fantasy* allow participants to create new personalities, environments, or stories of fantasy. Here, individuals can take on the persona of an imaginative or factual being and act out roles like members of a spontaneous improvisational theater.
- *Communities of Relationship* center on intense personal experiences and generally adhere to masking identities and anonymity. Examples include cancer survivors and rape victims. Here, participants discuss the pain associated with

Arthur Armstrong is a consultant in McKinsey & Company's New York City office. John Hagel III is a principal in McKinsey & Company's Silicon Valley office in California. An earlier version of this article appeared in the McKinsey Quarterly *(Number 3, 1995) under the title "Real Profits from Virtual Communities."*

these experiences, talk about how to deal with personal issues, and exchange information about medical research and treatments.

Lastly, the authors point to significant management challenges in supporting, designing, and operating online communities as well as addressing new roles that may prove important in these online endeavors.

The notion of community has been at the heart of the Internet since its inception. For many years, scientists have used the Internet to share data, collaborate on research, and exchange messages. In essence, scientists formed interactive research communities that existed not on a physical campus but on the Internet. Within the last few years, millions of computer users worldwide have begun to explore the Internet and commercial online services such as Prodigy and America Online. Many have joined one or more of the communities that have sprung up to serve consumer needs for communication, information, and entertainment. One of the oldest virtual communities is the Well, launched in 1985 by a group of high-tech enthusiasts located primarily near San Francisco. (See the exhibit "Visit an Electronic Community.") Over the past decade, thousands of computer users have communicated with one another through the Well and, over time, developed strong personal relationships off-line.

Commercial enterprises—relative newcomers to the online world—have been slow to understand and make use of the unique community-building capabilities of the medium. Usually, businesses on the Internet today do little more than advertise their wares on the World Wide Web in the hope that somebody will buy something. For instance, flower distributors, booksellers, liquor companies, durable-goods manufacturers, and other businesses have sites on the World Wide Web where visitors can obtain information about the company and its products and send electronic messages to the company. Some of the more sophisticated sites allow visitors to play games and order products electronically. But rarely do these sites encourage communication among visitors to the site. (Meanwhile, most existing communities, such as the Well, are not business oriented; in fact, most strongly oppose the very idea of commercial activity on the Internet.)

By adapting to the culture of the Internet, however, and providing consumers with the ability to interact with one another in addition to the company, businesses can build new and deeper relationships with customers. We believe that commercial success in the online arena will belong to those businesses that organize electronic communities to meet multiple social and commercial needs. By creating strong online communities, businesses will be able to build customer loyalty to a degree that today's marketers can only dream of and, in turn, generate strong economic returns.

CONSUMERS' NEEDS FOR COMMUNITY

Electronic communities meet four types of consumer needs.

Communities of transaction primarily facilitate the buying and selling of products and services and deliver information related to those transactions. They are not communities in the traditional social sense. Participants are encouraged to interact with one another in order to engage in a specific transaction that can be informed by the input of other members of the community. Visitors to communities of transaction may want to buy a used car or a vintage wine, and they may want to consult with other community members before doing so.

Virtual Vineyards, a Web-based service that sells wines, is a community of transaction. The Virtual Vineyards site offers visitors information on wines and lists special deals on attractively priced offerings. Most of the wines that are listed are from small vineyards and are usually difficult to obtain. Visitors can purchase the wines directly from Virtual Vineyards, using an online form, or they can call the online service. Although visitors can post e-mail to the organizer of the site (and wine neophytes can post questions to the Cork Dork), they cannot yet trade information with one another. Adding that capability might add value for the site's visitors, making it a true community.

The organizer of a community of transaction does not need to be a vendor. Community organizers may simply bring together a critical mass of buyers and sellers to facilitate certain types of transactions. For example, a community organizer might offer electronic classified ads or provide a "marketspace" where everything from used construction machinery to financial investment products and services could be bought and sold.

Communities of interest bring together participants who interact extensively with one another on specific topics. These communities involve a higher degree of interpersonal communication than do communities of transaction. One community of interest is GardenWeb, where visitors can share ideas with other gardeners through GardenWeb forums; post requests for seeds and other items on the Garden Exchange; and post queries on electronic bulletin boards. GardenWeb also provides direct electronic links to other Internet gardening resources, including directories of sites relating to gardening. Participants communicate and carry out transactions with one another, but their interactions are limited to gardening. They do not discuss topics such as car care or parenting—topics which bring together people in other communities of interest. Nor do they share intensely personal information.

One of the most successful communities of interest is the Motley Fool, an electronic forum that two charismatic brothers, David and Tom Gardner, host on America Online. The Gardners began the Motley Fool for people interested in personal financial investment. They developed a portfolio of stock investments and invited people to comment on the choices made. The Motley Fool has become an engaging blend of information and entertainment. For example, in an area known as Today's Pitch, the organizers recently offered a short tutorial on why insider trading by managers of a company may be an important indicator of potential changes in stock value. They then provided a selection of companies in which insider trading had been particularly active and invited community participants to bet on which company would have the largest change in stock value over the next several weeks. The winner received several hours of free online time on America Online.

The Motley Fool has also aggressively leveraged user-generated content. Because the number of users and the extent of their participation have grown, the Motley Fool now offers extensive message boards organized by company, industry, and investment strategy. The forum also provides opportunities for participants to chat. The Motley Fool is one of the most rapidly growing communities within America Online, and it has spun off new communities that focus on entertainment (Follywood), sports (Fooldome), and popular culture and politics (Rogue).

Many people online today participate in *communities of fantasy*, where they create new environments, personalities, or stories. On America Online, a participant can pretend to be a medieval baron at the Red Dragon Inn. In this fantasy area, visitors exercise their imagination and participate (through typed, electronic chat) in the creation of an ongoing story of life at the inn. On ESPNet, an Internet-based sports community, participants can indulge their need for fantasy by creating their own sports teams (using the names of real players), which then compete against teams created by other participants. Winners are determined based on the performance of the real players during the season. Participants' real identities are not important in many of these communities, but interaction with others is at the heart of the appeal.

Finally, groups of people may feel a need to come together in *communities of relationship* around certain life experiences that often are very intense and can lead to the formation of deep personal connections. In communities of relationship, people often are aware of one another's actual identities—exceptions being communities formed around addictions (there is even a community of Internet addicts!), whose participants may prefer anonymity. The Cancer Forum on CompuServe, for instance, provides support for cancer patients and their families. Participants talk about how they deal with the disease and exchange information on medical research, pain medication, test results, and protocols. The forum's library features literature on cancer, which participants can download. However, the primary value of this sort of community is that it gives people the chance to come together and share personal experiences. Other communities of relationship on the Internet include groups focused on divorce, widowhood, and infertility.

Clearly, the four sorts of community are not mutually exclusive. When consumers shop for goods and services, they often seek advice from others before they buy, essentially blending the needs met by communities of transaction with those met by communities of interest. But currently, most communities target only one of the four needs. In so doing, they are missing an opportunity to exploit the online medium fully. Imagine an online toy store that allows visitors only to enter, buy a toy, and then exit, without giving them the opportunity to connect with one another—an experience that might encourage them to return. Now consider Parents Place, an Internet-based community for parents. Parents can turn to the community for advice on such matters as whether an infant should be put on a schedule for meals and sleep. Parents Place also has a shopping mall equipped with catalogs, stores, and services such as online diaper ordering. Price and selection being equal, it is more likely that parents will shop at Parents Place than at a competing site that allows only for transactions.

Organizers offer participants the greatest range of services when they address all four needs within the same community. In practice, this may not be possible, but community organizers should strive to meet as many of the four needs as they can. By doing so, they will be able to develop new and stronger relations with participants. A travel community, for instance, could allow visitors to search for information about museums and special events in, say, London, and even to purchase airline tickets and make hotel reservations (community of transaction). The site could offer bulletin boards filled with tips from people who have traveled to London recently; it also could offer the opportunity to chat with travel experts, residents of London, and others (community of interest). Travelers might be invited to join a game hosted by an airline running a special deal (community of fantasy). The site even could make it possible for single travelers, such as elderly widows and widowers, to chat and perhaps find compatible travel companions for a trip to London (community of relationship).

By fostering relationships and networks of interest, organizers can make their communities highly competitive. First movers can build a critical mass of participants that has the potential to make it difficult for new entrants to lure customers away. When Apple Computer introduced its online service, eWorld, to compete with America Online, CompuServe, and Prodigy, media and industry reviews generally agreed that it was an appealing environment and easy to use. But eWorld was not popular with consumers, who were frustrated to discover that when they entered chat areas, they could find no one to chat with, and when they accessed bulletin boards, they found few postings. A community full of half-empty rooms offers visitors a very unsatisfactory experience. The value of participating in a community lies in users' ability to access a broad range of people and resources quickly and easily.

CREATING VALUE IN COMMUNITIES

What will be the likely sources of economic value in electronic communities? Most companies investing in an Internet presence today are doing so cautiously because they are uncertain about the payoff. Pundits point out that the only businesses currently making money on the Internet are those selling products and services to enable companies to develop their own sites. Certainly, even under the best of circumstances, electronic communities may take a decade to grow to sufficient scale to be significant contributors to the overall profitability of a large company.

In the short run, however, businesses that create communities that satisfy both relational and transactional needs will reap the benefits of greater customer loyalty and may gain important insights into the nature and needs of their

The Impact of Electronic Commerce on Marketing

Most marketers today focus narrowly on consumers' needs within the parameters of their product category; at best, a marketer may analyze a few related categories. But few marketers (outside of advertising-supported media organizations) try to analyze the business of companies in unrelated industries that are targeting the same customers.

Marketers must expand their horizons as electronic communities emerge. They must learn how to cross-sell the products and services of the many providers within their community. Consider the role of marketing at a toy manufacturer that plans to participate in the organization of a parenting community. Marketers first must understand the full range of products and services that the community needs to provide if it is to attract online parents. These could include parenting magazines; access to book publishers, health care providers, and life insurance companies; links to brokers offering college savings plans; and even the products of competing toy manufacturers. Second, marketers must learn new ways to interact with the providers of those additional products and services in order to reach customers.

Also, marketers must learn how to take advantage of the technology that allows customers to move seamlessly from information gathering—finding out about a product through an advertisement or another user's online recommendation—to completing the transaction. This technology will transform today's marketing into tomorrow's direct selling. Marketers who are not currently in the business of direct selling, such as those in many consumer-goods companies, will need to learn the skills of fulfillment.

They also must come to understand the strategic impact of electronic communities, which in many cases will threaten the existing distribution channels of dealers, brokers, and retailers. Questions about channel strategy that marketers must answer include: What electronic communities might our customers belong to now or soon? Who will be organizing those communities? How can we use them to strengthen our relationships with our target customers—not just through advertising but as a means to stimulate greater trial and usage, or even to sell directly to the consumer?

Communities affect the very nature of some products; they even can affect how marketers define their business. For a magazine publisher, is the product the online magazine or the online community? If the online community features content from competing publishers, what business is the community owner really in? New business definitions may emerge around the notion of owning a customer segment across the full range of its interests and needs, rather than focusing on owning products and services.

Finally, electronic communities will offer marketers a wealth of new and quite detailed information about their customers—even about individual customers. Marketers will need to learn how to use this information to anticipate a customer's needs and respond to them instantly. For example, if a greeting card company or a toy manufacturer knows the birthdays and ages of children in a given household, it could market to the parents two to three weeks before the birthdays. This means that marketers will need to wrestle with time-sensitive microsegmentation—marketing to the individual customer at specific points in time. Marketers therefore face several questions related to information: What kind of information can we capture in electronic communities? Are our information systems equipped to access and analyze this information? Are we organized to market both more broadly to specific customers and more narrowly to individual customers at particular points in time? Marketers who rise to meet these challenges will hold the business advantage.

customer base. In the long run, electronic communities are likely to create value in four different ways.

First, communities can charge *usage fees*. This is how online services such as America Online and Internet access providers such as Netcom make most of their revenues. (Typically, customers pay a fixed price to access the service for a certain number of hours per month; when customers use the service for additional hours, they are charged additional fees.) Time-based fees may make sense in the short run, given the relative absence of other sources of revenue. They make less sense in the long run. Communities will need to maximize the number of members and encourage them to spend increasingly more time online—posting messages on bulletin boards and chatting, for example—in order to make the community attractive to others. Usage fees do not encourage members to venture online and discourage them from lingering there. For this reason, we believe that most electronic communities will eventually turn away from usage fees.

Second, communities can charge users *content fees* for downloading an article or a picture from the service's library or for obtaining access to material. *Encyclopaedia Britannica* offers online access to its content and varies its fees depending on how much information the user wants. Bill Gates has been assembling the electronic rights to a vast library of photographic and artistic images over the last several years, and one way for him to derive value from those assets is through content fees.

Third, communities can draw revenues from *transactions and advertising*. Advertising is already a significant source of revenue for many popular Internet sites. In 1995, online revenue from placement of advertising amounted to roughly $50 million to $60 million; according to best estimates. (The actual amount spent is not yet systematically tracked.) Still, this amount pales in comparison with the $140 billion spent annually in the United States on advertising overall to reach consumers in the home. It is even more difficult to assess—or define—the volume of transactions conducted in online environments. For instance, should estimates include business-to-business transactions conducted over private electronic-data-interchange networks? Jupiter Communications, a research company, has suggested that the value of all shopping transactions that took place over the Internet or through online services in 1994 amounted to roughly $500 million.

For most communities, revenue from transactions probably will be slimmer than those from advertising. Community organizers could take a substantial share of advertising revenues (although if they choose to offer their communities through an online service such as America Online, with its existing audience of 5 million subscribers, they may have to share the revenues with the service), but they will have to share a much greater portion of transaction revenues with the manufacturers and distributors of goods and services to the community. Currently, online services such as CompuServe usually receive commissions of 3% to 5% on transactions—not much more than commissions taken by credit card companies. These limited commissions reflect the fact that once the retailer's margins are factored in, additional margins are slim. Community organizers may be able to increase their cut of transaction revenues if they bypass retailers entirely and strike deals directly with product and service vendors. By doing so, a community organizer can become, in effect, the merchandiser and distribution channel for products and services and can command a retailer's share of the revenues (as much as 50%).

Finally, some electronic communities may be in a position to take advantage of *synergies* with other parts of their business. For a software company such as Microsoft Corporation, that could mean saving the cost of physically distributing new software or software upgrades. For some companies, it may mean reducing customer service costs. Federal Express Corporation allows customers to track a package online. This is convenient for the customer and saves money for Federal Express because it reduces the number of expensive calls to customer service representatives. Companies can benefit by following this model and moving activities from the physical world to the electronic world. (See "Exploiting the Virtual Value Chain," by Jeffrey F. Rayport and John J. Sviokla, *HBR* November–December 1995.)

How communities adopt these four models of value creation will vary, depending on the blend of needs the community addresses. Consider again the travel community that meets multiple needs. This community will probably derive most of its value from transactions and advertising, but it also may charge an access fee. A community for substance abusers, on the other hand, will probably have to derive its value primarily or even entirely from fees, given that its members are interested in a mutual support network rather than in buying goods or services.

Yet even though communities will rely primarily on just one of the four models of value creation, innovative community organizers will blend models. A canny organizer of the community of substance abusers, for instance, might find other sources of value to subsidize the cost of managing the community. Perhaps synergies for providers of health care services could be identified, for example.

MANAGEMENT CHALLENGES

Before they can capture new sources of value, aspiring community organizers face a daunting array of issues, whether they are assessing strategies for competition or designing and managing the communities. Everyone needs to learn the new rules for managing in online communities.

Assessing Strategies for Competition

There are two strategic questions that a would-be community organizer must face up front: How large is the economic potential of the community and how intense is the competition likely to be?

The elements that make a community economically attractive include the potential for a large number of participants, the likelihood of frequent use and intense interaction among participants, the attractiveness the participants hold for advertisers, and the expectation that participants will want to engage in frequent or valuable transactions. When assessing those elements, managers might look to specialty-magazine advertising or product-category retail sales for indications of the overall economic potential of a target community. Additionally, they might explore whether the community they are considering could draw provocative gurus or personalities who would attract a broader range of participants and spur discussion on bulletin boards or chat lines.

When assessing potential competition, organizers must recognize that some communities may have "natural owners." For example, magazine publishers are likely to have a head start in some areas because of their strong understanding of particular groups of people (young women, for instance) or of a specific subject (such as boating). A boat manufacturer intent on launching a community could end up competing with a magazine in which its advertisements regularly appear. The magazine, for its part, could view the development of a community not simply as an opportunity but also as a mechanism for defending an existing business—because through an electronic community it would be able to collect, package, and offer to advertisers more detailed information about participants than it could before. If, however, the magazine fails to allow communication among members of its audience, or if it blocks participation by competing publishers, it will create opportunities for competitors. More fundamentally, natural owners of a community are those businesses that have a substantial economic incentive to exploit synergies between an online community and a preexisting business. For example, can the Walt Disney Company afford not to organize one of the leading online communities that target children?

Designing the Community

In order to decide how to structure their community, organizers must look at how they might segment the community over time. The finer the segmentation, the easier it will be to appeal to people's narrow (and probably more passionate) interests, but the smaller the community's size. For example, organizers of a travel community could divide the community by continent (Europe) or by type of travel (cruises). They could divide each continent into subcommunities for each country of interest (Italy) and sub-subcommunities for cities (Venice).

Another design dilemma the organizer faces is whether to locate the community directly on the Internet or within a proprietary service. On the one hand, a proprietary service provides, among other benefits not yet available on the Internet, a ready audience, a technology infrastructure, security for transactions, and billing processes. On the other hand, it also is a powerful business entity standing between the community organizer and subscribers. A proprietary service that builds a critical mass of subscribers and erects barriers to prevent those

Visit an Electronic Community

The Well
http://www.well.com

Virtual Vineyards
http://www.virtualvin.com

GardenWeb
http://www.gardenweb.com

Motley Fool
available on America Online

Red Dragon Inn
available on America Online

ESPNet
http://espnet.sportszone.com

Cancer Forum
available on CompuServe

Parents Place
http://www.parentsplace.com

subscribers from switching may be able to renegotiate what share of revenues it takes from participating communities. At an extreme, the proprietary service could "backward integrate" by establishing communities of its own to compete with the communities it serves. Or it might try to disintermediate certain communities. For example, it might bypass a successful personal financial-investment community and offer subscribers direct access to checking accounts, credit cards, or mutual funds at an attractive discount.

Operating the Community

Electronic communities will involve a number of new roles. The "producer" (general manager) or any community or subcommunity will play or oversee at least six roles, of which the first three are the most important.

The *executive moderator* will manage a large number of system operators ("sysops"), who in turn will moderate discussions on bulletin boards and chat lines. Sysops—such as the Gardner brothers—resemble radio or television talk-show hosts in that they are, at their best, conversation managers. They help to keep the discussion focused on the topic at hand, inject new topics or provocative points of view when discussion lags, and seed the discussion with appropriate facts or content. Sysops must be able to transform the random, low-quality interactions that one often finds on cyberspace chat lines and bulletin boards into engaging and informative forums that will keep people coming back for more.

Community merchandisers will identify goods and services that are likely to be attractive to community members, negotiate with the providers of those goods and services, and then market them creatively and unobtrusively to community members. The *executive editor* will develop a programming strategy for the community (including content, special events, and the overall look and feel of the community) and manage the external providers of content, information, and services.

That leaves the *archivist*, who will maintain and organize the content generated by participants over time; the *usage analyst*, who will study data on participants' behavior within the community and develop programming or editorial recommendations for the producer; and the *new-product developer*, who will keep the community fresh and distinct from its rivals.

Partnering to Compete

Organizers must decide whether to build communities by themselves or to form alliances. Given the broad range of distinctive skills needed to manage a community successfully, it may make sense for many businesses to work with partners. For example, a magazine publishing company intent on forming a community will know its subscribers' interests and possess a large body of content, but will it know how to foster interaction among members of the potential community? The magazine may look to a large society, such as the American Association of Retired Persons, or to a smaller society focused on a specific hobby (depending on the nature of the community) for help. It also may look to those manufacturers or service providers that understand the key transactional needs of the members.

The value of successful electronic communities will be in the intense loyalty they generate in their participants, which is what favors first movers into this area. The organization of successful electronic communities will depend on skills and the right iconoclastic mind-set, not capital. As a consequence, this arena may favor bold entrepreneurs with constrained resources over established corporate titans.

Those titans who are tempted to wait and buy later should be warned that this market will not wait for slow learners. The skills required to participate successfully will be hard to learn quickly; and the premiums required to buy successful businesses will be very high. We therefore believe that any business marketing to consumers should make the small investment required to "buy an option" on electronic communities so that it can better understand both the potential value of communities and the radical changes they may cause.

PART TWO

Theory Development

7

Organizational Learning and Communities of Practice: Toward a Unified View of Working, Learning, and Innovation*

John Seely Brown and Paul Duguid
Xerox Palo Alto Research Center and
Institute for Research on Learning, Palo Alto, California

In this chapter, Brown and Duguid indicate that there are significant differences between the way that work is documented versus the way it is actually performed. Building on Lave and Wenger's practice-based theory, Orr's investigation of knowledge-practice, and Daft and Weick's interpretive account of "enacting" organizations, Brown and Duguid suggest that learning is the natural connection between working and innovating. By focusing on what the authors term *canonical* and *noncanonical* practices, they further conclude, "the central issue in learning is about becoming a practitioner, not learning about practice." As the community fosters learning, working, and innovating, the organization has the potential to become an overarching "community-of-communities." This allows it to capitalize on the innovative energy, learning, and working that reside throughout the entire organization.

INTRODUCTION

Working, learning, and innovating are closely related forms of human activity that are conventionally thought to conflict with each other. Work practice

* Reprinted with permission from *Organization Science*, Vol. 2, No. 1 (February 1991): 40–57.

is generally viewed as conservative and resistant to change; learning is generally viewed as distinct from working and problematic in the face of change; and innovation is generally viewed as the disruptive but necessary imposition of change on the other two. To see that working, learning, and innovating are interrelated and compatible and thus potentially complementary, not conflicting forces requires a distinct conceptual shift. By bringing together recent research into working, learning, and innovating, we attempt to indicate the nature and explore the significance of such a shift.

The source of the oppositions perceived between working, learning, and innovating lies primarily in the gulf between precepts and practice. Formal descriptions of work (e.g., "office procedures") and of learning (e.g., "subject matter") are abstracted from actual practice. They inevitably and intentionally omit the details. In a society that attaches particular value to "abstract knowledge," the details of practice have come to be seen as nonessential, unimportant, and easily developed once the relevant abstractions have been grasped. Thus education, training, and technology design generally focus on abstract representations to the detriment, if not exclusion of actual practice. We, by contrast, suggest that practice is central to understanding work. Abstractions *detached from practice* distort or obscure intricacies of that practice. Without a clear understanding of those intricacies and the role they play, the practice itself cannot be well understood, engendered (through training), or enhanced (through innovation).

We begin by looking at the variance between a major organization's formal descriptions of work both in its training programs and manuals and the actual work practices performed by its members. Orr's (1990a, 1990b, 1987a, 1987b) detailed ethnographic studies of service technicians illustrate how an organization's view of work can overlook and even oppose what and who it takes to get a job done. Based on Orr's specific insights, we make the more general claim that reliance on espoused practice (which we refer to as *canonical practice*) can blind an organization's core to the actual, and usually valuable practices of its members (including *noncanonical practices*, such as "work arounds"). It is the actual practices, however, that determine the success or failure of organizations.

Next, we turn to learning and, in particular, to Lave and Wenger's (1990) practice-based theory of learning as "legitimate peripheral participation" in "communities of practice." Much conventional learning theory, including that implicit in most training courses, tends to endorse the valuation of abstract knowledge over actual practice and as a result to separate learning from working and, more significantly, learners from workers. Together Lave and Wenger's analysis and Orr's empirical investigation indicate that this knowledge-practice separation is unsound, both in theory and in practice. We argue that the composite concept of "learning-in-working" best represents the fluid evolution of learning through practice.

From this practice-based standpoint, we view learning as the bridge between working and innovating. We use Daft and Weick's (1984) interpretive account of "enacting" organizations to place innovation in the context of changes in a community's "way of seeing" or interpretive view. Both Orr's and Lave and Wenger's research emphasize that to understand working and learning, it is necessary to focus on the formation and change of the communities in which work takes place. Taking all three theories together, we argue that, through their constant adapting to changing membership and changing circumstances, evolving communities of practice are significant sites of innovating.

1. WORKING

a. Canonical Practice

Orr's (1990a, 1990b, 1987a, 1987b) ethnography of service technicians (reps) in training and at work in a large corporation paints a clear picture of the divergence between espoused practice and actual practice, of the ways this divergence develops, and of the trouble it can cause. His work provides a "thick" (see Geertz 1973), detailed description of the way work actually progresses. Orr contrasts his findings with the way the same work is thinly described in the corporation's manuals, training courses, and job descriptions.[1]

The importance of such an approach to work in progress is emphasized by Bourdieu (1973), who distinguishes the *modus operandi* from the *opus operatum*—that is, the way a task, as it unfolds over time, looks to someone at work on it, while many of the options and dilemmas remain unresolved, as opposed to the way it looks with hindsight as a finished task. (Ryle [1954] makes a similar point.) The *opus operatum*, the finished view, tends to see the action in terms of the task alone and cannot see the way in which the process of doing the task is actually structured by the constantly changing conditions of work and the world. Bourdieu makes a useful analogy with reference to a journey as actually carried out on the ground and as seen on a map ("an abstract space, devoid of any landmarks or any privileged centre" [p. 2]). The latter, like the *opus operatum*, inevitably smooths over the myriad decisions made with regard to changing conditions: road works, diversions, Memorial Day parades, earthquakes, personal fatigue, conflicting opinions, wrong-headed instructions, relations of authority, inaccuracies on the map, and the like. The map, though potentially useful, *by itself* provides little insight into how *ad hoc* decisions presented by changing conditions can be resolved (and, of course, each resolved decision changes the conditions once more). As a journey becomes more complex, the map increasingly conceals what is actually needed to make the journey. Thick description, by contrast, ascends from the abstraction to the concrete circumstances of actual practice, reconnecting the map and the mapped.

Orr's study shows how an organization's maps can dramatically distort its view of the routes its members take. This "misrecognition," as Bourdieu calls it, can be traced to many places, including pedagogic theory and practice. Often it has its more immediate cause in the strategy to downskill positions. Many

---

[1] For a historical overview of anthropology of the workplace, see Burawoy (1979).

organizations are willing to assume that complex tasks can be successfully mapped onto a set of simple, Tayloristic, canonical steps that can be followed without need of significant understanding or insight (and thus without need of significant investment in training or skilled technicians). But as Bourdieu, Suchman (1987a), and Orr show, actual practice inevitably involves tricky inter-polations between abstract accounts and situated demands. Orr's reps' skills, for instance, are most evident in the improvised strategies they deploy to cope with the clash between prescriptive documentation and the sophisticated, yet unpredictable machines they work with. Nonetheless, in the corporation's eyes practices that deviate from the canonical are, by definition, deviant practices. Through a reliance on canonical descriptions (to the extent of overlooking even their own noncanonical improvisations), managers develop a conceptual outlook that cannot comprehend the importance of noncanonical practices. People are typically viewed as performing their jobs according to formal job descriptions, despite the fact that daily evidence points to the contrary (Suchman 1987b). They are held accountable to the map, not to road conditions.[2]

In Orr's case, the canonical map comes in the form of "directive" documentation aimed at "single point failures" of machines. Indeed, the documentation is less like a map than a single predetermined route with no alternatives: it provides a decision tree for diagnosis and repair that assumes both predictable machines and an unproblematic process of making diagnoses and repairs through blindly following diagnostic instructions. Both assumptions are mistaken. Abstractions of repair work fall short of the complexity of the actual practices from which they were abstracted. The account of actual practice we describe below is anything but the blind following of instructions.

The inadequacies of this corporation's directive approach actually make a rep's work more difficult to accomplish and thus perversely demands more, not fewer, improvisational skills. An ostensible downskilling and actual upskilling therefore proceed simultaneously. Although the documentation becomes more prescriptive and ostensibly more simple, in actuality the task becomes more improvisational and more complex. The reps develop sophisticated noncanonical practices to bridge the gulf between their corporation's canonical approach and successful work practices, laden with the dilemmas, inconsistencies, and unpredictability of everyday life. The directive documentation does not "deprive the workers of the skills they have"; rather, "it merely reduces the amount of information given them" (Orr 1990a, 26). The burden of making up the difference between what is provided and what is needed then rests with the reps, who in bridging the gap actually protect the organization from its own shortsightedness. If the reps adhered to the canonical approach, their corporation's services would be in chaos.

---

[2] Not all the blame should be laid on the managers' desk. As several anthropologists, including Suchman (1987a) and Bourdieu (1977) point out, "informants" often describe their jobs in canonical terms though they carry them out in noncanonical ways. Lave (1988) argues that informants, like most people in our society, tend to privilege abstract knowledge. Thus they describe their actions in its terms.

Because this corporation's training programs follow a similar downskilling approach, the reps regard them as generally unhelpful. As a result, a wedge is driven between the corporation and its reps: the corporation assumes the reps are untrainable, uncooperative, and unskilled; whereas the reps view the overly simplistic training programs as a reflection of the corporation's low estimation of their worth and skills. In fact, their valuation is a testament to the depth of the rep's insight. They recognize the superficiality of the training because they are conscious of the full complexity of the technology and what it takes to keep it running. The corporation, on the other hand, blinkered by its implicit faith in formal training and canonical practice and its misinterpretation of the rep's behavior, is unable to appreciate either aspect of their insight.

In essence, Orr shows that in order to do their job the reps must—and do— learn to make better sense of the machines they work with than their employer either expects or allows. Thus they develop their understanding of the machine not in the training programs, but in the very conditions from which the programs separate them—the authentic activity of their daily work. For the reps (and for the corporation, though it is unaware of it), learning-in-working is an occupational necessity.

b. Noncanonical Practice

Orr's analyses of actual practice provide various examples of how the reps diverage from canonical descriptions. For example, on one service call (Orr 1990b, 1987b) a rep confronted a machine that produced copious raw information in the form of error codes and obligingly crashed when tested. But the error codes and the nature of the crashes did not tally. Such a case immediately fell outside the directive training and documentation provided by the organization, which tie errors to error codes. Unfortunately, the problem also fell outside the rep's accumulated, improvised experience. He summoned his technical specialist, whose job combines "troubleshooting consultant, supervisor, and occasional instructor." The specialist was equally baffled. Yet, though the canonical approach to repair was exhausted, with their combined range of noncanonical practices, the rep and technical specialist still had options to pursue.

One option—indeed the only option left by canonical practice now that its strategies for repair had been quickly exhausted—was to abandon repair altogether and to replace the malfunctioning machine. But both the rep and the specialist realized that the resulting loss of face for the company, loss of the customer's faith in the reps, loss of the their own credit within their organization, and loss of money to the corporation made this their last resort. Loss of face or faith has considerable ramifications beyond mere embarrassment. A rep's ability to enlist the future support of customers and colleagues is jeopardized. There is evidently strong social pressure from a variety of sources to solve problems without exchanging machines. The reps' work is not simply about maintaining machines; it is also and equally importantly, about maintaining social relations:

"A large part of service work might better be described as repair and maintenance of the social setting" (Orr 1990b, 169). The training and documentation, of course, are about maintaining machines.

Solving the problem *in situ* required constructing a coherent account of the malfunction out of the incoherence of the data and documentation. To do this, the rep and the specialist embarked on a long story-telling procedure. The machine, with its erratic behavior, mixed with information from the user and memories from the technicians, provided essential ingredients that the two aimed to account for in a composite story. The process of forming a story was, centrally, one of diagnosis. This process, it should be noted, *begins* as well as ends in a communal understanding of the machine that is wholly unavailable from the canonical documents.

While they explored the machine or waited for it to crash, the rep and specialist (with contributions from the ethnographer) recalled and discussed other occasions on which they had encountered some of the present symptoms. Each story presented an exchangeable account that could be examined and reflected upon to provoke old memories and new insights. Yet more tests and more stories were thereby generated.

> The key element of diagnosis is the situated production of understanding through narration, in that the integration of the various facts of the situation is accomplished through a verbal consideration of those facts with a primary criterion of coherence. The process is situated, in Suchman's terms, in that both the damaged machine and the social context of the user site are essential resources for both the definition of the problem and its resolution. . . . They are faced with a failing machine displaying diagnostic information which has previously proved worthless and in which no one has any particular confidence this time. They do not know where they are going to find the information they need to understand and solve this problem. In their search for inspiration, they tell stories (Orr 1990b, 178–179).

The storytelling process continued throughout the morning, over lunch, and back in front of the machine, throughout the afternoon, forming a long but purposeful progression from incoherence to coherence: "The final troubleshooting session was a five hour effort. . . . This session yielded a dozen anecdotes told during the troubleshooting, taking a variety of forms and serving a variety of purposes" (Orr 1990b, 10).

Ultimately, these stories generated sufficient interplay among memories, tests, the machine's responses, and the ensuing insights to lead to diagnosis and repair. The final diagnosis developed from what Orr calls an "antiphonal recitation" in which the two told different versions of the same story: "They are talking about personal encounters with the same problem, but the two versions are significantly different" (Orr 1987b, 177). Through storytelling, these separate experiences converged, leading to a shared diagnosis of certain previously encountered but unresolved symptoms. The two (and the ethnographer) had constructed a communal interpretation of hitherto uninterpretable data and individual experience. Rep and specialist were now in a position to modify previous stories and build a more insightful one. They both increased their own understanding and added to their community's collective knowledge. Such stories are passed around, becoming part of the repertoire available to all reps. Orr reports hearing a concise, assimilated version of this particular false error code passed among reps over a game of cribbage in the lunch room three months later (Orr 1990b, 181ff.). A story, once in the possession of the community, can then be used—and further modified—in similar diagnostic sessions.

c. Central Features of Work Practice

In this section, we analyze Orr's thick description of the rep's practice through the overlapping categories, "narration," "collaboration," and "social construction"—categories that get to the heart of what the reps do and yet which, significantly, have no place in the organization's abstracted, canonical accounts of their work.

Narration

The first aspect of the reps' practice worth highlighting is the extensive narration used. This way of working is quite distinct from following the branches of decision tree. Stories and their telling can reflect the complex social web within which work takes place and the relationship of the narrative, narrator, and audience to the specific events of practice. The stories have a flexible generality that makes them both adaptable and particular. They function, rather like the common law, as a usefully underconstrained means to interpret each new situation in the light of accumulated wisdom and constantly changing circumstances.

The practice of creating and exchanging of stories has two important aspects. First of all, telling stories helps to diagnose the state of a troublesome machine. Reps begin by extracting a history from the users of the machine, the users' story, and with this and the machine as their starting point, they construct their own account. If they cannot tell an adequate story on their own, then they seek help—either by summoning a specialist, as in the case above, or by discussing the problem with colleagues over coffee or lunch. If necessary, they work together at the machine, articulating hunches, insights, misconceptions, and the like, to dissect and augment their developing understanding. Storytelling allows them to keep track of the sequences of behavior and of their theories, and thereby to work towards a coherent account of the current state of the machine. The reps try to impose coherence on an apparently random sequence of events in order that they can decide what to do next. Unlike the documentation, which tells reps *what* to do but not *why*, the reps' stories help them develop causal accounts of machines, which are essential when documentation breaks down. (As we have suggested, documentation, like machines, will always break down, however well it is designed.) What the reps do in their storytelling is develop a causal map out of their experience to replace the impoverished directive route that they have been furnished by the corporation. In the absence of such support, the reps Orr studied cater to their own needs as well as they can. Their narratives yield a story of the machine fundamentally different from the prescriptive account provided by the documentation, a story that is built in response to the particulars of breakdown.

Despite the assumptions behind the downskilling process, to do their job in any significant sense, reps need these complex causal stories and they produce and circulate them as part of their regular noncanonical work practice. An important part of the reps' skill, though not recognized by the corporation, comprises the ability to create, to trade, and to understand highly elliptical, highly referential, and to the initiated, highly informative war stories. Zuboff (1988) in her analysis of the skills people develop working on complex systems describes similar cases of storytelling and argues that it is a necessary practice for dealing with "smart" but unpredictable machines. The irony, as Orr points out, is that for purposes of diagnosis the reps have no smart machines, just inadequate documentation and "their own very traditional skills."

It is worth stressing at this point that we are not arguing that communities simply can and thus should work without assistance from trainers and the corporation in general. Indeed, we suggest in our conclusion that situations inevitably occur when group improvisation simply cannot bridge the gap between what the corporation supplies and what a particular community actually needs. What we are claiming is that corporations must provide support that corresponds to the real needs of the community rather than just to the abstract expectations of the corporation. And what those needs are can only be understood by understanding the details and sophistications of actual practice. In Orr's account, what the reps needed was the means to understand the machine causally and to relate this causal map to the inevitable intricacies of practice. To discern such needs, however, will require that corporations develop a less formal and more practice-based approach to communities and their work.

The second characteristic of storytelling is that the stories also act as repositories of accumulated wisdom. In particular, community narratives protect the reps' ability to work from the ravages of modern idealizations of work and related downskilling practices. In Orr's example, the canonical decision trees, privileging the decontextualized over the situated, effectively sweep away the clutter of practice. But it is in the face of just this clutter that the reps' skills are needed. Improvisational skills that allow the reps to circumvent the inadequacies of both the machines and the documentation are not only developed but also preserved in community storytelling.

Jordan's (1989) work similarly draws attention to the central, dual role of informal stories. She studied the clash between midwifery as it is prescribed by officials from Mexico City and as it is practiced in rural Yucatan. The officials ignore important details and realities of practice. For instance, the officials instruct the midwives in practices that demand sterile instruments though the midwives work in villages that lack adequate means for sterilization. The midwives' noncanonical practices, however, circumvent the possibility of surgical operations being carried out with unsterile instruments. These effective practices survive, despite the government's worryingly decontextualized attempts to replace them with canonical practices, through storytelling. Jordan notes that the two aspects of storytelling, diagnosis and preservation, are inseparable. Orr also suggests that "The use of storytelling both to preserve knowledge and to consider it in subsequent diagnoses coincides with the narrative character of diagnosis" (Orr 1990b, 178). We have pulled them apart for the purpose of analysis only.

Collaboration

Based as it is on shared narratives, a second important aspect of the reps' work is that it is obviously communal and thereby *collaborative*. In Orr's example, the rep and specialist went through a collective, not individual process. Not only is the learning in this case inseparable from working, but also individual learning is inseparable from collective learning. The insight accumulated is not a private substance, but socially constructed and distributed. Thus, faced with a difficult problem reps like to work together and to discuss problems in groups. In the case of this particular problem, the individual rep tried what he knew, failed, and there met his limits. With the specialist he was able to trade stories, develop insights, and construct new options. Each had a story about the condition of the machine, but it was in telling it antiphonally that the significance emerged.

While it might seem trivial, it is important to emphasize the collaborative work within the reps' community, for in the corporation's eyes their work is viewed individually. Their documentation and training implicitly maintain that the work is individual and the central relationship of the rep is that between an individual and the corporation:

> The activities defined by management are those which one worker will do, and work as the relationship of employment is discussed in terms of a single worker's relationship to the corporation. I suspect the incidence of workers alone in relations of employment is quite low, and the existence of coworkers must contribute to those activities done in the name of work.... The fact that work is commonly done by a group of workers together is only sometimes acknowledged in the literature, and the usual presence of such a community has not entered into the definition of work (Orr 1990a, 15).

In fact, as Orr's studies show, not only do reps work with specialists, as in the example given here, but throughout the day they meet for coffee or for meals and trade stories back and forth.

Social Construction

A third important aspect of Orr's account of practice, and one which is interfused with the previous two and separated here only to help in clarification, involves *social construction*. This has two parts. First and most evident in Orr's example, the reps constructed a shared understanding out of bountiful conflicting and confusing data. This constructed understanding reflects the reps' view of the world. They developed a *rep's* model of the machine, not a trainer's, which had already proved unsatisfactory, nor even an engineer's, which was not available to them (and might well have been unhelpful, though Orr interestingly points out that reps cultivate connections throughout the corporation to help them circumvent the barriers to understanding built by their documentation and training). The reps' view, evident in their stories, interweaves generalities about "this model" with particularities about "the site" and "this machine."

Such an approach is highly situated and highly improvisational. Reps respond to whatever the situation itself—both social and physical—throws at them, a process very similar to Levi-Strauss's (1966) concept of *bricolage*: the ability to "make do with 'whatever is to hand'" (p. 17). What reps need for *bricolage* are not the partial, rigid models of the sort directive documentation provides, but help to build, *ad hoc* and collaboratively, robust models that do justice to particular difficulties in which they find themselves. Hutchins, in his analysis of navigation teams in the U.S. Navy (in press, 1991), similarly notes the way in which understanding is constructed within and distributed throughout teams.

The second feature of social construction, as important but less evident than the first, is that in telling these stories an individual rep contributes to the construction and development of his or her own identity as a rep and reciprocally to the construction and development of the community of reps in which he or she works. Individually, in telling stories the rep is becoming a member. Orr notes, "this construction of their identity as technicians occurs both in doing the work and in their stories, and their stories of themselves fixing machines show their world in what they consider the appropriate perspective" (Orr 1990b, 187). Simultaneously and interdependently, the reps are contributing to the construction and evolution of the community that they are joining—what we might call a "community of interpretation," for it is through the continual development of these communities that the shared means for interpreting complex activity get formed, transformed, and transmitted.

The significance of both these points should become apparent in the following sections, first, as we turn to a theory of learning (Lave and Wenger's) that, like Orr's analysis of work, takes formation of identity and community membership as central units of analysis; and second as we argue that innovation can be seen as at base a function of changes in community values and views.

2. LEARNING

The theories of learning implicated in the documentation and training view learning from the abstract stance of pedagogy. Training is thought of as the *transmission* of explicit, abstract knowledge from the head of someone who knows to the head of someone who does not in surroundings that specifically exclude the complexities of practice and the communities of practitioners. The setting for learning is simply assumed not to matter.

Concepts of knowledge or information transfer, however, have been under increasing attack in recent years from a variety of sources (e.g., Reddy 1979). In particular, learning theorists (e.g., Lave 1988; Lave and Wenger 1990) have rejected transfer models, which isolate knowledge from practice, and developed a view of learning as social construction, putting knowledge back into the contexts in which it has meaning (see also Brown, Collins, and Duguid 1989; Brown and Duguid, in press; Pea 1990). From this perspective, learners can in one way or another be seen to construct their understanding out of a wide range of materials that include ambient social and physical circumstances and the histories and social relations of the people involved. Like a magpie with a nest, learning is built out of the materials on hand and in relation to the structuring resources of local conditions. (For the importance of including the structuring resources in any account of learning, see Lave 1988.) What is learned is profoundly connected to the conditions in which it is learned.

Lave and Wenger (1990), with their concept of *legitimate peripheral participation (LPP),* provide one of the most versatile accounts of this constructive view of learning. LPP, it must quickly be asserted, is *not* a method of education. It is an analytical category or tool for understanding learning across different methods, different historical periods, and different social and physical environments. It attempts to account for learning, not teaching or instruction. Thus this approach escapes problems that arise through examinations of learning from pedagogy's viewpoint. It makes the conditions of learning, rather than just abstract subject matter, central to understanding what is learned.

Learning, from the viewpoint of LPP, essentially involves becoming an "insider." Learners do not receive or even construct abstract, "objective," individual knowledge; rather, they learn to function in a community—be it a community of nuclear physicists, cabinetmakers, high school classmates, street-corner society, or, as in the case under study, service technicians. They acquire that particular community's subjective viewpoint and learn to speak its language. In short, they are enculturated (Brown, Collins, and Duguid 1989). Learners are acquiring not explicit, formal "expert knowledge," but the embodied ability to behave as community members. For example, learners learn to tell and appreciate community-appropriate stories, discovering in doing so, all the narrative-based resources we outlined above. As Jordan (1989) argues in her analysis of midwifery, "To acquire a store of appropriate stories and, even more importantly, to know what are appropriate occasions for telling them, is then part of what it means to become a midwife" (p. 935).

Workplace learning is best understood, then, in terms of the communities being formed or joined and personal identities being changed. The central issue in learning is *becoming* a practitioner not learning *about* practice. This approach draws attention away from abstract knowledge and cranial processes and situates it in the practices and communities in which knowledge takes on significance. Learning about new devices, such as the machines Orr's technicians worked with, is best understood (and best achieved) in the context of the community in which the devices are used and that community's particular interpretive conventions.

Lave and Wenger argue that learning, understanding, and interpretation involve a great deal that is not explicit or explicable, developed and framed in a crucially *communal* context.

Orr's study reveals this sort of learning going on in the process of and inseparable from work. The rep was not just an observer of the technical specialist. He was also an important participant in this process of diagnosis and storytelling, whose participation could legitimately grow in from the periphery as a function of his developing understanding not of some extrinsically structured training. His legitimacy here is an important function of the social relations between the different levels of service technician, which are surprisingly egalitarian, perhaps as a result of the inherent incoherence of the problems this sort of technology presents: a specialist cannot hope to exert hierarchical control over knowledge that he or she must first construct cooperatively. "Occupational communities...have little hierarchy; the only real status is that of member" (Orr 1990a, 33).

a. Groups and Communities

Having characterized both working and learning in terms of communities, it is worth pausing to establish relations between our own account and recent work on groups in the workplace. Much important work has been done in this area (see, for example, the collections by Hackman [1990] and Goodman and Associates [1988]) and many of the findings support our own view of work activity. There is, however, a significant distinction between our views and this work. Group theory in general focuses on groups as canonical, bounded entities that lie within an organization and that are organized or at least sanctioned by that organization and its view of tasks. (See Hackman 1990, pp. 4–5.) The communities that we discern are, by contrast, often noncanonical and not recognized by the organization. They are more fluid and interpenetrative than bounded, often crossing the restrictive boundaries of the organization to incorporate people from outside. (Orr's reps can in an important sense be said to work in a community that includes both suppliers and customers.) Indeed, the canonical organization becomes a questionable unit of analysis from this perspective. And significantly, communities are emergent. That is to say their shape and membership emerges in the process of activity, as opposed to being created to carry out a task. (Note, by contrast, how much of the literature refers to the *design* or *creation* of new groups [e.g., Goodman and Associates 1988]. From our viewpoint, the central questions more involve the *detection* and *support* of emergent or existing communities.)

If this distinction is correct then it has two particularly important corollaries. First, work practice and learning need to be understood not in terms of the groups that are ordained (e.g., "task forces" or "trainees"), but in terms of the communities that emerge. The latter are likely to be noncanonical (though not necessarily so) while the former are likely to be canonical. Looking only at canonical groups, whose configuration often conceals extremely influential interstitial communities, will not provide a clear picture of how work or learning is actually organized and accomplished. It will only reflect the dominant assumptions of the organizational core.

Second, attempts to introduce "teams" and "work groups" into the workplace to enhance learning or work practice are often based on an assumption that without impetus from above, an organization's members configure themselves as individuals. In fact, as we suggest, people work and learn collaboratively and vital interstitial communities are continually being formed and reformed. The reorganization of the workplace into canonical groups can wittingly or unwittingly disrupt these highly functional noncanonical—and therefore often invisible—communities. Orr argues:

> The process of working and learning together creates a work situation which the workers value, and they resist having it disrupted by their employers through events such as a reorganization of the work. This resistance can surprise employers who think of labor as a commodity to arrange to suit their ends. The problem for the workers is that this community which they have created was not part of the series of discrete employment agreements by which the employer populated the work place, nor is the role of the community in doing the work acknowledged. *The work can only continue free of disruption if the employer can be persuaded to see the community as necessary to accomplishing work* (Orr 1990, 48, emphasis added).

b. Fostering Learning

Given a community-based analysis of learning so congruent with Orr's analysis of working, the question arises, how is it possible to foster learning-in-working? The answer is inevitably complex, not least because all the intricacies of context, which the pedagogic approach has always assumed could be stripped away, now have to be taken back into consideration. On the other hand, the ability of people to learn *in situ*, suggests that as a fundamental principle for supporting learning, attempts to strip away context should be examined with caution. If learners need access to practitioners at work, it is essential to question didactic approaches, with their tendency to separate learners from the target community and the authentic work practices. Learning is fostered by fostering access to and membership of the target community of practice, not by explicating abstractions of individual practice. Thus central to the process are the recognition and legitimation of community practices.

Reliance on formal descriptions of work, explicit syllabuses for learning about it, and canonical groups to carry it out immediately set organizations at a disadvantage. This approach, as we have noted, can simply blind management to the practices and communities that actually make things happen. In particular, it can lead to the isolation of learners, who will then be unable to acquire the implicit practices required for work. Marshall (in Lave and Wenger 1990) describes a case of apprenticeship for butchers in which learning was extremely restricted because, among other things, "apprentices...could not watch journeymen cut and saw meat" (p. 19). Formal training in cutting and sawing is quite different from the understanding of practice gleaned through informal observation that copresence makes possible and absence obviously excludes. These trainees were simply denied the chance to become legitimate peripheral participants. If training is designed so that learners cannot observe the activity of practitioners, learning is inevitably impoverished.

Legitimacy and peripherality are intertwined in a complex way. Occasionally, learners (like the apprentice butchers) are granted legitimacy but are denied peripherality. Conversely, they can be granted peripherality but denied legitimacy. Martin (1982) gives examples of organizations in which legitimacy is explicitly denied in instances of "open door" management, where members come to realize that, though the door is open, it is wiser not to cross the threshold. If either legitimacy or peripherality is denied, learning will be significantly more difficult.

For learners, then, a position on the periphery of practice is important. It is also easily overlooked and increasingly risks being "designed out," leaving people physically or socially isolated and justifiably uncertain whether, for instance, their errors are inevitable or the result of personal inadequacies. It is a significant challenge for design to ensure that new collaborative technologies, designed as they so often are around formal descriptions of work, do not exclude this sort of implicit, extendable, informal periphery. Learners need legitimate access to the periphery of communication—to computer mail, to formal and informal meetings, to telephone conversations, etc., and, of course, to war stories. They pick up invaluable "know how"—not just information but also manner and technique—from being on the periphery of competent practitioners going about their business. Furthermore, it is important to consider the periphery not only because it is an important site of learning, but also because, as the next section proposes, it can be an important site for innovation.

3. INNOVATING

One of the central benefits of these small, self-constituting communities we have been describing is that they evade the ossifying tendencies of large organizations. Canonical accounts of work are not only hard to apply and hard to learn. They are also hard to change. Yet the actual behaviors of communities of practice are constantly changing both as newcomers replace old timers and as the demands of practice force the community to revise its relationship to its environment. Communities of practice like the reps' continue to develop a rich, fluid, noncanonical world view to bridge the gap between their organization's static canonical view and the challenge of changing practice. This process of development is inherently innovative. "Maverick" communities of this sort offer the core of a large organization a means and a model to examine the potential of alternative views of organizational activity through spontaneously occurring experiments that are simultaneously informed and checked by experience. These, it has been argued (Hedberg, Nystrom and Starbuck 1976; Schein 1990), drive innovation by allowing the parts of an organization to step outside the organization's inevitably limited core world view and simply try something new. Unfortunately, people in the core of large organizations too often regard these noncanonical practices (if they see them at all) as counterproductive.

For a theoretical account of this sort of innovation, we turn to Daft and Weick's (1984) discussion of interpretive innovation. They propose a matrix of four different kinds of organization, each characterized by its relationship to its environment. They name these relationships "undirected viewing," "conditioned viewing," "discovering," and "enacting." Only the last two concern us here. It is important to note that Daft and Weick too see the community and not the individual "inventor" as the central unit of analysis in understanding innovating practice.

The *discovering organization* is the archetype of the conventional innovative organization, one which responds—often with great efficiency—to changes it detects in its environment. The organization presupposes an essentially prestructured environment and implicitly assumes that there is a correct response to any condition it discovers there. By contrast, the *enacting organization* is proactive and highly interpretive. Not only does it respond to its environment, but also, in a fundamental way, it creates many of the conditions to which it must respond. Daft and Weick describe enacting organizations as follows:

> These organizations construct their own environments. They gather information by trying new behaviors and seeing what happens. They experiment, test, and stimulate, and they ignore precedent, rules, and traditional expectations (Daft and Weick 1984, p. 288).

Innovation, in this view, is not simply a response to empirical observations of the environment. The source of innovation lies on the interface between an organization and its environment. And the process of innovating involves actively constructing a conceptual framework, imposing it on the environment, and reflecting on their interaction. With few changes, this could be a description of the activity of inventive, noncanonical groups, such as Orr's reps, who similarly "ignore precedent, rules, and traditional expectations" and break conventional boundaries. Like storytelling, enacting is a process of interpretive sense making and controlled change.

A brief example of enacting can be seen in the introduction of the IBM Mag-I memory typewriter "as a new way of organizing office work" (Pava cited in Barley 1988). In order to make sense and full use of the power of this typewriter, the conditions in which it was to be used had to be reconceived. In the old conception of office work, the potential of the machine could not be realized. In a newly conceived understanding of office practice, however, the machine could prove highly innovative. Though this new conception could not be achieved without the new machine, the new machine could not be fully realized without the conception. The two changes went along together. Neither is wholly either cause or effect. Enacting organizations differ from discovering ones in that in this reciprocal way, instead of waiting for changed practices to emerge and responding, they enable them to emerge and anticipate their effects.

Reregistering the environment is widely recognized as a powerful source of innovation that moves organizations beyond the paradigms in which they begin their analysis and within which, without such a reformation, they must inevitably end it. This is the problem which Deetz and Kersten (1983) describe as closure: "Many organizations fail because...closure prohibits adaptation to current social conditions" (p. 166). Putnam (1983) argues that closure-generating structures appear to be "fixtures that exist independent of the processes that create and transform them" (p. 36). Interpretive or enacting organizations, aware as they are that their environment is not a given, can potentially adopt new viewpoints that allow them to see beyond the closure-imposing boundary of a single world view.

The question remains, however, how is this reregistering brought about by organizations that seem inescapably trapped within their own world view? We are claiming that the actual noncanonical practices of interstitial communities are continually developing new interpretations of the world because they have a practical rather than formal connection to that world. (For a theoretical account of the way practice drives change in world view, see Bloch 1977.) To pursue our connection with the work of the reps, closure is the likely result of rigid adherence to the reps' training and documentation and the formal account of work that they encompass. In order to get on with their work, reps overcome closure by reregistering their interpretation of the machine and its ever changing milieu. Rejection of a canonical, predetermined view and the construction through narration of an alternative view, such as Orr describes, involve, at heart, the complex intuitive process of bringing the communicative, community schema into harmony with the environment by reformulating both. The potential of such innovation is, however, lost to an organization that remains blind to noncanonical practice.

An enacting organization must also be capable of reconceiving not only its environment but also its own identity, for in a significant sense the two are mutually constitutive. Again, this reconceptualization is something that people who develop noncanonical practices are continuously doing, forging their own and their community's identity in their own terms so that they can break out of the restrictive hold of the formal descriptions of practice. Enacting organizations similarly regard both their environment and themselves as in some sense unanalyzed and therefore malleable. They do not assume that there is an ineluctable structure, a "right" answer, or a universal view to be discovered; rather, they continually look for innovative ways to impose new structure, ask new questions, develop a new view, become a new organization. By asking different questions, by seeking different *sorts* of explanations, and by looking from different points of view, different answers emerge—indeed different environments and different organizations mutually reconstitute each other dialectically or reciprocally. Daft and Weick (1984) argue, the interpretation can "shape the environment more than the environment shapes the interpretation" (p. 287).

Carlson's attempts to interest people in the idea of dry photocopying—xerography—provide an example of organizational tendencies to resist enacting innovation. Carlson and the Batelle Institute, which backed his research, approached most of the major innovative corporations of the time—RCA, IBM, A. B. Dick, Kodak. All turned down the idea of a dry copier. They did not reject a flawed machine. Indeed, they all agreed that it worked. But they rejected the *concept* of an office copier. They could see no use for it. Even when Haloid bought the patent, the marketing firms they hired consistently reported that the new device had no role in office practice (Dessauer 1971). In some sense it was necessary both for Haloid to reconceive itself (as Xerox) and for Xerox's machine to help bring about a reconcentualization of an area of office practice for the new machine to be put into manufacture and use.

What the evaluations saw was that an expensive machine was not needed to make a record copy of original documents. For the most part, carbon paper already did that admirably and cheaply. What they failed to see was that a copier allowed the proliferation of copies and of copies of copies. The quantitative leap in copies and their importance independent of the original then produced a qualitative leap in the way they were used. They no longer served merely as records of an original. Instead, they participated in the productive interactions of organizations' members in a unprecedented way. (See Latour's [1986] description of the organizational role of "immutable mobiles.") Only in use in the office, enabling and enhancing new forms of work, did the copier forge the conceptual lenses under which its value became inescapable.

It is this process of seeing the world anew that allows organizations reciprocally to see themselves anew and to overcome discontinuities in their environment and their structure. As von Hippel (1988), Barley (1988), and others point out, innovating is not always radical. Incremental improvements occur throughout an innovative organization. Enacting and innovating can be conceived of as at root sense-making, congruence-seeking, identity-building activities of the sort engaged in by the reps. Innovating and learning in daily activity lie at one end of a continuum of innovating practices that stretches to radical innovation cultivated in research laboratories at the far end.

Alternative world views, then, do not lie in the laboratory or strategic planning office alone, condemning everyone else in the organization to submit to a unitary culture. Alternatives are inevitably distributed throughout all the different communities that make up the organization. For it is the organization's communities, at all levels, who are in contact with the environment and involved in interpretive sense making, congruence finding, and adapting. It is from any site of such interactions that new insights can be coproduced. If an organizational core overlooks or curtails the enacting in its midst by ignoring or disrupting its communities of practice, it threatens its own survival in two ways. It will not only threaten to destroy the very working and learning practices by which it, knowingly or unknowingly, survives. It will also cut itself off from a major source of potential innovation that inevitably arises in the course of that working and learning.

4. CONCLUSION: ORGANIZATIONS AS COMMUNITIES OF COMMUNITIES

The complex of contradictory forces that put an organization's assumptions and core beliefs in direct conflict with members' working, learning, and innovating arises from a thorough misunderstanding of what working, learning, and innovating are. As a result of such misunderstandings, many modern processes and technologies, particularly those designed to downskill, threaten the robust working, learning, and innovating communities and practice of the workplace. Between Braverman's (1974) pessimistic view and Adler's (1987) optimistic one, lies Barley's (1988) complex argument, pointing out that the intent to downskill does not *necessarily* lead to downskilling (as Orr's reps show). But the intent to downskill may first drive noncanonical practice and communities yet further underground so that the insights gained through work are more completely hidden from the organization as a whole. Then later changes or reorganizations, whether or not intended to downskill, may disrupt what they do not notice. The gap between espoused and actual practice may become too large for noncanonical practices to bridge.

To foster working, learning, and innovating, an organization must close that gap. To do so, it needs to reconceive of itself as a community-of-communities, acknowledging in the process the many noncanonical communities in its midst. It must see beyond its canonical abstractions of practice to the rich, full-blooded activities themselves. And it must legitimize and support the myriad enacting activities perpetrated by its different members. This support cannot be intrusive, or it risks merely bringing potential innovators under the restrictive influence of the existing canonical view. Rather, as others have argued (Nystrom and Starbuck 1984; Hedberg 1981; Schein 1990) communities of practice must be allowed some latitude to shake themselves free of received wisdom.

A major entailment of this argument may be quite surprising. Conventional wisdom tends to hold that large organizations are particularly poor at innovating and adapting. Tushman and Anderson (1988), for example, argue justifiably that the *typical*, large organization is unlikely to produce discontinuous innovation. But size may not be the single determining feature here. Large, *atypical*, enacting organizations have the potential to be highly innovative and adaptive. Within an organization perceived as a collective of communities, not simply of individuals, in which enacting experiments are legitimate, separate community perspectives can be amplified by interchanges among communities. Out of this friction of competing ideas can come the sort of improvisational sparks necessary for igniting organizational innovation. Thus large organizations, *reflectively structured*, are perhaps particularly well positioned to be highly innovative and to deal with discontinuities. If their internal communities have a reasonable degree of autonomy and independence from the dominant world view, large organizations might actually accelerate innovation. Such organizations are uniquely positioned to generate innovative discontinuities incrementally, thereby diminishing the disruptiveness of the periodic radical reorganization that Nadler calls "frame breaking"

(Nadler 1988). This occurs when conventional organizations swing wholesale from one paradigm to another (see also Bartunek 1984). An organization whose core is aware that it is the synergistic aggregate of agile, semiautonomous, self-constituting communities and not a brittle monolith is likely to be capable of extensible "frame bending" well beyond conventional breaking point.

The important interplay of separate communities with independent (though interrelated) world views may in part account for von Hippel's (1988) account of the sources of innovation and other descriptions of the innovative nature of business alliances. Von Hippel argues that sources of innovation can lie outside an organization among its customers and suppliers. Emergent communities of the sort we have outlined that span the boundaries of an organization would then seem a likely conduit of external and innovative views into an organization. Similarly, the alliances Powell describes bring together different organizations with different interpretive schemes so that the composite group they make up has several enacting options to choose from. Because the separate communities enter as independent members of an alliance rather than as members of a rigid hierarchy, the alternative conceptual viewpoints are presumably legitimate and do not get hidden from the core. There is no concealed noncanonical practice where there is no concealing canonical practice.

The means to harness innovative energy in any enacting organization or alliance must ultimately be considered in the design of organizational architecture and the ways communities are linked to each other. This architecture should preserve and enhance the healthy autonomy of communities, while simultaneously building an interconnectedness through which to disseminate the results of separate communities' experiments. In some form or another the stories that support learning-in-working and innovation should be allowed to circulate. The technological potential to support this distribution—e-mail, bulletin boards, and other devices that are capable of supporting narrative exchanges— is available. But narratives, as we have argued, are embedded in the social system in which they arise and are used. They cannot simply be uprooted and repackaged for circulation without becoming prey to exactly those problems that beset the old abstracted canonical accounts. Moreover, information cannot be assumed to circulate freely just because technology to support circulation is available (Feldman and March 1981). Eckert (1989), for instance, argues that information travels differently within different socio-economic groups. Organizational assumptions that given the "right" medium people will exchange information freely overlook the way in which certain socio-economic groups, organizations, and in particular, corporations, implicitly treat information as a commodity to be hoarded and exchanged. Working-class groups, Eckert contends, do pass information freely and Orr (1990a) notes that the reps are remarkably open with each other about what they know. *Within* these communities, news travels fast; community knowledge is readily available to community members. But these communities must function within corporations that treat information as a commodity and that have superior bargaining power in negotiating the terms of exchange. In such unequal conditions, internal communities cannot reasonably be expected to surrender their knowledge freely.

As we have been arguing throughout, to understand the way information is constructed and travels within an organization, it is first necessary to understand the different communities that are formed within it and the distribution of power among them. Conceptual reorganization to accommodate learning-in-working and innovation, then, must stretch from the level of individual communities of practice and the technology and practices used there to the level of the overarching organizational architecture, the community-of-communities.

It has been our unstated assumption that a unified understanding of working, learning, and innovating is potentially highly beneficial, allowing, it seems likely, a synergistic collaboration rather than a conflicting separation among workers, learners, and innovators. But similarly, we have left unstated the companion assumption that attempts to foster such synergy through a conceptual reorganization will produce enormous difficulties from the perspective of the conventional workplace. Work and learning are set out in formal descriptions so that people (and organizations) can be held accountable; groups are organized to define responsibility; organizations are bounded to enhance concepts of competition; peripheries are closed off to maintain secrecy and privacy. Changing the way these things are arranged will produce problems as well as benefits. An examination of both problems and benefits has been left out of this chapter, whose single purpose has been to show where constraints and resources lie, rather than the rewards and costs of deploying them. Our argument is simply that for working, learning, and innovating to thrive collectively depends on linking these three, in theory and in practice, more closely, more realistically, and more reflectively than is generally the case at present.

ACKNOWLEDGMENTS

This chapter was written at the Institute for Research on Learning with the invaluable help of many of our colleagues, in particular Jean Lave, Julian Orr, and Etienne Wenger, whose work, with that of Daft and Weick, provides the canonical texts on which we based our commentary.

REFERENCES

Adler, P. S. (1987), "Automation and Skill: New Directions," *International Journal of Technology Management* 2 [5/6], 761–771.

Barley, S. R. (1988), "Technology, Power, and the Social Organization of Work: Towards a Pragmatic Theory of Skilling and Deskilling," *Research in the Sociology of Organizations*, 6, 33–80.

Bartunek, J. M. (1984), "Changing Interpretive Schemes and Organizational Restructuring: The Example of a Religious Order," *Administrative Science Quarterly*, 29, 355–372.

Bloch, M. (1977), "The Past and the Present in the Present," *Man*[NS], 12, 278–292.

Bourdieu, P. (1977), *Outline of a Theory of Practice*, trans R. Nice. Cambridge: Cambridge University Press. (First published in French, 1973.)

Braverman, H. (1974), *Labor and Monopoly Capitalism: The Degradation of Work in the Twentieth Century*, New York: Monthly Review Press.

Brown, J. S. and P. Duguid, (in press), "Enacting Design," in P. Adler (ed.), *Designing Automation for Usability*, New York: Oxford University Press.

Brown, J. S., A. Collins, and P. Duguid (1989), "Situated Cognition and the Culture of Learning," *Education Research*, 18, 1, 32–42. (Also available in a fuller version as IRL Report 88-0008, Palo Alto, CA: Institute for Research on Learning.)

Burawoy, M. (1979), "The Anthropology of Industrial Work," *Annual Review of Anthropology*, 8, 231–266.

Daft, R. L. and K. E. Weick (1984), "Toward a Model of Organizations as Interpretation Systems," *Academy of Management Review*, 9, 2, 284–295.

Deetz, S. A. and A. Kersten (1983), "Critical Models of Interpretive Research," in L. L. Putnam and M. E. Pacanowsky (eds.), *Communication and Organizations: An Interpretive Approach*, Beverly Hills, CA: Sage Publications.

Dessauer, J. H. (1971), *My Years with Xerox: The Billions Nobody Wanted*, Garden City, NJ: Doubleday.

Eckert, P. (1989), *Jocks and Burnouts*, New York: Teachers College Press.

Feldman, M. S. and J. G. March (1981), "Information in Organizations as Signal and Symbol," *Administrative Science Quarterly*, 26, 171–186.

Geertz, C. (1973), *Interpretation of Cultures: Selected Essays*, New York: Basic Books.

Goodman, P. and Associates (1988), *Designing Effective Work Groups*, San Francisco: Jossey-Bass.

Hackman, J. R. (ed.) (1990), *Groups that Work (and Those that Don't)*, San Francisco: Jossey-Bass.

Hedberg, B. (1981), "How Organizations Learn and Unlearn," in P. C. Nystrom and W. H. Starbuck (eds.), *Handbook of Organizational Design, Vol. 1: Adapting Organizations to their Environments*, New York: Oxford University Press.

——, P. C. Nystrom, and W. H. Starbuck (1976), "Designing Organizations to Match Tomorrow," in P. C. Nystrom and W. H. Starbuck (eds.), *Prescriptive Models of Organizations*, Amsterdam, Netherlands: North-Holland Publishing Company.

Hutchins, E. (1991), "Organizing Work by Adaptation," *Organization Science*, 2, 1, 14–39.

——(in press), "Learning to Navigate," in S. Chalkin and J. Lave (eds.), *Situated Learning*, Cambridge: Cambridge University Press.

Jordan, B. (1989), "Cosmopolitical Obstetrics: Some Insights from the Training of Traditional Midwives," *Social Science and Medicine*, 28, 9, 925–944. (Also available in slightly different form as *Modes of Teaching and Learning: Questions Raised by the Training of Traditional Birth Attendants*, IRL report 88-0004, Palo Alto, CA: Institute for Research on Learning.)

Latour, B. (1986), "Visualization and Cognition: Thinking with Eyes and Hands," *Knowledge and Society*, 6, 1–40.

Lave J. (1988), *Cognition in Practice: Mind, Mathematics, and Culture in Everyday Life*, New York: Cambridge University Press.

——and E. Wenger (1990), *Situated Learning: Legitimate Peripheral Participation*, IRL report 90-0013, Palo Alto, CA: Institute for Research on Learning. (Also forthcoming [1990] in a revised version, from Cambridge University Press.)

Levi-Strauss, C. (1966), *The Savage Mind*, Chicago: Chicago University Press.

Martin, J. (1982), "Stories and Scripts in Organizational Settings," in A. H. Hastorf and A. M. Isen (eds.), *Cognitive and Social Psychology*, Amsterdam: Elsevier.

Nadler, D. (1988), "Organizational Frame Bending: Types of Change in the Complex Organization," in R. H. Kilman, T. J. Covin, and associates (eds.), *Corporate Transformation: Revitalizing Organizations for a Competitive World*, San Francisco: Jossey-Bass.

Nystrom, P. C. and W. H. Starbuck (1984), "To Avoid Organizational Crises, Unlearn," *Organizational Dynamics*, Spring, 53–65.

Orr, J. (1990a), "Talking about Machines: An Ethnography of a Modern Job," Ph.D. Thesis, Cornell University.

——(1990b), "Sharing Knowledge, Celebrating Identity: War Stories and Community Memory in a Service Culture," in D. S. Middleton and D. Edwards (eds.), *Collective Remembering: Memory in Society*, Beverley Hills. CA: Sage Publications.

——(1987a), "Narratives at Work: Story Telling as Cooperative Diagnostic Activity," *Field Service Manager*, June, 47–60.

——(1987b), *Talking about Machines: Social Aspects of Expertise*, Report for the Intelligent Systems Laboratory, Xerox Palo Alto Research Center, Palo Alto, CA.

Pea, R. D. (1990), *Distributed Cognition*, IRL Report 90-0015, Palo Alto, CA: Institute for Research on Learning.

Putnam, L. L. (1983), "The Interpretive Perspective: An Alternative to Functionalism," in L. L. Putnam and M. E. Pacanowsky (eds.), *Communication and Organizations: An Interpretive Approach*, Beverley Hills, CA: Sage Publications.

Reddy, M. J. (1979), "The Conduit Metaphor," in Andrew Ortony (ed.), *Metaphor and Thought*, Cambridge: Cambridge University Press, 284–324.

Ryle, G. (1954), *Dilemmas: The Tarner Lectures*, Cambridge: Cambridge University Press.

Schein, E. H. (1990), "Organizational Culture," *American Psychologist*, 45, 2, 109–119.

Schön, D. A. (1987), *Educating the Reflective Practitioner*, San Francisco: Jossey-Bass.

——(1984), *The Reflective Practitioner*, New York: Basic Books.

——(1971), *Beyond the Stable State*, New York: Norton.

Scribner, S. (1984), "Studying Working Intelligence," in B. Rogoff and J. Lave (eds.), *Everyday Cognition: Its Development in Social Context*, Cambridge, MA: Harvard University Press.

Suchman, L. (1987a), *Plans and Situated Actions: The Problem of Human–Machine Communication*, New York: Cambridge University Press.

——(1987b), "Common Sense in Interface Design," *Techné*, 1, 1, 38–40.

Tushman, M. L. and P. Anderson (1988), "Technological Discontinuities and Organization Environments," in A. M. Pettigrew (ed.), *The Management of Strategic Change*, Oxford: Basil Blackwell.

van Maanen, J. and S. Barley (1984), "Occupational Communities: Culture and Control in Organizations," in B. Straw and L. Cummings (eds.), *Research in Organization Behaviour*, London: JAI Press.

von Hippel, E. (1988), *The Sources of Innovation*, New York: Oxford University Press.

Zuboff, S. (1988), *In the Age of the Smart Machine: The Future of Work and Power*, New York: Basic Books.

8

Communities of Practice, Social Capital and Organizational Knowledge*

Eric Lesser

Executive Consultant, IBM Institute for Knowledge Management

Laurence Prusak

Executive Director, IBM Institute for Knowledge Management

Communities of practice play a critical role as the building blocks for creating, sharing, and applying organizational knowledge. Lesser and Prusak propose that communities of practice are "formed by individuals who need to associate themselves with others facing similar issues and challenges within the organization. They exist without formal charters or operational mandates." As these informal organizations become recognized by organizations, both knowledge and human capital can be leveraged. Addressing this potential, Lesser and Prusak point to social capital as "the web of social relationships that influences individual behavior and thereby affects economic growth." The authors propose that communities of practice serve as the primary vehicle for building social capital. This is illustrated by exploring the structural, relational, and cognitive dimensions of communities of practice and their implications for managers attempting to bridge the gap between creating, sharing, and applying knowledge.

* Reprinted with permission from *Information Systems Review*, The Korean Society of Management Information Systems, Vol. 1, No. 1 (June 1999): 3–10.

INTRODUCTION

Within all organizations, there exists a formal structure that is described by boxes, arrows, documented policies, and procedures. This formal structure may be contrasted with a less formal environment that is more based on self-organized group interaction and individual relationships. Behind every organization chart lies informal clusters and networks of employees who work together—sharing knowledge, solving common problems and exchanging insights, stories and frustrations. When appropriately supported by the formal organization these "communities of practice," as they are often called, play a critical role: they are the major building blocks in creating, sharing, and applying organizational knowledge.

Organizations ranging from British Petroleum to the World Bank have begun to invest time, energy, and money in supporting their communities of practice, viewing these communities as vehicles for managing their organizational knowledge. A common question asked by these organizations is "How should we best allocate our resources to assist these informal communities, manage knowledge and ultimately derive value for the rest of the organization?" Before this question can be answered, a prior question must be addressed: What are the mechanisms by which communities of practice impact knowledge creation, sharing, and use?

When we consider this question, we converge on a related topic emerging in the economic and sociological literatures: social capital. Social capital, as we will discuss later, refers to the social resources individuals within a community draw upon and provide value to themselves and their organizations. These social resources include common identity, familiarity, trust, and a degree of shared language and context among individuals. These resources manifest themselves in a variety of ways, including reducing the time it takes to locate an expert within an organization, minimizing the costs associated with validating expertise, and reducing the time and effort associated with developing and monitoring an agreement between individuals in an organization. All of these activities enable an organization to better manage its knowledge resources. Much like financial or human capital, social capital can be fostered and tapped as needed to enable individuals to perform their jobs more efficiently and effectively.

In this chapter, we hypothesize that communities of practice are valuable to organizations because they contribute to the development of social capital, which in turn is a necessary condition for knowledge creation, sharing, and use. Drawing upon the literature, and our own experience, we will attempt to demonstrate the linkages between communities of practice, social capital and knowledge management. Also, we will explore implications for managers attempting to undertake knowledge management efforts and identify methods for leveraging communities within their own organization.

COMMUNITIES OF PRACTICE

Communities of practice are defined as collections of individuals bound by informal relationships that share similar work roles and a common context.[1] Each of the words in this definition merits close consideration. First, the term "community" highlights the personal basis upon which relationships are formed. The word further suggests that communities of practice are not constrained by typical geographic, business unit, or functional boundaries, but rather by common tasks, contexts, and work interests.

Second, the word "practice" implies "knowledge in action."[2] The concept of "practice" as used here, is the representation of how individuals *actually* perform their jobs on a day-to-day basis, as opposed to more formal policies and procedures that reflect the way work *should* be performed. Further, the term "practice" refers to the dynamic process through which individuals learn how to do their jobs by actually performing tasks and interacting with others performing similar tasks. Etienne Wenger, an authority on the subject, states that,

> Learning reflects our participation in communities of practice. If learning is a matter of engagement in socially defined practices, the communities that share these practices play an important role in shaping learning. The communities that matter are not always the most easily identifiable, because they often remain informal.[3]

Communities of practice differ notably from conventional units of organization, such as teams or work groups. Teams and groups have a task orientation, are often launched for a specific purpose, and have formal requirements for membership. Communities, by contrast, have an informal membership that is often fluid and self-organizing in nature. John Seely Brown from Xerox PARC and Paul Duigid at the University of California at Berkeley, two leading researchers in this field, state that,

> Group theory, in general, focuses on groups as canonical (reliant on formal rules and tasks), bounded entities that lie within an organization, and that are organized, or at least sanctioned by that organization and its view of tasks. The communities (of practice) that we discern, are by contrast, often noncanonical and not formally recognized by the organization. They are more fluid and interpenetrative than bounded... And significantly, communities are emergent. That is to say their share and membership emerges in the process of activity, as opposed to being created to carry out a task.[4]

Communities of practice exist within all organizations. These range from the "peer groups" of drilling specialists within British Petroleum[5] to poverty specialists at the World Bank to the insurance claims processors documented in Etienne Wenger's recent book, *Communities of Practice: Learning, Meaning and Identity*.[6] They are formed over time by individuals with a need to associate themselves with others facing similar issues and challenges within an organization. In most organizations, they exist without formal charters or organizational mandates. However, many companies are beginning to recognize that these communities can be supported and leveraged to benefit the "membership" of communities and the organization as a whole.

SOCIAL CAPITAL

Social capital has recently gained acceptance in the eyes of both sociologists and economists. In the past, significant attention has been paid to the development of "human capital," how individuals obtain the education, skills, and background necessary to be productive in a competitive labor market. However, sociologists such as James Coleman, Ron Burt, and Mark Granovetter argue that there is much more to explaining the differences in individual success than individual characteristics alone. This school of thought argues that "even in new institutional economics, there is a failure to recognize the importance of concrete personal relationships and networks of relations...in generating trust, in establishing expectations, and in creating and enforcing norms."[7] To address these failures in standard economic theory, the concept of social capital, the "web of social relationships that influences individual behavior and thereby affects economic growth,"[8] was developed. Social capital theory has been used to explain a number of phenomena, ranging from social policy issues in inner city housing projects to economic development in Northern Italy.[9]

In a recent article, "Social Capital, Intellectual Capital, and the Organizational Advantage" Janine Nahapiet at the University of Oxford and Sumantra Ghoshal at the London Business School have attempted to link social capital at the organizational level with the organization's ability to manage its knowledge resources. They define social capital as,

> "the sum of the actual and potential resources embedded within, available through, and derived from the network of relationships possessed by an individual or social unit."[10]

The authors further identify social capital as having three interrelated dimensions: structural, relational and cognitive.[11] The structural dimension refers to the formation of informal networks that enable individuals to identify others with potential resources. These networks include relationships with "strong ties" (those with multiple contacts on a regular basis) and "weak ties" (individuals whose contact occurs less frequently). Overall, the structural dimension of social capital reflects the need for individuals to reach out to others within an organization to seek out resources that they may not have at their own disposal.

While having a network of individuals is a critical part in developing social capital, equally as important are the interpersonal dynamics between individuals within the network. This relational dimension addresses issues around trust, shared norms and values, obligations, expectations, and identification that are critical in developing social capital among members of a group. Francis Fukuyama, in his recent book entitled *Trust*, states,

> "Trust is the expectation that arrives within a community of regular, honest, and cooperative behavior, based on commonly shared norms on the part of other members of that community... Social capital is the capability that arises from the prevalence of trust in a society or in certain parts of it. It can be embodied in the smallest and most basic social group, the family, as well as the largest of all groups, the nation and in all the other groups in between. Social capital differs from other forms of human capital insofar as it is usually created and transmitted through cultural mechanisms like religion, tradition, or historical habit."[12]

This relational dimension recognizes that social capital is developed and fostered when individuals believe that their actions will be appropriately reciprocated, and that individuals will meet their expected obligations.

The final dimension in the authors' construct is the cognitive dimension. The cognitive dimension addresses the need for a common context and language to build social capital. Without a common understanding or "vocabulary," it is difficult to construct the connections necessary to create and foster social capital. Building a common context can be done through two mechanisms. The first mechanism is the shared use of common objects and artifacts. These objects, such as documents, procedure manuals, and memos provide a shared reference point that others can quickly understand. Another technique is the use of stories that convey a sense of shared history and context which is retransmitted and carried on by others in the organization.

Nahapiet and Ghoshal developed a model that illustrates how these three dimensions influence four variables that mediate the creation and sharing of intellectual capital (what we refer to as organizational knowledge). These four variables include: access to parties for combining/exchanging intellectual capital, the anticipation of value through combining/exchanging intellectual capital, the motivation of individuals to combine/share intellectual capital, and the ability for the organization to change according to the needs of its outside environment.[13] They hypothesize that increasing the amount of social capital within an organization will positively influence the intermediate variables and subsequently impact the creation and sharing of organizational knowledge.

In a follow-up study, Ghoshal and Wenpin Tsai test this theoretical construct in a large multinational electronics company.[14] Using product innovation as a proxy for knowledge creation and sharing, the authors found that social capital had significant effects on the levels of resource exchange and combination within the organization. While this study was limited to the results of one organization, it further reinforced the concept that social capital has a significant impact on the way organizations create and share knowledge.

LINKING SOCIAL CAPITAL AND COMMUNITIES OF PRACTICE

If we assume that the presence of social capital has a positive impact on knowledge creation, sharing and use, then how do communities of practice serve as a vehicle for building social capital? Using the three dimensions described previously (structural, relational, and cognitive) we can illustrate how communities play a critical role in fostering the development of social capital.

Structural Dimension

Communities of practice provide the opportunity for individuals to develop a network of individuals who have similar interests. This manifests itself in several ways. First, the community serves as an intra-network clearinghouse by identifying those with relevant knowledge and helping individuals within the community make connections with one another. This is particularly valuable as the organization grows and goes "virtual" and individuals find it increasingly difficult to know "who knows what." Second, the community acts as a reference mechanism, quickly enabling individuals to evaluate the knowledge of other members without having to contact each individual within the network. Lastly, the community of practice can help connect individuals from outside the network to those who are already identified as community members. This function can be critical, especially for new employees who are looking to identify individuals who hold the firm-specific knowledge needed to be successful in their new roles.

Relational Dimension

Communities of practice foster the interpersonal interactions necessary to build a sense of trust and obligations critical to building social capital. By being able to bring people together to create and share relevant knowledge, the community creates the condition where individuals can "test" the trustworthiness and commitment of other community members. Through this process, the community builds its own form of "informal currency," with norms and values that are commonly held and terms and conditions of "payment" that are generally accepted. It is through these repeated interactions that individuals can develop empathy for the situations of others and can develop the rapport with individuals in the community.

Cognitive Dimension

Because they tend to be organized around a common issue or theme, communities of practice are instrumental in maintaining the shared "vernacular" used by their members. First, communities of practice help shape the actual terminology used by group members in everyday work conversations. In addition, they generate and share the knowledge objects or "artifacts" that are used by community members. Equally as important, communities generate stories that communicate the norms and values of the community and of the organization as a whole. These stories enable new members to take cues from more experienced personnel and allow the development of a community memory that perpetuates itself long after the original community members have departed.

IMPLICATIONS FOR MANAGERS

Communities of practice play an instrumental role in developing the structural, relational, and cognitive dimensions of social capital. These dimensions, in turn, lead to an increased ability to manage organizational knowledge. Managers seeking to increase the level of social capital via these communities of practice should consider the following rules of thumb:

Identify communities of practice that influence critical goals within the organization. Within a given organization, there may be a large number of communities. Many of these will exist independently. When identifying communities to which resources should be applied, the organization should select those that have a direct impact on the organization's strategic objectives. In a pharmaceutical company, for example, a community of practice focused on regulatory approval issues might be a primary target for initial community assistance. In a software development company, a community of Java developers might be a likely candidate.

Provide communities with the means to meet face-to-face. In many geographically dispersed organizations, communities of practice are challenged and constrained by the lack of opportunity to make the direct connections that foster each of the three dimensions of social capital. Allowing people to meet each other enables them to more quickly build the network of contacts within the community, foster interactions that allow for trust building, and share knowledge artifacts and stories that build a common context among participants. Without these face-to-face encounters, the process of community building becomes less effective and less likely to benefit the organization as a whole.

Provide tools that enable the community to identify new members and maintain contact with existing members. Technology can play an important role in supporting communities of practice. Tools such as personal web pages, directories of expertise, and knowledge maps can help individuals locate others with similar interests and experiences, fostering the network component of social capital. Same-time collaborative tools such as chat rooms and videoconferences can help community members maintain connections, and foster interactions that lead to increased trust and context sharing. In addition, knowledge repositories can play an important role in helping community members maintain and refine their stock of knowledge "artifacts," and can enable community members to quickly and easily access representations of the community memory.

Identify key "experts" within the community and enable them to provide support to the larger group. Within most communities, there often exists a select group of individuals whom others in the community seek out for their expertise. These "experts" play a critical role in the community. Not only do they provide organizational wisdom, but they function as intermediaries, directing individuals to others in the network who may have even more relevant knowledge. These experts are often not recognized within the formal organization—performing this function in parallel with their normal day-to-day work. We have seen leading organizations begin to identify these individuals, and give them time and resources to more efficiently create and share community knowledge with others in the organization.

Remember that the capital, in social capital, implies an investment model with an expected return. Communities of practice are naturally present in all organizations. However, for these communities to exploit the type of social capital required to effectively create, share, and use organizational knowledge, they often require outside investment from the formal organization as a whole. Such investments can enable existing communities to be more effective, efficient and/or innovative. Investment may take many forms, ranging from money for face-to-face meetings, technology to support distributed communities, to enabling experts to spend time providing assistance to others in the network. These are all tangible investments and, when focused appropriately, can pay dividends in terms of stronger, more vibrant communities.

CONCLUSION

Communities of practice play a critical role in the day-to-day activities of organizations. One of their key functions is to build social capital among its members, which in turn enables their members to more effectively manage their organizational knowledge. In this paper, we have attempted to illustrate the important linkages between communities of practice and social capital. Further, we have provided managers with some guidelines on how to best support the growth of social capital within communities. We hope that these insights will help organizations further their ability to manage their knowledge and lead to improved organizational performance.

ENDNOTES

1. Snyder, William M., "Communities of Practice: Combining Organizational Learning and Strategy Insights to Create a Bridge to the 21st Century," *Presented at the 1997 Academy of Management Conference*, p. 3.

2. Ibid, p. 4.

3. Wenger, Etienne, "Communities of Practice: The Social Fabric of a Learning Organization," *Healthcare Forum Journal* (39:4) July/August, 1996, p. 24.

4. Brown, John S. and Paul Duguid, "Organizational Learning and Communities of Practice: Toward a Unified View of Working, Learning and Innovation," *Organization Science* (2:1), February, 1991, p. 49.

5. Prokesh, Steven, "Unleashing the Powers of Learning: An Interview with British Petroleum's John Browne," *Harvard Business Review* (75:5), September–October, 1997, pp. 146–168.

6. Wenger, Etienne. *Communities of Practice: Learning, Meaning and Identity.* (Cambridge, UK: Cambridge University Press, 1998).

7. Coleman, James, "Social Capital in the Creation of Human Capital," *American Journal of Sociology*, (94 Supplement), p. 97.

8. Pennar, Karen, "The Ties That Lead to Prosperity," *Business Week*, December 15, 1997, p. 154.

9. Ibid, p. 154.

10. Nahapiet, Janine and Sumantra Ghoshal, "Social Capital, Intellectual Capital and the Organizational Advantage," *Academy of Management Review* (23:2), April, 1998, p. 243.

11. Ibid, p. 251.

12. Fukuyama, Francis, *Trust: The Social Virtues and the Creation of Prosperity*, (New York: Penguin Books, 1995), p. 26.

13. Op. Cit., Nahapiet and Ghoshal, p. 251.

14. Tsai, Wenpin and Sumantra Ghoshal, "Social Capital and Value Creation: The Role of Intrafirm Networks," *Academy of Management Journal*, (41:4), August, 1998, p. 464.

9

Linking Competitive Advantage with Communities of Practice*

Jeanne Liedtka
University of Virginia

In this chapter, Jeanne Liedtka uses communities of practice and the management themes of learning, participative leadership, collaboration, strategic thinking, and total quality management to highlight a broad-based competitive advantage called *metacapabilities*. Metacapabilities prevent issues that can lead to complacency and failure by allowing organizations to adapt to environmental and marketplace change. When metacapabilities are woven into communities, organizations have the ability to capitalize on the underlying strategy of each theme's core value and shared meaning. Liedtka proposes that this can be realized through:

- Learning new sets of skills on an ongoing basis.
- Conversing, learning, and working more efficiently by collaborating across formal organizational structures.
- Redesigning processes and continuously enhancing both efficiency and quality from the customer's perspective.
- Responding to local opportunities and maintaining broad market intent through strategic thinking.
- Fostering continuous co-evolution of individual and organizational meaning through participative leadership amid changing market realities.

This article makes the argument that important themes from a number of characteristically separate literatures in the field of management—organizational behavior, operations management, corporate strategy, and business ethics—converge in their support to provide a view of organizations as communities of practice that are built on an underlying ethic of care. I assert that such com-

* From *Journal of Management Inquiry*, Vol. 8, No. 1 (March 1999): 5–16. Copyright © 1999 by Sage Publications, Inc. Reprinted by permission of Sage Publications, Inc.

munities have the potential to prosper in today's marketplace through creating and sustaining powerful new sources of competitive advantage, termed *metacapabilities*.

The themes I examine are those of organizational learning, collaboration, participative leadership, quality, reengineering, and strategic thinking. I deal first with the larger frame, arguing that new thinking in the field of strategy suggests the value of looking across these seemingly disparate topics for the common threads with which we can weave a broader view of the qualities of competitively successful organizations. Then, I trace the relevant themes developed in each field individually and consider their implications for the types of organizations that need to be created to support them. After synthesizing these, I next turn to the business ethics field and work on the ethic of care to identify the values base that seems likely to further the development of such organizations. Finally, I attempt to advance an integrative view and its implications for research and practice.

A Capability Based View of Competitive Advantage

Competing on capabilities is a concept that has become the focus of significant practitioner and scholarly attention in the strategy field. It provides a useful lens to draw together a wide-ranging set of discussions underway in other management disciplines. This view gives increased attention to obtaining and sustaining competitive advantage through the development of a distinctive set of organizational capabilities, rather than through traditional strategies based on industry positioning and fit. Stalk, Evans, and Shulman (1992) note:

> The essence of strategy is not the structure of a company's products and markets but the dynamics of its behavior. And the goal is to develop the hard-to-imitate organizational capabilities that distinguish a company from its competitors in the eyes of customers. (p. 62)

Capabilities are "complex bundles of skills and accumulated knowledge, exercised through organizational processes, that enable firms to coordinate activities and make use of their assets" (Day, 1994, p. 37). Here the essence of advantage focuses on the development of processes rather than particular products or markets. This approach argues that the pace and unpredictability of change has rendered inflexible and vulnerable strategies based on narrowly focused definitions of products and markets; therefore, sustaining competitive advantage relies on the development of a broad-based set of capabilities that are transportable across products and markets.

The strategy literature argues that only certain processes are seen as having the potential to confer advantage. Processes are strategically significant to the extent that they provide superior value to customers, are hard to imitate, and render the organization more adaptable to change (Day, 1994). The first two qualities—value creation and inimitability—have been much discussed in the strategy field. Yet, any particular set of skills that are valuable and hard to imitate will also be difficult to change. Karl Weick has noted that adaptation precludes adaptability. The drivers of past success can lead to complacency and failure to adapt in the face of environmental change, making the third quality of continuous adaptation critical. Although this quality has received less attention from strategists, it has received significant attention from those writing in the areas of learning and quality. Recently, authors in the field of strategy have argued that achieving on-going adaptability requires the creation of a set of metacapabilities (Liedtka, 1996a). Metacapabilities contribute the kinds of skills and knowledge that underlie the process of capability building itself. Only by coupling metacapabilities with a particular set of business-specific capabilities can all three conditions for competitive advantage—value creation, inimitability, adaptability—be satisfied.

A set of themes of significant interest to practicing managers and scholars today—learning, participative leadership, collaboration, quality, reengineering, and strategic thinking—can be usefully thought of as representing different kinds of related metacapabilities. Each of these metacapabilities allows organizations to deal with change in competitively superior ways. For example, the ability to learn new sets of skills on an ongoing basis has been argued by some to represent the only sustainable source of advantage for the future. Similar to this, collaboration allows organizations to converse, learn, and work more efficiently across the silos that have characterized organizational structures. The ability to redesign processes and continuously enhance their efficiency and quality from the customer's perspective represent critical metacapabilities for value creation across all products and technologies. Strategic thinking, practiced at all organizational levels, allows an organization to respond more readily to local opportunity while maintaining a coherent broader intent. Participative leadership fosters the continuous coevolution of individual and organizational meaning and purpose amid changing market realities.

Taking this view, the interest in these topics suggests an increasing recognition by practitioners of the inherent value of these underlying process capabilities across very different organizational contexts and strategies. It also suggests that one potential explanation for the widely acknowledged failure to successfully implement many of these potentially valuable initiatives lies with the emphasis on techniques that has accompanied their attempted use. If these metacapabilities are truly bundles of skills and knowledge that are process-driven, they defy piecemeal implementation of individual best practices. They cannot be grafted one behavior at a time onto existing ways of thinking and behaving. Instead, they rely on larger context, in which core values and processes align in self-sustaining and mutually supportive ways.

Communities of Practice

One potentially useful metaphor for describing such a larger supportive context is that of a *community of practice*. The term is borrowed from learning theorists Lave and Wenger (1991) who define it as an activity system about which participants share understandings concerning what they are doing and what that means in their lives and for their community. Thus, they are united in both action and in the meaning that that action has, both for themselves and for the larger collective. (p. 98)

Lave and Wenger argue that such communities are fundamentally and simultaneously concerned with producing both practical outcomes for customers and learning for members. Lave and Wenger believe that the nature of learning requires participation in the doing, the sharing of perspectives about the doing itself, and the mutual development of both the individual and the collective's capabilities in the process. Thus, it is in the social interaction of the community, not in the individual heads and hands of its producing members, that the community's practice exists and evolves. With its emphasis on individual learning, organizational purpose, and systems outcomes, such a community appears especially well-suited for ongoing value creation in a time of change. The challenge in the creation of such a community becomes one of preserving, supporting, and enriching the development of each individual's uniqueness within the context of the community, and then linking this uniqueness with community purpose rather than subordinating the individual in the name of community-building.

Thus, to see a business organization as a community of practice is to see it as held together by a shared concern for both the outcomes it achieves for stakeholders (be they customers or shareholders) and the personal development and learning of its members. In fact, it sees these two as inseparable, in that increased capabilities at the organizational level flow from development at the individual level. The business organization as community of practice is process-focused at a systems level. The quality of what they do is fundamental to that for which they stand. That is, the work itself matters. Agreement around the how of process and the why of purpose are the foundation of their shared meanings. Informed dialogue among members is central to the ongoing coevolution of meaning and capabilities. Because the work itself is central to a view of business as a community of practice, and because meaning, purpose, and learning is tied to the doing, everything of importance that happens is personal, and hence, local.

Much of the power of the community of practice metaphor lies with its ability to move beyond the traditional dichotomies that we have often accepted in the management field: The decoupling of who we are from what we do—the work from the person; the juxtaposition of shareholders versus employees; the tension between caring for and respecting individuals, and insisting that they change. Most prominently, a focus on a community of practice refuses to see the interests of the individual at odds with that of the organization and vice-versa. In doing so, it challenges the organization to find that shared purpose that links individual development with institutional direction in a far more reciprocal way than the old dictum of "What's good for the firm is good for the employee." It issues an invitation to join a community, rather than a contractual transaction to buy one's labor for 8 hours a day.

Communities of practice evolve, they are not created. As such, they resist management as we generally think of it. They are not a form of formal structure, like a team or a department. They exist in the minds of their members in the connection that they have with each other and with the larger institution in which they reside. Researchers in the field of management have only begun to observe and describe them in the context of research and development teams (Stewart, 1996) or other kinds of knowledge work. Other writers that use somewhat different terminology have argued that building community is the obvious and more powerful successor to building teams (Nirenberg, 1994/1995). Still others have used the term *community of purpose* (Warren, 1996) or *learning community* (Senge, 1990) to describe a similar concept. All of these perspectives share a belief that the creation of community relies on a set of shared meanings that are intimately bound up with the practice of the work itself, the purpose that such work serves and for whom, and the ongoing development of its individual members.

EXAMINING THE INDIVIDUAL THEMES

Let us look briefly at the individual themes that we have alluded to thus far to test the usefulness of this community of practice metaphor against the specific views that their leading proponents advocate.

The Learning Organization

Peter Senge's concept of the learning organization has received enormous attention from both practitioners and academics. Senge's premise is straightforward: Given the pace and unpredictability of change in today's business environment, the ability to learn and to gain leverage from that learning within an organization are the critical skills for ensuring future success. Senge argues that creating such an organization requires mastering five disciplines: (a) systems thinking, which sees the whole system and recognizes interdependencies within it; (b) personal mastery, concerned with personal vision and growth; (c) mental models, balancing inquiry and advocacy modes; (d) building shared vision, finding commonality of purpose that builds on each individual's personal vision; and (e) team learning, establishing collective intelligence through dialogue. Thus, Senge asserts that members of learning organizations must see beyond the narrow confines of their task and function to the larger system. Organizational learning and development must connect with and be based on personal development and vision. Members must be able to talk and work together in mutually developmental ways.

Building such skills, Senge argues, requires a belief that people want to contribute to something that they see as important and to an environment not dominated by self-interest. Openness in two forms—the freedom to speak one's mind and the willingness to challenge one's own thinking—are key. Using conflict productively rather than suppressing it is central to his thinking. Localized decision making that gives people a sense of responsibility for their actions is also critical. The encouragement of risk taking—and forgiveness when it fails—plus a focus on the whole person (and the end of "the war between work and home" [p. 306] as he describes it) are two other requirements that Senge cites. Finally, new kinds of leadership that involve designing, stewarding, and teaching are called into play.

Total Quality Management

Total quality management (TQM) has been embraced even more widely than learning organizations by business practitioners and academics writing in the field of operations. Interestingly, much of the underlying practice of TQM as described by W. Edwards Deming (1992) in his "Fourteen Principles for Transformation," echoes themes similar to Senge's. A similar emphasis on developing the personal capabilities of individual workers is his precondition for achieving quality. He argues that education and self-improvement is key for everyone:

> Quality begins with intent.... Empowerment includes selection of people, their placement, their training to give everyone, including production workers, a chance to advance their learning and to contribute to the best of their talents. It means removing the barriers to pride of workmanship. (p. 51)

The biggest barrier to pride of workmanship, he argues, is our market-based view of employees: "People, whether in management or on the factory floor, have become, to management, a commodity.... Management may hire them at the price posted, or may not, depending on need" (p. 77).

He advocates a view of arms-around, rather than arms-length in dealing with suppliers. Deming (1992) also stresses the need to "drive fear out of the workplace; no one can put in his best performance unless he feels secure" (p. 59). His leader, like Senge's, is a colleague and counselor, rather than a judge. He is a leader who looks to subordinates to define their own needs, one "who will spend hours with everyone of his people. They will know what kind of help they need" (p. 117).

Another central focus of TQM is its unwavering emphasis on the customer. Each individual customer is the ultimate arbiter of quality. This shifts the process of quality management from an exclusively internal operational focus, to being based on an intimate knowledge of the needs and expectations of others—the customer, in this case.

Other writers in the field of quality have echoed the importance of relationships in the service, as well as the production sector. Berry, Zeithaml, and Parasuraman (1990) note that "An interactive community of coworkers who collaborate, overcome, and achieve together is a powerful antidote to service burn-out" (p. 33).

Another immensely popular initiative in the operations area that shares TQM's focus on both customers and processes is the concept of reengineering, or process redesign, described by Hammer and Champy (1993) in *Reengineering the Corporation.* In this book, they make an argument that initiatives, like teamwork and empowerment, fail because they are not linked to the drivers of a business—the business processes themselves. Such initiatives are "the consequences of process redesign, and can only be achieved in that context" (p. 203). Thus, the ability to focus on the basic work processes, rather than departmental or hierarchial boundaries, is the central tenet.

According to Hammer and Champy (1993), one of the fundamental causes of the failure of redesign efforts is neglecting the values and beliefs of workers: "Management must pay attention to what goes on in people's heads as well as what happens on their desks" (p. 204) in the redesign process.

Unlike TQM, however, Hammer and Champy situate the 1993 version of reengineering firmly in a traditional hierarchial notion of management. They assert that it must be a top-down process that is heavily outsider (i.e., consultant) driven. They argue for a ratio of one outsider for every two or three insiders, as necessary for achieving successful redesign. There are two reasons that make this necessary, they argue: (a) front-line workers "lack the broad perspective that reengineering demands," and (b) "business processes inevitably cross organizational boundaries so no middle level manager had the authority to insist that such a process be transformed" (p. 208). This approach clearly raises problems in an environment of continuous change in which organizations must develop a capability to reengineer themselves. For instance, Senge (1990) and Deming (1992) would both argue that a focus on building a broader perspective and a willingness to cooperate across boundaries at all levels of the organization would be a far wiser investment than an ongoing stream of reengineering consultants.

Taken together, the quality and reengineering movements highlight the critical importance of a set of skills for customer-focused process redesign. The question becomes how to embed these skills within the organization, rather than outside of it. Although Hammer and Champy are describing what they see as the inevitability of parochialism and turf protection at the front line, emerging themes around strategic thinking and collaboration in other fields embrace new possibilities in these areas.

Strategic Thinking

In the strategy field, influential authors like Henry Mintzberg (1994), Ralph Stacey (1992), and Gary Hamel and C. K. Prahalad (1994) are advocating a shift in emphasis from strategic planning to strategic thinking. Their litany of indictments against the types of planning processes in place at most large multinational firms is long, and it mirrors the faults that Senge (1990) and Deming (1992) find with traditional management approaches, such as breeding bureaucracy, choking initiative and creativity, and favoring analytics over invention and incremental change over substantive change.

Strategy theorists assert that strategic thinking practiced at every organizational level ought to replace—or at minimum inform—strategic planning. Strategic thinkers, like Senge's (1990) learners, have a broad field of view and see both the whole and the connections between its pieces. They are driven by a strategic intent or a larger vision that includes a sense of where the future connects and disconnects with the past and where it demands anew in the present. The process of strategic thinking is an experimental one that makes use of both creative thinking to design options and critical thinking to test these options. Thus, organizations who want strategic thinking must encourage risk taking and be tolerant of mistakes. Finally, the strategic thinker remains open to emerging opportunities both in service to the defined intent and in question in regard to the continuing appropriateness of that intent. The successful implementation of strategic thinking requires that individuals, at every level, have the decision-making scope and resources to act on the opportunities they see that fall within the boundaries of their role in the larger system. They also must have the courage and support to challenge conventional wisdom.

Individual level strategic thinking is not enough, however. Other writers in the strategy field have argued that coherent strategy making at the corporate level requires a capacity for strategic conversation—a dialogue among members of the organization in which the rationale behind individual strategies is shared and a larger organizational purpose is forged (Liedtka & Rosenblum, 1996; Westley, 1990). Thus, organizational members must have a forum to converse freely with each other in a way that allows them to reach consensus on a shared vision of the future (Burgelman, 1991).

As with the initiatives discussed earlier, the themes of developing a systems perspective, a shared purpose, appropriate decision scope, and open communication are central to creating a capability for strategic thinking.

Collaboration

Successful implementation of the process-driven customer-focused strategies that have been discussed thus far will require a boundary crossing capability that has become another important focus for writers in the management field. All organizational structures create boundaries that are simultaneously functional and dysfunctional—they support some kinds of activities and inhibit others. Recognizing this, organizations have increasingly looked to a capacity for collaboration, rather than structure, as the solution to optimizing the processes and outcomes of the larger system, rather than its pieces. Many authors have approached this topic from the perspective of teamwork, be it cross-functional, self-managed internal teams, or strategic alliances and partnerships that cross firm boundaries. The topics that we have already discussed—learning, quality, reengineering, and strategic thinking—all require collaboration in order to succeed.

The literature in this area is voluminous, long-established, and less dominated by a few powerful voices than the other topics discussed thus far. Yet, it again echoes similar themes. For instance, Gray (1989) has stressed the need for perspective-taking and a shared understanding of context in facilitating collaboration. Katzenbach and Smith (1994), in their widely cited book on *The Wisdom of Teams*, assert that to perform successfully as a team, group members need both to develop a certain mix of individual skills (e.g., technical expertise, problem solving skills, and interpersonal skills) and to operate within a larger context that includes a commitment to a common purpose, a specific set of performance goals, and a mutual accountability for team members. Dubnicki (1991) asserts that although the specific skills that allow groups to excel will vary over time, they must be complemented by an ongoing set of relationship competencies. Sessa (1994) reviews the literature in the area of conflict resolution and argues that the conflict that can arise within a work group can improve, rather than reduce, group effectiveness when managed properly.

Thus, the themes of the existence of shared purpose, relationship competencies, the productive use of conflict, and an optimism concerning the cooperative behavior of others, are repeated here.

Participative Leadership

Closely linked with the topic of collaboration is the theme of participative leadership. In discussing the implications for management of new developments in the field of chaos theory, Margaret Wheatley (1992) focuses on the topic of managerial control, long central to the leadership literature. Wheatley argues that leaders lead best by maintaining the focus of organizational members, rather than through hands-on control. She believes that meaning is the source of coherence, and order in the midst of chaos comes from "a clear core of values and vision, kept in motion through continuing dialogue" (p. 133). The resulting sense of purpose creates a capacity for self-reference among individuals. The criteria for choice, then, evolves from an individual's knowledge of self and community.

Robert Greenleaf (1977), one of the early and prominent proponents of a similar view of leaders, saw them as serving, rather than commanding, followers. He argued that the primary question that such servant leaders ask themselves was whether those served grew as people. Did they become freer, wiser, and more autonomous? Similar to this, James MacGregor Burns (1978), whose influential work on leadership is widely considered a classic in the field, defined leadership as "engagement with each other to raise one another to higher levels of motivation and morality." Following more recently in this tradition, Rost (1991) reviews decades of work in the leadership field and concludes that leadership is a community phenomenon linked with mutual purpose and the intention to change. Drath and Palus (1994) consider the leader's central role to involve meaning making: a process in which "private meaning is transformed into public meaning." They assert that such leaders do not operate out of a view that followers are standing still and in need of motivation to get them moving. Rather, followers are already in motion, and the leader's task is to help them reconstruct their current meaning in a way that allows them to refocus and change. To succeed, such views of leadership require an organization with many of the same qualities that we have already noted: shared purpose, respect for the individual, a capacity for dialogue, and a willingness to put a dominating self-interest aside.

CONVERGING THEMES

Looking across these individual discussions, the popular initiatives examined do not appear to be at cross purposes with each other. Instead, they emerge as complementary. Taken together, they call for an organization with a distinctive set of qualities that mirror closely those of the community of practice. These include:

- A shared sense of meaning and purpose that flows from the personal to the organizational, rather than one that is imposed from the top down. Members of such organizations are not motivated primarily by self-interest, nor do they see their self-interest at odds with that of the community.
- A view held by each individual of themselves as embedded within a larger system of value creation for customers, along with a recognition of the dynamics and interdependencies within that system. Outcomes are important, and the outcomes of central focus are those that the system, as a whole, produces for the customer.
- An emphasis on business processes, rather than on hierarchy or structure boundaries, which take on less consequence.
- A developmental focus, at both personal and organizational levels. This perspective sees continuous learning and growth of the individual as the cornerstone of the growth of corporate capabilities.
- A capacity for dialogue is perhaps the most striking chord across the themes visited. This implies an openness to sharing one's thoughts, a willingness to listen and understand the perspectives of others, and to challenge one's own, as well as others' thinking. This includes an ability to use conflict productively and to seek better solutions, rather than to debate existing alternatives. Talk is fundamental to the development of individuals and organizations, and to the creation of shared purpose and meaning.
- Local decision making that is appropriately located in the hands of those with the perspective, information, and ownership of the relationship is key. Above all else, work is personal, and meaningful relationships evolve out of personal contact with specific individuals.
- A sense of commitment and ownership among organizational members that includes a level of trust and optimism about their relationship with each other. The commitment is to purpose and to each other; the ownership is of outcomes and the means to achieve them.

These qualities describe a way of seeing, of focusing attention, of talking with each other, and of making decisions that must be sustained by a core of values consistent with these practice. For the most part, today's organizations take market values as their core; they feel and behave like internal markets, rather than communities. If initiatives like TQM and organizational learning require communities to create and sustain them, they will not take in firms whose values mimic those of its marketplace. Worse yet, in an organization whose fundamental values reflect those of the marketplace and lack a genuine concern and respect for the individual as an end rather than merely a means, these more participative initiatives may well represent only a more sophisticated and manipulative version of management as usual. Some have argued that honestly authoritarian and profit-driven management is ethically superior to the pretense of superficial involvement (Keeley, 1995).

Paradoxically, an authentic commitment to organizations as communities rather than as markets may enable the creation of capabilities that lead to a competitive advantage in a real marketplace characterized by change.

THEMES FROM THE FIELD OF BUSINESS ETHICS

As we look for a tradition of values consistent with a sense of community that honors the individual, we look to yet another management literature: the field of business ethics. Yet, here we find that much of the literature has focused on the individual as an autonomous moral agent, with an attendant rule-based focus centered on principles of justice and freedom rather than on the creation of community. Exceptions to this emphasis are found in the more relational focus taken by advocates of stakeholder theory (Freeman, 1984), communitarians (Etzioni, 1988), virtue-based theorists (Hartman, 1996), and feminist theorists (Liedtka, 1996b).

Each of these latter schools of thought has argued for a view of ethics that is embedded within its social context and fundamentally concerned with relationships. This focus on ethics as primarily relational rather than individual finds its theoretical precedents in the contextual ethics tradition of Aristotle, Adam Smith, Alistair McIntyre, and Habermas. Kittay and Meyers (1987) note:

> The interest in alternatives to a deductive, calculative approach to moral decision making, with its strong emphasis on individual autonomy, may be traced back to Aristotle and Hume and finds expression in a number of contemporary moral philosophers who stress the importance of virtue, rather than justice, in moral life.... For Aristotle, moral judgement springs from a moral character attuned to circumstantial and contextual features.... Aristotle stresses the social embeddedness of the human being, a political animal by nature.... Alistair McIntyre and Bernard Williams are among the contemporary moral philosophers who call for a return to the notions of virtue, of moral character, and of a personal point of view to counteract the excessive formalism, the calculative ratiocination, and the impersonal perspective of the dominant moral traditions of Kant, on the one hand, and utilitarianism, on the other. (p. 8)

Creating the Good Community

Writing out of the Aristotelian tradition, Hartman (1996) has argued for a focus on creating the good community, rather than on the individual as an independent agent. He asserts that the good community is evidenced by commons-preserving behavior that results from "dispositions that are not narrowly selfish." Such a community allows its members to both express and develop their preferences, as the individual and the community coevolve. It welcomes differing views for the sake of both moral progress and personal freedom.

Hartman argues that the characteristics of such a morally good community mirror those of Hirshman's (1970) exit, voice, and loyalty: an ability to leave, broad freedom to speak and participate, and a preference for exercising voice over exit that derives from an emotional attachment. The sources of that attachment he does not describe. Of what might these broad guidelines that Hartman alludes to, that result in emotional attachment, actually consist?

The Ethic of Care

One set of answers to this question comes from feminist moral theorists who have worked for more than a decade to explicate a set of relational ethics. Carole Gilligan (1982) first described it as an ethic of care that focuses on the self as connected to others. The ethic of care is often compared with the stereotypically masculine ethic of justice. The latter focuses on defining the self as separate, and it uses rights to protect boundaries between the self and other; care moves from its view of the connected self to an emphasis on relationships and the responsibilities that they entail. Gilligan's metaphor of the web to represent feminine thinking has been juxtaposed against the use of hierarchy to represent masculine thinking.

The ethic of care takes as one of its distinctive elements an attention to particular others in actual contexts (Held, 1993). Though it situates the individual within a larger community, an ethic of care does not subjugate the needs of that individual to the community. Instead, it seeks to find commonality of purpose among them. Care is situational in its orientation; it does not prescribe standardized moral rules across contexts. Thus, care includes a commitment to dialogue as the primary means of moral deliberation (Benhabib, 1992).

Finally, care is always local, with one's ability to care bounded by one's reach. Noddings (1984) argues that caring represents a personal investment that must always remain at the level of *I*; caring at the more abstract level of *we* is an illusion. This quality of particularity is essential—caring lives in the relationship between me, an individual, and you, another individual. Without this particularity the caring connection is lost, and we must relabel the new process. In Nodding's terminology, the process can no longer be considered caring; it is now called problem solving. The significance of the differentiation between caring and problem solving goes far beyond semantics. The process of defining generalized problems and decoupling these from the lived experiences of particular individuals who we see ourselves as having relationships with is antithetical to care.

The Practice of Care

Tronto (1993) has described care as a practice, raising parallels with our community of practice. Like Lave and Wenger (1991), Tronto uses the term *practice* to emphasize a concern with both thought and action that is directed toward some end and dependent on the resources of time, skill, and material goods. Along with other scholars (Held, 1993; Ruddick, 1989), Noddings (1984) has used the relationship between a mother and her child to illustrate, at its deepest level, what it means to care. Thus, the essence of caring becomes a focus on nurturing the development of the one for which he or she cares. Contrary to a stereotypical view that caring fosters dependence, care's aim is the opposite— to care means to respect the other's autonomy and to work to enhance the cared-for's ability to make his or her own choices well. If, as Flanagan (1982) states, the "motor of cognitive development is contradiction," (p. 500) caring may well be comprised more of tough love than of indulgence. Anthropologist Mary Catherine Bateson (1989) observes:

> The best care-taker offers a combination of challenge and support.... To be nur-turant is not always to concur and comfort, to stroke and flatter and appease; often, it requires offering a caring version of the truth, grounded in reality. Self-care should include the cold shower as well as the scented tub. Real caring requires setting priorities and limits. Even the hard choices of triage have their own tenderness. (p. 155)

Central to developing an enhanced ability to choose well is the recognition that choices are made within the context of a community. Learning to care is essential to my ability to take my place in the community. The community, in insisting that its members develop a capacity to care, helps both the individuals and the larger community in the process. The existence of a transcending mutual purpose that seeks to accommodate and respect and, of necessity, sometimes bound the personal projects of individuals within the community's goals is critical. Bereft of a strong regard for particularity, communities can smother difference and subordinate individuals.

In the long term, individual caring is only sustainable within caring systems (Kahn, 1993). The personal investment required to care is substantial, and the risks of burnout are ever present. Caring, although a particular relationship between individuals, is situated within the context of a community, derives its shared focus from the needs of that community, and is only sustainable with the support of that community. Care becomes self-reinforcing within that context.

Thus, for an organization to care in the sense that feminist ethicists have used the term, such caring would need to be focused on individuals as ends in and of themselves, not merely as means to the community's purpose. The focus would need to be local, in that it ultimately involves particular individuals caring for other particular individuals within their reach, and it would need to be growth enhancing for the cared-for, in that it moves them toward the use and develop-ment of their full capacities within the context of their self-defined needs and aspirations and in service to the larger community of care.

Caring in the Business Context

The ethic of care has generally been viewed as ill-fitted to the realities of the marketplace, and the literature in business ethics has—until very recently—

devoted little attention to any discussion of the ethic of care (White, 1992). However, it is consistent with a view of business organizations as communities, not as markets, as reflected in the themes of learning, participative leadership, quality, strategic thinking, and collaboration reviewed in this essay.

The ethic of care, then, provides a highly relevant set of ethical values for an organization viewed as a community of practice. Its emphasis on ethics as concerned with practice, in which thought and action intersect, is key to its usefulness. Its emphasis on meeting the developmental needs of particular individual members as the central moral activity is also consistent, as is its belief that in meeting these individual needs, the community itself will develop and prosper. Thus, common purpose flows from the individual to the organizational through dialogues in which a common meaning evolves. Helping individual members fulfill their personal projects, as well as those projects concerning the larger community, requires providing an environment in which it is safe to think for oneself, speak freely, and experiment locally. To care is to take the perspective of the other, to understand their meaning, and to provide both challenge and support to facilitate their growth.

In caring, organizational members do so within a larger community, but they concentrate within their area of reach. Such a view sees an organization as composed of the overlapping circles of the reach of its members. The potential for chaos in the absence of shared agreement on purpose and practices is obvious. Yet, in a community of practice that is based on an underlying ethic of care, shared meaning and purpose continuously evolve to provide a self-reference that creates both coherence at the institutional level and responsive caring at the local level.

Such a community has a strong moral foundation of values that (a) respects each individual's unique capacity to grow and, in doing so, to contribute to the community's purpose, (b) recognizes each member's responsibility to help those within their reach to develop their abilities, (c) conveys an obligation to engage in honest dialogue with each other, and (d) includes an uncoerced agreement to subordinate short-term self-interest in return for the benefits of full participation in the life of the community.

If we believe in the arguments supporting the marketplace value of the meta-capabilities that we have discussed, such a community will gain, not sacrifice, competitive success in making these promises to its members.

Workplace Democracy Versus an Ethic of Care

The aforementioned discussion evokes themes that have been discussed in the literature on workplace democracy for decades, particularly in its focus on broadening participation in decision-making processes and its belief in the viability of the simultaneous pursuit of both individual interests and the common good. Like the founders of the American democratic system, both rest on a belief in what James Madison referred to as the "virtue and intelligence" of the common man, and in what James Morone (1990) has called the "central demo- cratic wish: the direct participation of a united people pursuing a shared com- munal interest." However, this democratic ideal has proven difficult to realize in both the public and private arena. I believe that an ethic of care, although incorporating these democratic beliefs, has some advantages over workplace democracy approaches within the realities of the imperatives facing private enterprise.

As students of American history have often noted, the ideal of direct participation in governance must, in practice, often be reduced to the reality of democratic processes based on representation rather than direct participation. Participation through representation, however, does not produce the outcomes of interest to us here; namely, it does not produce a sense of shared meaning, self-reference, and ownership. Instead, such a process is more likely to create factions rather than communities and to result in negotiation of competing interests rather than the pursuit of the common good. Thus, workplace democracy, in practice, has often had a legalistic cast that focuses on issues like worker representation on boards of directors or on union representa- tion (Ritzky, 1994). The likelihood of these approaches resulting in what Mans- bridge (1983) has called adversarial democracy, rather than the democratic ideal of a united people, is significant. An ethic of care, on the other hand, preserves respect for the individual, but in a process that relies more on "a voice than a vote," to borrow from Max DePree. Reach cannot be achieved through repre- sentation.

As Viggiani (1997) has noted, attempts to reconcile effective and efficient business practices with democratic processes create significant tensions around the structuring of accountabilities, achieving productivity, and dealing with per- ceptions of equality. She suggests that democratic hierarchies, characterized by formal roles and responsibilities, coupled with forums for dialogue, all within the context of a clear shared commitment to democratic values, may instead be necessary. An ethic of care accomplishes these hierarchies by honoring and clarifying individual roles and accountabilities, within permeable boundaries and the context of shared community purpose.

Finally, an ethic of care takes as central something that democracy only hints at—a focus on individual development. If the capacity for innovation and for enhancing value creation on an ongoing basis is critical for business success, a value system that allows individuals to opt out of the often uncomfortable process of personal growth will be irreconcilable with competitive realities. The inclusive processes advocated here would give organizational members broad- ened voice and enhanced choices; however, the choice to stand still would not be among them.

In my view, an ethic of care, although embracing many of the same values as workplace democracy, incorporates these in practices more suited to the context of capitalist enterprise.

IMPLICATIONS FOR RESEARCH

I have described here a possibility. This possibility suggests that a hypothetical organization that reflects the qualities of a community of practice, based on an ethic of care, ought to be able to create and sustain competitive advantage in a changing marketplace more effectively than its competitors who rely on traditional thinking about the nature of business organizations. It will be able to do this through the creation of a set of metacapabilities that allow it to think strategically, learn, collaborate, and redesign processes on an on-going basis in competitively superior ways.

The validity and usefulness of this proposition can only be tested by attention to a broad set of themes that cross a variety of management literatures and disciplines. The identification of existing organizations that evidence these qualities and an assessment of their values, capabilities, and practice would be a logical next step in developing this idea. This would require a more careful and detailed explication of the qualities that we have attributed to our hypothetical community of practice here. Another approach would be the detailed exploration of organizations who have succeeded in their implementation of one of the initiatives discussed here, with a focus on moving beyond an understanding of the best practice and into a deeper analysis of the values and culture that support it. Both of these tasks are beyond the scope of this chapter.

What lies within the scope of this chapter is the assertion that such endeavors would be a fruitful use of scholars' time. Many in the academic community have been justifiably skeptical of the waves of fads that seem to sweep with ever increasing regularity through the world of management practice. In the failure of these fads, we see confirmation of the more deliberate, empirically grounded work that we do in our individual disciplines. Yet, a possibility exists that these apparently unrelated initiatives signal a willingness to experiment with fundamentally new approaches to business organization. Unfortunately, a narrow technique-driven approach to the implementation of these new approaches, without consideration of the larger supporting context, appears unlikely to succeed in significant change. The community of practice metaphor draws our attention to the fundamental role of values, context, and meaning in the practice of management. It highlights the need for alignment and coherence among these factors, if we are to create vibrant communities in our workplaces. If we, as scholars, are to be catalysts of such positive change in both the competitive effectiveness and the moral quality of business organizations, rather than the chroniclers of its failure, we must take a broader lens to our work as well. We, too, are a potentially powerful community of practice.

REFERENCES

Bateson, M. C. (1989). *Composing a Life.* New York: Penguin.

Benhabib, S. (1992). *Situating the Self: Gender, Community, and Postmodernism in Contemporary Ethics.* New York: Routledge.

Berry, L., Zeithaml, V., & Parasuraman, A. (1990). Five imperatives for improving service quality. *Sloan Management Review, 31*(4), 29–38.

Burgelman, R. (1991). Intraorganizational ecology of strategy making and organizational adaptation: Theory and field research. *Organizational Science, 2*(3), 239–262.

Burns, J. M. (1978). *Leadership.* New York: Harper & Row.

Day, G. (1994, October). The capabilities of market-driven organizations. *Journal of Marketing, 58,* 37–52.

Deming, W. E. (1992). *Out of the Crisis.* Cambridge, MA: MIT Center for Advanced Engineering Study.

Drath, W., & Palus, C. (1994). *Making Common Sense.* Greensboro, NC: Center for Creative Leadership.

Dubricki, C. (1991, May/June). Building the high performance management team. *Healthcare Forum Journal,* 19–24.

Etzioni, A. (1988). *The Moral Dimension: Toward a New Economics.* New York: Free Press.

Flanagan, O. (1982, April). Virtue, sex, and gender: Some philosophical reflections on the moral psychology debate. *Ethics,* 499–512.

Freeman, R. E. (1984). *Strategic Management: A Stakeholder Approach.* Boston: Pitman.

Gilligan, C. (1982). *In a Different Voice.* Cambridge, MA: Harvard University Press.

Gray, B. (1989). *Collaborating: Finding Common Ground for Multiparty Problems.* San Francisco: Jossey-Bass.

Greenleaf, R. (1977). *Servant Leadership.* New York: Paulist Press.

Hamel, G., & Prahalad, C. (1994). *Competing for the Future.* Boston: Harvard Business School Press.

Hammer, M., & Champy, J. (1993). *Reengineering the Corporation.* New York: Harper Business.

Hartman, E. (1996). *Organizational Ethics and the Good Life.* New York: Oxford University Press.

Held, V. (1993). *Feminist Morality: Transforming Culture, Society, and Politice.* Chicago: University of Chicago Press.

Hirshman, A. (1970). *Exit, Voice, and Loyalty: Responses to Decline in Firms, Organizations, and States.* Cambridge, MA: Harvard University Press.

Kahn, W. (1993). Caring for the caregivers: patterns of organizational caregiving. *Administrative Science Quarterly, 38,* 539–563.

Katzenbach, J. R., & Smith, D. K. (1994). *The Wisdom of Teams.* New York: Harper Business.

Keeley, M. (1995). The trouble with transformational leadership. *The Business Ethics Quarterly, 5*(1), 67–98.

Kittay, E., & Meyers, D. (1987). *Women and Moral Theory.* Totowa, NJ: Rowman & Littlefield.

Lave, J., & Wenger, E. (1991). *Situated Learning.* Cambridge, MA: Cambridge University Press.

Liedtka, J. (1996a). Collaborating across lines of business for competitive advantage. *Academy of Management Executive,* 10(2), 20–34.

Liedtka, J. (1996b). Feminist morality and competitive reality: A role for an ethic of care? *Business Ethics Quarterly,* 6(2), 179–200.

Liedtka, J., & Rosenblum, J. (1996). Shaping conversations: Making strategy, managing change. *California Management Review,* 39(1), 141–157.

Mansbridge, J. (1983). *Beyond Adversary Democracy.* Chicago: University of Chicago Press.

Mintzberg, H. (1994). *The Rise and Fall of Strategic Planning.* New York: Free Press.

Morone, J. (1990). *The Democratic Wish.* New York: Basic Books.

Nirenberg, J. (1994/1995, Winter). From team building to community building. *National Productivity Review,* 51–62.

Noddings, N. (1984). *Caring: A Feminine Approach to Ethics and Moral Education.* Berkeley: University of California Press.

Ritzky, G. (1994, June). Workplace democracy: A passing phase? *Personnel Journal,* 1.

Rost, J. (1991). Leadership for the Twenty-First Century. London: Praeger.

Ruddick, S. (1989). *Maternal Thinking.* Boston: Beacon Press.

Senge, P. (1990). *The Fifth Discipline.* New York: Doubleday.

Sessa, V. (1994). Can conflict improve team effectiveness? *Issues and Observations,* 14(4), 1–5.

Stacey, R. (1992). *Managing the Unknowable.* San Francisco: Jossey-Bass.

Stalk, G., Evans, P., & Shulman, L. (1992, March/June). Competing on capabilities: The new rules of corporate strategy. *Harvard Business Review,* 70, 57–69.

Stwart, T. (1996). The invisible key to success. Fortune, August 5, 173–176.

Tronto, J. (1993). *Moral Boundaries: A Political Argument for an Ethic of Care.* New York: Routledge.

Viggiani, F. (1997). Democratic hierarchies in the workplace: Structural dilemmas and organized action. *Economic and Industrial Democracy,* 18(2), 231–260.

Warren, R. (1996). Business as a community of purpose. *Business Ethics: A European Review,* 5(2), 87–96.

Westley, F. (1990). Middle managers and strategy: micro dynamics of inclusion. *Strategic Management Journal,* 11, 337–351.

Wheatley, M. (1992). *Leadership and the New Science.* San Francisco: Berrett-Koehler.

White, T. (1992). Business, ethics, and Carol Gilligan's "two voices." *Business Ethics Quarterly,* 2(1), 51–59.

10

Communities of Practice at an Internet Firm: Netovation[i] vs. On-Time Performance*

Robin Teigland

In this chapter, Teigland seeks to understand how individuals in one Internet firm interact in communities of practice and how individual work performance is associated with these communities. In the beginning of the chapter, the author presents a concise yet conclusive review of communities of practice. Next, she works through a series of conceptual frameworks and propositions that confirm the importance of knowledge flows across boundaries as well as the extent to which individuals rely on high levels of personal interaction and social contact. After working through a statistical analysis of network theory, Teigland points to a number of easily recognized conclusions on innovation, creativity, and performance:

- The firm is a vehicle that brings together members from different professional communities of practice, transcending boundaries and exchanging knowledge with internal and external communities.
- The ability to manage knowledge flows that are represented within these professional communities presents considerable challenges for the organization.

Lastly, Teigland outlines a series of challenges that must be overcome for firms to successfully capitalize on their core competence as well as their employees' internal and external community-specific knowledge.

Seldom does a day go by in which one does not read about the New Economy in which newly established firms such as Amazon.com, Buy.com, and eBay are rapidly becoming household names. Yet, despite all the publicity and information about these firms, we are still a long way from understanding the workings of

* Copyright © 2000, The Institute of International Business at the Stockholm School of Economics and Robin Teigland.

these firms as well as the New Economy. Many of the management theories that we have at our disposal today were developed in the pre-Internet era and may no longer be applicable. For example, we have a very limited understanding of how individuals in these new age firms exchange knowledge or how the Internet is affecting knowledge flows across firm boundaries. Related to the emergence of these Internet firms is the rapidly growing interest in knowledge management by both academics and practitioners. In numerous firms, management has appointed Chief Knowledge Officers or Chief Learning Officers as well as implemented extensive knowledge management programs. However, often these programs do not live up to expectations and only serve as a cost to the bottom line. One of the reasons for this is that these programs often do not meet the knowledge needs of the employees. This often occurs because management designs the programs based on a poor understanding of how employees actually conduct their work. Thus, the purpose of this chapter is to tie the two areas above together by focusing on knowledge management within the setting of an Internet-based firm. The primary intent is to understand how individuals access knowledge in their everyday work in an Internet-intensive environment. The second intent is to then take this research one step further by linking an individual's knowledge access behavior to an individual's work-related performance.

With the above in mind, we performed an exploratory study of Icon Medialab (Icon), a company considered to be on the "bleeding edge" of the knowledge-intensive companies typical of the New Economy. Icon specializes in technologically complex digital communications solutions for large multinationals as well as for start-ups based on radically new business models. Icon's products include business-to-business, business-to-consumer, and consumer-to-business Internet-based solutions. A major objective for Icon management is to ensure not only the development and use of the latest Internet technology, but also the reuse of this technology in subsequent projects. However, this is a difficult challenge since the pace of technological development is so rapid with products often becoming outdated within six months or less from development. A second reason for choosing Icon is that its employees in all functions are not only extremely adept at using new Internet-based communication media such as bulletin boards, chatrooms, e-mail, etc. but they also use these to a high degree in their everyday work. One of the primary reasons for this is that the average firmwide age was 29.9 years. In addition, as is common with New Economy strategies, Icon focuses on an extremely rapid global expansion. Thus, within two years of its inception in 1996, the company had grown to 240 employees with offices in eight countries.

Our first step was to conduct a substantial number of interviews of various functions and levels at Icon. We then administered a detailed questionnaire to every employee in the firm aimed at developing an understanding of the sources of knowledge that each individual used in the course of his or her everyday work. With this data, we were then able to build a rich picture of an individual's knowledge networks inside the firm, and more interestingly of an individual's networks that reached across the boundaries of the firm. We then linked these knowledge flow patterns to individual performance on various dimensions in order to provide clear evidence regarding the value of these knowledge flows.

This chapter is organized as follows. In the following section, we review briefly the literature on knowledge management before entering a discussion of the Communities of Practice literature. This literature provides the foundation for our conceptual model, and the specification of six hypotheses linking knowledge flows to individual performance. Section three describes the research methodology and provides a brief description of Icon Medialab. Section four reports on the results of the empirical study while the last section provides a discussion of the results and the implications of the research for theory and practice.

BACKGROUND

Companies are increasingly faced with shrinking product life cycles, the need for integration across an increasing diversity of technologies in products and services, and increasing levels of competition from new competitors crossing not only geographical but industry borders as well (Boland & Tenkasi 1995; Purser et al. 1992). All of this has put increasing pressure on firms to do a better job of gaining access to new knowledge in their business environment while at the same time leveraging their existing knowledge within the boundaries of the firm (Bartlett & Ghoshal 1989; Doz & Hamel 1997; Drucker 1990; Hedlund & Nonaka 1993).

As a result, there has been an increasing number of scholars in recent years who claim that knowledge is perhaps the only "true" source of competitive advantage for a firm (Drucker 1991; Spender & Grant 1996). Due to the focus on knowledge at the firm level, some scholars of this knowledge-based view of the firm have preferred to study organizational learning or the acquisition and creation of organizational knowledge (e.g., routines, rules, procedures, etc.) (Spender 1989; Nonaka 1991, 1994). However, recently there has been an increasing interest in the individual and the manner in which his or her knowledge contributes to the knowledge of a firm.

Building on Simon (1945) and Williamson (1975), one of the basic assumptions of the knowledge-based view is that individuals are limited by their bounded rationality on two dimensions (Connor & Prahalad 1996): (1) neurophysiological and (2) language limits. The first dimension, neurophysiological limits, describes individuals as limited by the amount of information that they can receive, store, retrieve, and process without committing any error. Thus, all the firm's knowledge cannot be found in any one person's head and as a result, it is distributed across its members. Thus, the firm acts as an enabler of coordinated action among individuals. In addition, knowledge must flow between individuals without losing its meaning in order for the firm to serve its purpose. Yet, this flow is complicated by the second dimension of bounded rationality—that individuals have language limits due to their inability to articulate all of their knowledge or feelings. In other words, tacit knowledge is a result of bounded rationality (Conner & Prahalad 1996). Bound by both a physical and social context and embodied in the language and behaviors of those using it, tacit knowledge is not receptive to being made explicit or codified. Thus, it is more costly and more difficult to transfer to others who do not share the same language and behaviors.

Kogut & Zander (1992, 1995) argue that a firm should be understood as a social community in which its members have a shared identity. As individuals work together over time, they develop shared mental models, a common language, and common behaviors. This shared identity lowers the costs of communication between the firm's members and results in explicit and tacit rules of coordination as routines are built over time. In addition, a common language enables members to codify their tacit knowledge. Relative to individuals outside the firm, employees can then easily access and reuse this codified knowledge as they share the same communication code and mental models as those who codified it (Nonaka & Takeuchi 1995). In this manner, it is relatively easy for employees to search the company for advice or existing solutions (Constant et al. 1996).

In addition, it has been argued that the most effective means to transfer tacit knowledge is actually *not* to codify it, but rather to transfer it through an implicit mode. Reber (1993) defines transfer through implicit mode as "the acquisition of knowledge (that) takes place largely independently of conscious attempts to learn and largely in the absence of explicit knowledge about what was acquired." The firm facilitates this implicit transfer mode since its members have developed shared mental models, a common language, and common behaviors. One conceptual lens through which this implicit knowledge transfer can be studied is the evolving Community of Practice body of research, which is the subject of the next section.

Communities of Practice

The two limitations of bounded rationality that were described above lead to an endless number of gaps between the canonical and noncanonical practices in an individual's everyday work (Brown & Duguid 1991). One of the first studies to observe this was the ethnographic study of Xerox service technicians during the late 1980s when it was observed that there was a variance between the organization's formal description of work and the way in which the actual work was performed. When the technicians were faced with problems for which the formal structure often did not provide solutions, they relied on the organization's informal systems for help, such as storytelling, conversation, mentoring, and experiential learning (Brown & Duguid 1991; Orr 1990; Snyder 1997; Wenger 1997). Individuals collaborated with each other through an emergent and fluid structure of relationships and engaged in patterns of exchange and communication to reduce the uncertainty of their tasks (Pava 1983; Purser et al. 1992). Thus, the procedures required to fulfill the tasks were developed informally as the workers performed their tasks, demanding the creation and use of knowledge along the way (Purser et al. 1992; Stebbins & Shani 1995).

These informally established groups of collaborating individuals have been coined communities of practice. Communities of practice have no real boundaries and are in a constant state of evolution as members come and go and commitment levels fluctuate. This fluidity creates difficulties when management wants to pin down communities of practice, determine their boundaries, and develop some form of recipe to manage them. Indeed, it is argued that this is not possible due to the pure informal nature of communities of practice (Wenger 1998). Thus, we must satisfy ourselves at this point with a definition that captures this fluidity and intangibility.

> A group of people informally and contextually bound who are applying a common competence in the pursuit of a common enterprise (Brown & Duguid 1991; Lave & Wenger 1991; Snyder 1997; Wenger 1998).

To begin explaining this definition, we will start with a simple definition of community and practice. A community implies a form of collaboration or collectivism, a group of people bound together. Practice can be thought of as the sustained pursuit of an enterprise or an undertaking that is contextually bound in an historical and social sense. For the Xerox service technicians described above, their practice was satisfying customers through the reparation of copier machines. For a group of pharmaceutical researchers spread across a number of companies, it may be trying to find the cure for cancer. Within an organization, individuals belong to several communities of practice. Thus, an individual may belong to one community of practice that performs the same job (e.g., Xerox tech reps), one that works together on a shared task (e.g., software developers), or one that develops a product (e.g., engineers, marketers, and manufacturing specialists) (Brown & Gray 1997).

Through three aspects, "narration, social construction, and collaboration," employees become members of and build communities of practice within their organization (Brown & Duguid 1991). First, through the narration of stories, employees help each other to make sense of non-canonical or unexpected circumstances. Used in this manner, stories are more flexible than strict documentation such as training manuals since they provide the ability to interpret each new situation (Brown & Duguid 1991). The second aspect of a community of practice is the collaboration that occurs between its members. With knowledge-intensive tasks, often no one individual can solve problems on his or her own due to the inability to know everything. By relying on their community, individuals can perform their work without needing to know everything. In addition, many employees are confronted with information overload. Through asking someone in the community for help, time does not have to be spent sorting though piles of information for relevant documents (Wenger 1998). Through collaboration and storytelling, the members of a community of practice socially construct their world, the third aspect of a community of practice. Both a tacit and explicit means of communication and working are developed that enable the community to perform its practice in a satisfying manner. The explicit includes it own language and vocabulary, codified procedures, documents, regulations, etc. But more interestingly, the tacit is the invisible, the implicit relations, cues, unarticulated etiquette, etc.—the invisible glue that holds the community together (Boland & Tenkasi 1995; Brown & Duguid 1991; Wenger 1998). Thus, the members become bound together by the context of the situation and in an informal manner, creating the social fabric of the organization (Brown & Duguid 1991).

The effective creation and transfer of knowledge within a community of practice is dependent on the extent of commitment and genuine participation of its members and on the strength of personal relationships among them. Thus, a strong foundation of trust and respect is required. This foundation is built through the mutual engagement of community members. In addition, research has shown that when members of a community of practice did not feel a high level of shared trust and commitment, their capacity to share knowledge and skills was reduced (Snyder 1997).

In order to return to the focus of the present research document, it is important to make a few points based on the above discussion. The first is that the community of practice research argues that the most effective means to develop and transfer tacit knowledge is not through formal systems and structures, but rather through informal collaborative activities (Schon 1983; Snyder 1996, 1997). Thus, the focus is placed on the *informal*. Indeed, management in many companies is now focusing on supporting communities of practice within company walls with the hope of increasing the company's competitive advantage or improving the organizational learning process (Boland & Tenkasi 1995; Brown & Duguid 1998; Davenport & Prusak 1998). The second point is that an individual can also belong to communities that extent *across* a firm's boundaries, such as the larger professional community to which he or she belongs (Venkatraman & Henderson 1998). However, to date there has been very limited research focused on interorganizational communities of practice.

A third interesting aspect is the application of the communities of practice thinking to the virtual world. Through the rapid introduction of the Internet, the potential for non-face-to-face, lateral written communications that take place across time and space has been greatly facilitated (Hinds & Kiesler 1995). As a result, many organizations are in the process of implementing electronic communities to promote knowledge sharing between organizational individuals (Alavi and Leidner 1999; Davenport & Prusak 1998; Fulk & DeSanctis 1995). In addition, there are electronic communities that extend across organizational boundaries in which individuals can participate (Hagel and Armstrong 1997). Often these electronic communities are self-organized and participating individuals can communicate with thousands of others anywhere across the globe, regardless of demographic characteristics, organizational setting, or local culture (Sproull & Faraj 1995; Faraj & McClure-Wasko 1999). However, again there is a limited amount of research on electronic communities.

Operationalizing Communities of Practice

While the amount of papers and articles focusing on communities of practice continues to grow, few researchers have attempted to understand the relation between communities of practice and performance. This is understandable because they are—by definition—extremely hard to pin down. Any individual can potentially be involved in numerous communities of practice, varying from one's immediate workgroup to a set of Internet contacts on the other side of the world. Moreover, the process of defining the membership of communities of practice apparently takes away their very essence, because they thrive on their informal nature. Bearing this in mind it is not surprising that the community of practice literature is populated with ethnographies and case studies rather than surveys or experiments.

Our approach in this chapter is to bring the community of practice thinking down to the level of the individual. Rather than attempt to define the community of practices within and across the firm's boundaries, we instead work on the basis that an individual's performance at work is associated with the extent to which he or she is a member of various communities of practice, including those facilitated by electronic means. Thus, by measuring the patterns of communication of the individual with various groups of people, and through various different forums, one can predict to some degree his or her performance. In the next section we formally develop this idea into a series of testable propositions.

CONCEPTUAL FRAMEWORK AND PROPOSITIONS

As discussed earlier, competitive advantage is built on the firm's ability to acquire new knowledge from outside the boundaries of the firm while at the same time leveraging the existing knowledge within the firm. However, this leaves us with a vague idea regarding on which level knowledge acquisition and leverage occur because it can potentially occur at all levels—the individual, the group, the business unit, and the firm. As suggested by Hedlund (1994), it is the ability to transfer knowledge *between* levels of analysis (e.g., from the individual-level to the firm level and vice versa) that is valuable, and indeed one of the major characteristics that makes the firm unique.

In this chapter we are concerned with two levels of analysis: the individual and the community of practice. The logic here is that individuals are able to draw from their communities of practice to solve problems they encounter in the course of their work, and that they also contribute back to these communities in a reciprocal manner. Thus, the extent to which an individual is actively involved in communities of practice will *ceteris paribus* be associated with a superior performance at work.

But as we have already noted, there are significant methodological problems in studying communities of practice. Our primary concern is that the concept is typically defined in such a way that all informal interactions, inside or outside the firm, could represent participation in communities of practice. If this broad definition is accepted, then the concept becomes very difficult to research in a rigorous manner because nothing is excluded. The theory, in other words, cannot be falsified.

The approach taken here, as hinted above, is to move down to the level of the individual and to then examine the way in which that individual acquires new knowledge to address work-related problems. Some knowledge, as we will see, is gained through access to "codified" sources such as the Internet or company databases, but most is gained through interaction with other people in the firm and outside. Our premise, in other words, is that the frequency and quality of the interaction an individual has with specific groups of individuals is a manifestation of the communities of practice he or she is involved with. And that such interactions will have a positive impact on his or her individual-level performance.

The conceptual framework in Figure 10.1 illustrates our approach. Individual level performance, we argue, is a function of the various ways knowledge is acquired by the individual, and the sources of that knowledge can be divided into (1) internal vs. external sources, and (2) tacit vs. codified sources. In addition

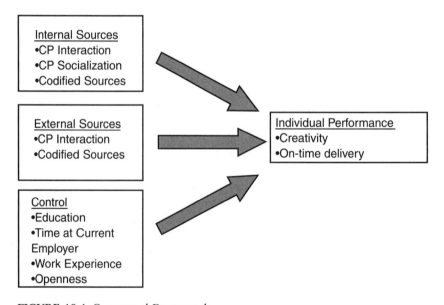

FIGURE 10.1 Conceptual Framework

there are many other factors contributing to individual level performance, some of which are empirically examined as controls.

Proposition Development

The first proposition follows directly from the discussion about the nature of communities of practice inside the firm. As stated above, individuals within organizations are thought to be members of numerous communities of practice. Researchers claim that the creation and exchange of tacit knowledge occurs in the interaction between the individual and other community members when solving work-related problems. Being an active member of communities within the organization implies a high degree of collaboration and interaction with other members through primarily face-to-face but also non-face-to-face interactions. A high degree of interactions with other community members should therefore lead to a greater individual development of task-related knowledge and thus higher performance. Thus we have our first proposition.

> Proposition 1: The higher the level of individual personal interaction with communities within the firm, the higher the level of individual performance.

For an individual to truly become a member of a community of practice and access the community's knowledge, it is argued that he or she must not only have a high degree of interaction, but also become an "insider" through the development of trust with other members of the community (Lave & Wenger 1991). Through a high level of trust, the member learns of other members' mistakes and breakthroughs through storytelling and narration of work-related happenings. While trust is difficult to measure, and particularly so when the community in question is not clearly specified, one manifestation of it is in the existence of social contacts outside of work. Thus:

> Proposition 2: Social contacts with community members from work leads to a higher level of individual performance.

The two propositions above are concerned with an individual's participation in communities of practice within the boundaries of the organization. However, it is central to the concept of communities of practice that they also spread across organizational boundaries, through professional or technical relationships. These communities may involve members from the suppliers, customers, or even friends working on similar tasks in other companies. A high degree of interaction with members of communities that cross organizational boundaries can be expected to broaden the individual's knowledge through the exchange of knowledge from outside the firm. Thus, much in the same manner as proposition 1, proposition 3 thus becomes the following:

> Proposition 3: The higher the level of individual personal interaction with members of communities that spread across organizational boundaries, the higher the level of performance.

Propositions four and five are concerned with the acquisition of knowledge through codified sources. The spread of the Internet and the development of intranets are factors that have led to this explosion of rapidly accessible codified knowledge. While communities of practice are understood to be the channels for the development and exchange of primarily tacit knowledge, the use of codified sources of data such as company documents facilitates an individual when solving work-related tasks. For example, access to an internal document can help an individual to avoid reinventing the wheel, thus facilitating the completion of a work-related task. This codification and documentation of knowledge within the firm is one of the main thrusts of management in organizations in order to ensure the transfer and application of knowledge throughout the firm.

> Proposition 4: The higher the use of internal codified sources of information, the higher the level of individual performance.

In addition to company specific codified knowledge, individuals also have access to numerous sources of codified knowledge outside the firm. In today's fast-changing world, the knowledge required to solve a new, challenging task may not exist inside the firm, thus the individual may have to search outside the firm for help.

> Proposition 5: The higher the use of external codified sources of information, the higher the level of performance.

Finally, we put forward the rather general proposition that the extent to which the above approaches to knowledge acquisition affect performance will be contingent on the nature of the task being performed. Space limitations prevent us from getting into a detailed discussion, but one would expect *ceteris paribus* that the less routine, the more intellectually challenging, and the more fast-changing the work, the more important it would be to have ready access to personal and codified sources of knowledge. In terms of the specifics of this study, we have therefore separated out those individuals who work in software programming and web design from those doing other tasks (such as administration, sales, and management), on the basis that the former group are likely to rely more on knowledge acquisition from a variety of sources to undertake their work effectively. Thus:

> Proposition 6: The relationships put forward in propositions 1–5 will be stronger for "technical" employees (software programmers, web designers) than for other employees.

Many other factors are also expected to be associated with individual performance. In this study we measured the education level of the individual, the amount of time he or she has spent with Icon Medialab, and their general work experience. In addition we also measured their perceptions of how "open" the work environment is at Icon because it is a factor that is likely to affect their propensity to exchange information with others.

Finally, it is worth observing here that individual-level performance is not a unidimensional construct. At the very least, we would expect to see a split between "exploration" and "exploitation" (March 1991) where exploration would be manifested as creativity or the development of novel solutions, while exploitation would be manifested in the ability to get work done on time and on budget. However, given the exploratory nature of this research we have not specified any *a priori* expectations regarding the type of performance associations we expect to see.

METHODS

Sample and Analysis

The research was undertaken in a single firm, Icon Medialab. While our objective in the future is to broaden the investigation to other firms, it makes sense to begin in a single case and then to reevaluate on the basis of the findings from that study. As already mentioned, the choice of Icon was motivated primarily on the basis that it is a quintessential "IT intensive" firm, in which a large proportion of the employees are working on a day-to-day basis with the latest Internet technology. Many of these employees, it turns out, are interacting frequently with "communities" of "techies" whom they have never met. As such, this setting represents a fascinating test of the communities of practice concept.

It should be noted that Icon is based in Stockholm. This was not only convenient, but Stockholm is also quite an opportune location for studying such a firm because Sweden is at the forefront of digital communications technology. The country has one of the highest penetration rates in the world of mobile telephones and Internet subscriptions per capita, and Stockholm is a recognized high-technology "cluster." Icon is one of many recent start-up Internet firms in the area (founded 1996), and one of the world's best 350 small companies according to Forbes (Forbes 1998). A description of the company follows.

Two phases of data collection and analysis were conducted. The first phase was conducted at the Swedish office, in which thirty in-depth field interviews were held from May 1998 to June 1998. People at different areas of the company (e.g., corporate management, business development, sales, and different production competencies) were interviewed for one-and-a-half to two hours each. Interviews with management were conducted first in order to understand the formal structures that had been put in place to facilitate knowledge acquisition mechanisms. Extensive written material was also collected from the companies.

The second phase of the data collection involved a questionnaire sent to all 242 employees of Icon Medialab at their local offices. Questionnaires were then sealed in individual envelopes and returned to us either by mail or directly. Of the 242 questionnaires, 203 usable questionnaires were collected, an 84 percent response rate. Throughout the data collection process, individuals were assured that their responses would be kept confidential and that all results would be presented on an aggregated level. In addition to these individual questionnaires, each of the managing directors of the eight subsidiaries and seven managers at the Stockholm office were asked to complete a questionnaire relating to the performance of the individuals at their office. The average age of the respondents was 29.9 years with an average of 385 days employed at Icon and 4.8 years experience in their competence. The sample was 30 percent women.

In terms of the split between functions, there were 72 respondents working in technically oriented functions (e.g., programmers, web-page designers) and 131 working in the non-technically oriented functions (e.g., sales, administration). As discussed in the previous section, this split is important in terms of understanding the types of communities of practice individuals are likely to develop.

Measures

Dependent Variables

Several different approaches exist for measuring performance, including both subjective and objective measurements. For the purposes of this study we used two different subjective dependent variables that measure individual performance, creativity, and on-time performance. As discussed above, these measures represent the two dimensions of performance of exploration and exploitation where exploration is manifested as creativity or the development of novel solutions and exploitation manifested as the ability to get work done on time and on budget (March 1991). While it is somewhat difficult to distinguish between these two measures, we do feel that it is important to measure both since it is often difficult to develop solutions that are highly creative but that are also on budget and on-time.

1. *Creativity*—Individuals were asked to answer 3 questions that created a creativity scale (Sjöberg & Lind 1994). These were based on a seven-point scale from 1, "strongly disagree," to 7, "strongly agree" (three items, $\alpha = 0.64$).
2. *On-time performance*—The final performance measure asked respondents to answer to what degree they felt they delivered their work on-time on a seven-point scale from 1, "strongly disagree," to 7, "strongly agree" (two items, $\alpha = 0.66$).

In addition, we asked the managers in each of the offices to rate the performance of each individual reporting to him or her on two different items: ability to meet superior's objectives and to develop creative solutions. While the two items were strongly correlated with each other ($r = 0.75$), the correlation with the various self-reported performance measures was very weak (between 0.05 and 0.28). After discussing this matter with several of these individuals, it became clear that the managers often had remarkably limited contact with many of their direct reports, and that they could not easily assess their performance. We therefore concluded that the self-reported performance measures were more valid, an observation that is consistent with a number of previous studies (e.g., Heneman 1974; Wexley et al. 1980).[ii]

Independent Variables

These variables included the different dimensions of the knowledge acquisition processes and we have chosen to split them on the external vs. internal dimension. The external mechanisms consisted of two measures. The first measures which relates to proposition 5, *Codified—external*, asked respondents to answer on a seven-point scale the frequency of use of external knowledge sources. These sources included traditional sources such as externally produced books or journals in addition to recently developed sources such as Internet web pages or Internet discussion forums (five items, $\alpha = 0.73$). The second measure, *External community interaction*, was measured on a four-point scale relating to the degree of interaction on work-related matters with customers and friends. Respondents were asked how often they initiated the interaction as well as how often the external party initiated the interaction (four items, $\alpha = 0.80$) and relates to proposition 3. The second group of variables, internal mechanisms, consisted of 7 different measures. The first measure relating to proposition 4, *Codified—internal*, asked respondents to answer on a seven-point scale the frequency of use of internal knowledge sources. These included using the company's intranet as well as materials such as documents that were produced internally by Icon (three items, $\alpha = 0.64$). The next measure, *Interaction with internal community*, that relates to proposition 1 was based on a four-point frequency scale on two dimensions. The first one was based on whether it was the respondent who initiated the interaction and the second one based on whether the other party initiated the interaction. This measure was built upon the interaction with others within the same function, others within one's workgroup, and others outside of one's workgroup (three items, $\alpha = 0.64$). For example, the workgroup of a programmer included art directors and web designers as these three functions comprised the production team for each project. Those outside of the programmer's workgroup included those in support functions (e.g., sales) or those in management functions (e.g., human resources). The final measure, *Social contact*, was measured through the level of social contact outside of work with any individual throughout the organization. This was measured on a simple 1–2 scale, 1 for no and 2 for yes (3 items, $\alpha = 0.86$) and relates to proposition 2.

Control Variables

These variables included level of education (1–5 scale), time employed at Icon (no. of days), related work experience (years),[iii] and openness. Openness was created to measure the level of openness at Icon perceived by the individual on a seven-point scale from 1, "strongly disagree," to 7, "strongly agree" (11 items, $\alpha = 0.65$). Summary statistics for the control variables and the other variables are presented in Table 10.1.

TABLE 10.1 Descriptive Statistics and Correlations for All Variables[a]

Variable	Unit	Mean	s.d.	1	2	3	4	5	6	7	8	9	10
Self-evaluated performance													
1. Creativity	1–7 scale	5.06	1.04										
2. On-time performance	1–7 scale	4.96	1.22	0.08									
Control													
3. Education	1–5 scale	2.98	1.03	0.10	−0.15*								
4. Related work experience	years	4.76	4.42	0.29***	0.20*	−0.04							
5. Employed at Icon	days	385.52	349.92	0.18*	−0.08	0.03	0.11						
6. Office openness	1–7 scale	5.13	0.63	0.27***	0.18**	−0.06	0.05	0.16*					
External													
7. Codified	1–7 scale	3.63	1.21	0.17*	0.00	−0.00	0.13	0.02	0.05				
8. External community interaction	1–4 scale	2.79	0.84	0.21**	0.04	0.07	0.17	0.14	0.14	0.13			
Internal													
9. Codified	1–7 scale	3.68	1.34	0.06	0.23**	0.04	0.18	−0.14	0.13	0.15*	0.17*		
10. Interaction with internal community	1–4 scale	3.12	0.62	0.15*	0.15*	0.11	0.02	0.09	0.29***	0.10	0.20**	0.08	
11. Social contact	1, no; 2, yes	1.36	0.41	0.27**	−0.06	0.05	−0.08	0.10	0.24***	0.12	0.14	0.09	0.27**

a. Range of N is 154–203.

 * p < 0.05.

 ** p < 0.01.

 *** p < 0.001.

The propositions were tested through a series of stepwise regression models. The stepwise approach was chosen primarily because of the small sample size and the relatively large number of independent variables. Also, the exploratory nature of the study makes it appropriate to work with a rather larger number of independent variables than would normally be the case. The plan in future iterations of this research will be to move towards a more carefully specified model.

Company Description

Icon Medialab was founded in March 1996 in response to the rapid growth of the Internet.[iv] The company's mission was to facilitate the creation of competitive advantage for its customers through the incorporation of the Internet in customer operations. Products and services included Internet homepages, intranets, extranets, and e-commerce solutions. Icon Medialab's clients ranged from the Swedish Postal Office and Compaq to British Petroleum and Volkswagen. The company posted sales of SEK 65 mln for the fiscal year ending April 1998 (SEK 13 mln in 1997) and at the time of this study had 242 employees with 46% of these in Sweden. The remaining employees were spread throughout offices of 10–25 employees in Spain, Finland, Denmark, Germany, Belgium, England, and the United States, with new offices planned for France and Norway.

A strategy of rapid global growth was developed by the founders at the company's inception. One of the means by which Icon hoped to achieve profitable growth was through the reuse of knowledge developed throughout its different projects. In fact, management set a target that more than 50% of all projects should include already proven successful products or services. Thus, Icon Medialab invested heavily in building its structural capital, with the key objectives to transfer and reuse knowledge complemented with follow-up and reporting.

In addition, Icon Medialab was unique in its representation of a mixture of competencies under the same organizational umbrella. These disciplines included Technology, Design, Usability Engineering, Statistics and Analysis, Media and Entertainment, and Business Strategy, representing the 6 sides of the "Icon Cube." Thus, Icon Medialab brought together art directors, behavioral scientists, copywriters, journalists, scriptwriters, animators, TV-producers, software programmers, management consultants, and web designers, with accounting, personnel, and administration completing the organization.

RESULTS

Descriptive Statistics

Before moving to the results of the regression analysis, it is important to describe the patterns of knowledge acquisition among the Icon employees, and

TABLE 10.2 Comparison of Means

Variable	Nontech.	Tech.	t
External			
8. Codified—external[a]	3.43	4.00	3.30**
9. Interaction with external community[b]	2.96	2.46	−4.00***
Internal			
10. Codified—internal[a]	3.95	3.20	−3.90***
11. Interaction with internal community[b]	3.07	3.15	−0.88
12. Social contact outside work[c]	1.36	1.34	−0.35

a. 1—yearly or less, 2—four times a year, 3—once a month, 4—once a week, 5—two times a week, 6—once a day, 7—several times a day.

b. 1—rarely or never, 2—once a month, 3—two times a week, 4—a few times a day.

c. 1—no, 2—yes.

** $p < 0.01$.

*** $p < 0.001$.

in particular whether there are any significant differences between technical employees and others (cf. proposition 6). Table 10.2 presents a comparison of the means of the use of different sources of knowledge for the two groups at Icon. While there is no significant difference in the level of internal community interaction and social contact outside of work, Codified—internal sources, Codified—external sources, and Interaction with the external community do differ significantly. The technically oriented people tended to use external codified sources of information more than the non-technically oriented people while the opposite is true for the internal codified sources. Based on our scale, technically oriented people used external codified sources once a week on average, while the non-technically oriented people used these sources between one to two times a month. With regard to internal codified sources, non-technically oriented people accessed these about once a week and the technically oriented people closer to once a month. In addition, the level of interaction with the external community was higher for non-technically oriented people than for those who are technically oriented. Non-technically oriented people interacted with the external community an average of about two times a week while the non-technical people interacted about two times a month.

Propositions

Individual performance was measured using two different constructs, Creativity and On-time performance. In addition, we have reported two different models for each dependent variable—one for the whole sample, and one for just the technical employees. The purpose of this split is to see if the results differ significantly when one just considers technical employees.

TABLE 10.3 Results of Regression Analysis of the Relationship between Knowledge Acquisition Mechanisms and Self-Reported Creativity

Variable	Prop.	Model 1 Whole Sample		Model 2 Tech. Only	
		Var. Incl	Var. Excl.	Var. Incl	Var. Excl
Control					
4. Education		0.18*			−0.00
5. Work experience		0.31***			0.10
6. Time at Icon			0.03		−0.22
7. Office openness		0.30**		0.42*	
External knowledge					
8. Codified—external	5	0.15†		0.35*	
9. External community interaction	3		0.08		−0.22
Internal knowledge					
10. Codified—internal	4		0.08		0.11
11. Internal community interaction	1		0.07		0.06
12. Social contact outside work	2	0.17†		0.30†	
R2		0.28		0.51	
ΔR2		0.25		0.45	
F for ΔR2		7.97***		8.31**	

† $p < 0.10$.

* $p < 0.05$.

** $p < 0.01$.

*** $p < 0.001$.

Self-Reported Creativity—Whole Sample

In Table 10.3, limited support for propositions 5 and 2 is received for the whole sample size. Consistent with proposition 5, the coefficient of the use of External codified sources is positive ($p < 0.10$). In addition, the coefficient of Social contact outside of work is positive ($p < 0.10$) and is consistent with proposition 2. Thus, the higher the level of social contact and the higher the use of external codified sources, the higher the level of individual creative performance. In addition, the control variables were also highly significant: Education ($p < 0.05$), Office openness ($p < 0.01$), and Related work experience ($p < 0.001$).

Self-Reported Creativity—Technically Oriented

Table 10.3 also provides the results for only the technically oriented people. Stronger support is provided for proposition 5 since the coefficient for Codified external is more significant ($p < 0.05$) than in the above regression. Social contact is the same as above ($p < 0.10$), thus providing limited support for proposition 2. In addition, there was only one significant control variable, Openness ($p < 0.05$). Of interest, is that the adjusted R^2 is the highest for this regression than any of the others, 0.45.

Self-Reported On-Time Performance—Whole Sample

Support for proposition 4 is given in Table 10.4 as the coefficient is positively related ($p < 0.05$). Thus, on-time performance is positively related to the use of Codified internal sources. In addition, two control variables turned out negatively related to performance: Education ($p < 0.05$) and Time at Icon ($p < 0.10$). This regression had the weakest R^2 of the regressions, 0.11.

TABLE 10.4 Results of Regression Analysis of the Relationship between Knowledge Acquisition Mechanisms and Self-Reported On-Time Performance

Variable	Prop.	Model 1 Whole Sample		Model 2 Tech. Only	
		Var. Incl	Var. Excl	Var. Incl	Var. Excl
Control					
4. Education		−0.23*			−0.11
5. Work experience			0.04		−0.04
6. Time at Icon		−0.16†			−0.09
7. Office openness			0.08	0.28†	
External knowledge					
8. Codified—external	5		−0.04	−0.31*	
9. External community interaction	3		−0.10		−0.06
Internal knowledge					
10. Codified—internal	4	0.23*		0.55*	
11. Internal community interaction	1		0.11		0.26
12. Social contact outside work	2		−0.11		0.08
R2		0.13		0.48	
ΔR2		0.11		0.42	
F for ΔR2		5.25**		7.43**	

† $p < 0.10$.

* $p < 0.05$.

** $p < 0.01$.

*** $p < 0.001$.

TABLE 10.5 Support for Propositions

Proposition	Creativity		On-Time	
	Whole	*Tech.*	*Whole*	*Tech.*
1. Interaction with internal community				
2. Social contact outside work	$0.17^\dagger$	$0.30^\dagger$		
3. Interaction with external community				
4. Codified—internal			0.23^*	0.55^{**}
5. Codified—external	$0.15^\dagger$	0.35^*		-0.31^*

  † $p < 0.10$.
  * $p < 0.05$.
  ** $p < 0.01$.
  *** $p < 0.001$.

Self-Reported On-Time Performance—Technically Oriented

Table 10.4 shows that there is support for proposition 4 as the coefficient, Codified internal, is positively related to On-time performance ($p < 0.01$). In addition, proposition 5 was rejected as the coefficient, Codified external, was negatively related to performance ($p < 0.05$). Only one control, Openness ($p < 0.10$), appeared significant in this equation.

DISCUSSION AND IMPLICATIONS

Table 10.5 provides an overview of the support for the different propositions from the different regression models. Altogether we can see some support for propositions 2, 4, and 5. Moreover, what is interesting here is that we see such different results for the two dependent variables. Again, as discussed above, we have measured two dimensions of performance, creativity and on-time performance that represent exploration and exploitation, where exploration is manifested as creativity or the development of novel solutions and exploitation manifested as the ability to get work done on time and on budget (March 1991). Following is a discussion of the regression findings related to our qualitative findings.

Creativity

Taking creativity first, we see social contact outside work and the use of external codified sources of information (Internet communities and the like) as the significant predictors. Building on our qualitative findings, the impression one gets is that technical employees attach great importance to their external Internet-based relationships as sources of ideas and as ways of solving tricky problems. Several programmers even stated that they preferred to go first to their Internet community or use their private e-mail list for help instead of asking someone at their own company even if he or she was sitting at the next desk. This appeared to be for several reasons. The first was that by posting a question in an open forum, people were not obligated to help. Instead those who wanted to help could do so in a voluntary fashion. By reaching out to the community for help, one did not disturb a colleague at work who had his or her own schedule and deadlines to meet. Another reason was that people could access a much broader source of expertise than at their own company. Members of the communities worked at different types of companies all over the world; however, they worked on the same type of problem. Thus, it was felt that this enabled one to gain access to the latest thinking within one's field.

Another quite interesting reason for the use of electronic communities that we uncovered during the qualitative phase was that prestige played a significant role in which source one turned to for help. Several commented that programmers feared making mistakes or making themselves look stupid by asking others at Icon for help. So, they turned to the Internet where "no one knows if you're a monkey." Another aspect was that it was seen as prestigious if one belonged to some of the closed Internet communities. Some of these qualitative findings seem to be in accordance with Zipf's Law of Least Effort (1949), which argues that individuals when choosing a path towards a goal are more interested in minimizing effort than maximizing gain. This effort includes both physical as well as psychological effort. Thus, although asking another programmer within the company for help may result in a larger gain, it may cost the knowledge seeker more in terms of psychological effort, showing that he or she does not know the answer.[v]

To turn the discussion to the second predictor, Social contact, individuals became members of a tightly knit community of practice through extensive social contact outside of work. During this social contact, these individuals discussed the difficult problems encountered during the day, the responses received from the electronic community, and how they then attempted to solve the problem. The latest solutions or tips from both the outside communities and one's own work were passed between the members of the community. In this manner, these community members socially constructed their world through the narration of stories, turning incoherent data into coherent information. This enabled them to gain insights into the work they were performing, allowing them to be more creative in their daily work. What is interesting here then is that it is the combination of the use of an external community with one's internal community. As ideas cross community boundaries, resulting in the cross-fertilization of communities, knowledge is combined to foster creativity. Based on these findings and previous research, we then developed the term Netovation to describe this creative performance that was fostered through the use of the Internet (Teigland 1999).

On-Time Performance

In terms of achieving on-time performance, a very different picture emerges. Here, the use of internal codified sources of information is a positive predictor of on-time performance, while the use of external codified sources is a *negative* predictor. This is entirely in keeping with our intuitive expectations. Building relationships with external communities and creating unique or "elegant" solutions on the basis of those relationships works well when creativity is the objective, but it is a strong negative when on-time delivery matters. Gathering information from the outside takes time because first either the sources must be located or one must wait for someone to voluntarily help. And once the information or help is received, it must be assimilated into the context of both the problem and the company's way of doing things. This may take considerable time depending on the complexity of the information and the problem.

In addition, reciprocity within these electronic communities is necessary in order to become a true member. In other words, to be able to ask the other Internet community members for help, one must prove that one also gives back to the community through providing help to others when other members ask. This returning of help then results in the individual performing work for others outside the company, which then takes away time from the individual's internal responsibilities.

Thus, on-time performance can best be achieved by re-using existing solutions that can be accessed through the firm's intranet or company documents. To give an example from Icon, the company's intranet included a programming module database that included both a description for the sales force and a technical description for the programmers. Programming modules were building blocks of programming code that could be reused in a number of customer projects, such as a discussion forum, telephone book, and conference room booking system. In addition to a technical description, the module list also specified how many hours were required to develop the module. This information was added to help determine the pricing and planning of future projects.

Implications for Theory and Practice

This study raises a number of very interesting theoretical and practical issues. First, what do we make of the concept of the community of practice in the light of our findings? Some support was clearly found, in terms of the importance of work-related and social interaction with other community members. But there were also some surprises, notably the importance of so-called "Internet communities" as sources of knowledge for technical employees. This is a curious discovery because these "communities" exhibit many of the characteristics of communities of practice—reciprocity, identity, and so on—but the individuals involved have typically never met, and they work through what is by definition a *codified* exchange of information, which goes against other aspects of the theory. One programmer commented,

I've been really active in the Internet community for a long time. I'm in contact with a group of about 20 people who are experts at what they do. But I have never met them physically. But it doesn't matter because on the Internet we have always been friends. It's just like when you used to go snowboarding 10 years ago. If you were somewhere and saw another snowboarder, you said hi and then you'd hang out together in the evening. Just because we snowboarded and there were so few who did it. We were on the same level...we knew where we had one another.

The development of these electronic communities has added a spoke of a new dimension to the community of practice literature. Whether or not these electronic communities can be considered communities of practice is an issue currently being debated among scholars. According to Lave & Wenger (1991), socialization (i.e., face-to-face contact) among members is an important factor in the building of a community of practice. Nonaka & Takeuchi (1995) further explain that socialization requires the sharing of tacit knowledge that in turn requires a shared space among the community of practice members. Since communication through the Internet is textual among individuals who often are spread across the globe, it is argued that participating individuals do not have a shared space, thus there is no socialization, and more importantly, no sharing of tacit knowledge. Followers of this view would then argue that these Internet-based communities are not communities of practice in the "true" meaning of the term. As a result, we need to revisit certain aspects of the community of practice to better understand which theories are still valid and which need to be adapted to the new empirical contexts.

Secondly, our results provide some preliminary support for the idea that the firm is a vehicle that brings together members from different communities of practice that are more professionally oriented. Thus, a programmer may belong to a C++ community that spreads across many firms' boundaries while the other functions at Icon (e.g., management consultant, art director, etc.) do the same. Icon then brings together these different communities by hiring members and incorporates them into project teams. Professional knowledge flows across firm boundaries as individuals seek out help from their external professional communities. The firm then develops the knowledge as to how to coordinate these different professional individuals.

The third implication from our findings is that the building of the capability to manage these knowledge flows presents considerable challenges for a company's management. First as we found in our research, on-time performance was negatively correlated to the use of external codified sources, yet positively correlated to the use of internal codified sources. Too much external knowledge leads to missed deadlines and overrun budgets, while the reuse of internal knowledge leads to on-time performance. Based on our qualitative findings, the aspect of prestige including the "not-invented-here" syndrome—the desire to develop one's own solutions rather than reuse existing solutions—and Zipf's Law of Least Effort (1949) play a significant role in the choice of knowledge sources.

While it was found that this matter of prestige was strong within Icon, it may have its roots outside of Icon's borders in the global community, primarily

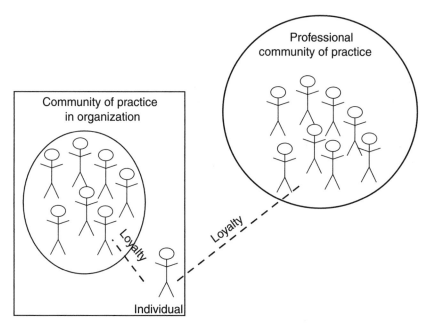

FIGURE 10.2 An Individual's Conflicting Loyalties

among the programmers. One programmer explained that he started working on one project because he really wanted to show Silicon Valley that other areas of the world could produce "bleeding edge" products as well. While on the one hand, programmers were inspired to make Icon the world's best company, on the other hand, programmers were pressured by their global community to produce the latest "cool" solution. In addition, programmers were under a form of social pressure from their external community to help fellow members solve their difficult problems, often attempting to "show off" in front of the others. This was found to lead to conflicting goals or loyalty for the programmers: best company vs. best profession (see Figure 10.2). Creating a "cool" solution or trying to impress a global community through solving another external member's difficult problem leads to longer hours worked, using unnecessary resources as well as causing delays in product delivery to the customer. However, it is this communication with communities that span organizational boundaries that leads to the cross-fertilization of communities that then fosters creativity. And it is this creativity that is essential for the continuous creation of a firm's competitive advantage.

Thus, the challenge for management is then to be able to align the use of both the internal and external knowledge sources with the company's competitive strategy. If the company is pursuing more of a knowledge creation over a knowledge reuse strategy, then a greater use of external sources over internal sources ensures creativity and the access to the latest solutions. However, if the strategic focus is on knowledge reuse, then too much external use leads to an inefficient use of resources. This is no new challenge, merely the exploration vs. exploitation balance in a new setting. What perhaps has intensified this challenge is that as the Internet technology develops so rapidly, management may have difficulty in keeping abreast of the developments, making it a challenge to know whether employees are working on necessary value-adding activities. One manager summed up this situation with reference to the programmers. "Programmers take us (management) hostage. We never know whether they're working on extra bells and whistles to impress their buddies or whether it's really a value-adding activity for the customer."

A second challenge for management is that when employees are active in their external communities, they are often involved in disclosing company knowledge to other external community members. As stated above, an unwritten code of conduct with fellow community members exists that includes reciprocity. In order for members to gain knowledge, they must provide knowledge to others. Those who do not give are cut off from the knowledge flows. Thus, management must be aware that knowledge is leaking through the boundaries of the firm to the external world through participation in these electronic communities, potentially diluting the firms' competitive advantage. Again, this is no new phenomenon (see Schrader 1991; von Hippel 1987; von Hippel & Schrader 1996); however, the ease with which this knowledge leakage can occur has been greatly facilitated with the spread of the Internet.

Finally, a third challenge is that when management hires a person, management is also "hiring" the employee's network as well. Thus, management must consider the potential employee's external network and how active this person is in his or her network. If the person is very active in his or her external network, then the individual's time may be spent on external activities. As shown above, this can lead to both positive and negative results for the company.

In terms of the limitations of this study, we acknowledge that there is a need to look at more than one firm and preferably with a larger sample of respondents before coming up with any definitive conclusions. The questionnaire suffers from common-method bias, so ideally we would also complement some of our measures with secondary data on (e.g., meetings attended, e-mails sent, hours on the web). But such a data-collection process would be extremely time-consuming and difficult to arrange.

Finally, it is important to acknowledge that our choice of communities of practice as our theoretical lens has its drawbacks. As noted several times, it is almost impossible to define communities of practice in an operational way, so one ends up falling back on measuring individual level patterns of interaction. And having moved in that direction, there are a number of other theoretical angles that could and perhaps should be incorporated, such as the vast literature on groups, environmental scanning, and organizational cognition. These are issues that will be considered in future research.

ACKNOWLEDGEMENT

I would like to acknowledge the extremely valuable help I received from Dr. Julian Birkinshaw in performing this research as well as the management at Icon Medialab who facilitated the data collection. In addition, I would like to thank Andy Schenkel and Joachim Timlon and all at IIB for their encouragement and comments as well as Ilkka Tuomi for his very insightful comments on a previous draft. Funding was provided by the CAMINO project at the Institute of International Business at the Stockholm School of Economics, whose generosity is greatly appreciated.

ENDNOTES

i. Netovation has been used to describe the use of the Internet as a source of creativity or innovation.

ii. It is worth noting in passing that the significant correlates with manager-rated performance were (a) age of employee, and (b) *lack of* socialization with other people outside of work. In other words, managers believe that older employees without social contacts with colleagues are the better performers!

iii. In order to avoid multicollinearity problems, we decided not to include age as it correlated highly with related work experience.

iv. The digital communication market is among the fastest growing markets ever. In a report by the International Data Corporation, the market for Internet services is predicted to grow from USD 2.5 billion in 1996 to USD 13.8 billion in 2000.

v. This also has some parallels to the work done by Edmondsson (1999) on team psychological safety. Team psychological safety is defined as the shared belief by the team that the team is safe for interpersonal risk taking, thus encouraging people to express their ideas without fearing that they will be rejected. This belief stems from mutual respect and trust among the team's members.

REFERENCES

Alavi, M. & Leidner, D. 1999. Knowledge management systems: Issues, challenges, and benefits. Communication of the Association for Information Systems 1, 1–28.

Bartlett, C. & Ghoshal, S. 1989. *Managing across Borders: The Transnational Solution.* Cambridge: Harvard Business School Press.

Boland, R. J. & Tenkasi, R. V. 1995. Perspective making and perspective taking in communities of knowing. *Organization Science*, 6, 350–372.

Brown, J. S. & Duguid, P. 1991. Organizational learning and communities of practice. *Organization Science*, 2, 40–57.

Brown, J. S. & Duguid, P. 1998. Organizing knowledge. *California Management Review*, 40, 90–111.

Brown, J. S. & Gray, E. S. 1997b. *Fast Company*, 1, 78–82.

Conner, K. R. & Prahalad, C. K. 1996. A resource-based theory of the firm: Knowledge versus opportunism. *Organization Science*, 7, 477–501.

Constant, D., Sproull, L. S., & Kiesler, S. 1996. The kindness of strangers: The usefulness of electronic weak ties for technical advice. *Organization Science*, 7, 119–135.

Davenport, T. H. & Prusak, L. 1998. *Working Knowledge*. Boston: Harvard Business School Press.

DeGeus, A. P. 1988. Planning as learning, *Harvard Business Review*, March–April, 70–74.

Doz, Y., Asakawa, K., Santos, J. E. P., & Williamson, P. J. 1997. The metanational corporation. Working paper, Insead, Fontainebleau.

Drucker, P. 1990. The emerging theory of manufacturing. *Harvard Business Review*, 94–102.

Edmondsson, A. 1999. Psychological safety and learning behavior in work teams. *Administrative Science Quarterly*, 44, 350–383.

Faraj, S. & McClure-Wasko, M. 1999. The web of knowledge: An investigation of self-organizing communities of practice on the net. Working paper, University of Maryland. Forbes. 1998, November.

Fulk, J. & DeSanctis, G. 1995. Electronic communication and changing organizational forms. *Organization Science*, 6, 337–350.

Hagel, J. & Armstrong, A. G. 1997. *Net Gain: Expanding Markets through Virtual Communties*. Boston: Harvard Business School Press.

Hedlund, Gunnar 1994. A model of knowledge management and the N-form corporation. *Strategic Management Journal*, 15.

Hedlund, G. & Nonaka, I. 1993. Models of knowledge management in the west and Japan. In P. Lorange, B. Chakravarthy, J. Roos and A. Van de Ven, (eds.), *Implementing Strategic Process*, 117–145. Blackwell Business.

Heneman, H. G. 1974. Comparisons of self and superior rating of managerial performance. *Journal of Applied Psychology*, 59, 638–642.

Hinds, P. & Kiesler, S. 1995. Communication across boundaries: Work, structure, and use of communication technologies in a large organization. *Organization Science*, 6, 373–393.

Kogut, B. & Zander, U. 1992. Knowledge of the firm, combinative capabilities and the replication of technology. *Organization Science*, 3, 383–397.

Kogut, B. & Zander, U. 1995. Knowledge of the firm and evolutionary theory of the multinational corporation. *Journal of International Business Studies*, 26, 625–644.

Lave, J. & Wenger, E. 1991. *Situated Learning: Legitimate Peripheral Participation*, Cambridge: Cambridge University Press.

March, J. G. 1991. Exploration and exploitation in organizational learning. *Organization Science*, 2, 71–87.

Nonaka, I. 1991. The knowledge-creating company. *Harvard Business Review*, November–December, 96–104.

Nonaka, I. 1994. A dynamic theory of organizational knowledge creation. *Organization Science*, 5, 14–37.

Nonaka, I. & Takeuchi, H. 1995. *The Knowledge-Creating Company*. New York: Oxford University Press.

Orr, J. 1990. *Talking about Machines: An Ethnography of a Modern Job.* Cornell University.

Purser, R. E., Pasmore, W. A., & Tenkasi, R. V. 1992. The influence of deliberations on learning in new product development teams. *Journal of Engineering and Technology Management,* 9, 1–28.

Reber, A. S. 1993. *Implicit Learning and Tacit Knowledge,* New York: Oxford University Press.

Schein, E. H. & Bennis, W. *Personal and Organizational Change via Group Methods.* New York: Wiley.

Schön, D. A. 1983. *The Reflective Practitioner: How Professionals Think in Action,* New York: Basic Books, Inc.

Simon, H. A. 1945. *Administrative Behaviour.* New York: The Free Press.

Sjöberg, L. & Lind, F. 1994. Work motivation in financial crisis: a study of prognosis factors. Stockholm School of Economics, Stockholm, Sweden.

Snyder, W. 1996. Organizational learning and performance: an exploration of linkages between organizational learning, knowledge, and performance. University of Southern California. Unpublished doctoral dissertation.

Snyder, W. 1997. Communities of practice: combining organizational learning and strategy insights to create a bridge to the 21rst century. Boston: Academy of Management Conference.

Spender, J.-C. 1989. *Industry Recipes: The Nature and Sources of Managerial Judgment.* Oxford: Basil Blackwell.

Spender, J.-C. 1996. Making knowledge the basis of a dynamic theory of the firm. *Strategic Management Journal.* 17(winter special issue), 45–62.

Spender, J.-C. & Grant, R. M. 1996. Knowledge and the firm: An overview. *Strategic Management Journal,* 17, 5–9.

Sproull, L. S. & Faraj, S. 1995. Atheism, sex and databases: The net as a social technology. In B. K. J. Keller, (ed.) *Public Access to the Internet.* Cambridge, MA: MIT Press.

Stebbins, M. W. & Shani, A. B. R. 1995. Organization design and the knowledge worker. *Leadership & Organization Development Journal,* 16, 23–30.

Teigland, R. 1999. Netovation: Linking cross-boundary knowledge flows to firm innovative performance in the internet industry. Working Paper 1999. Institute of International Business, Stockholm School of Economics.

Venkatraman, N. & Henderson, J. C. 1998. Real strategies for virtual organizing. *Sloan Management Review,* 40, 33–45.

Wenger, E. 1998. *Communities of Practice: Learning, Meaning, and Identity,* Cambridge: Cambridge University Press.

Wenger, E., Sep 17, 1997. Community of Practice Forum. Boston, 1997.

Wexley, K. N., Alexander, R. A., Greenawalt, J. P., & Couch, M. A. 1980. Attitudinal congruence and similarity as related to interpersonal evaluation in manager-subordinate dyads. *Academy of Management Journal,* 23(2), 320–330.

Williamson, O. E. 1975. *Markets & Hierarchies: Analysis and Antitrust Implications.* New York: The Free Press.

Zander, U. 1991. *Exploiting a technological edge—voluntary and involuntary dissemination of technology.* Published doctoral dissertation. Institute of International Business, Stockholm, Sweden.

Zipf, G. K. 1949. *Human Behavior and the Principle of Least Effort.* Cambridge, MA: Addison-Wesley.

11

Computer Networks as Social Networks: Collaborative Work, Telework, and Virtual Community*

Barry Wellman, Janet Salaff, Dimitrina Dimitrova, Laura Garton, Milena Gulia, Caroline Haythornthwaite
Centre for Urban and Community Studies, University of Toronto, Toronto, Canada

Computer-supported social networks (CSSNs) are the cornerstone of global connectivity, virtual communities, and computer-supported cooperative work (CSCW). Beginning with the U.S. Defense Department's ARPANET, scientific researchers began a quest for connecting social and workplace networks. Since then, the birth of personal computers and Intranets has grown rapidly, while the costs associated with access have decreased. Because the Web hosts communities of previously disconnected individuals searching for information, companionship, and social support, computer networks are expanding at an astonishing rate. Stemming from this economic and social phenomenon, the authors investigate online computer-mediated communication (CMC) and its relationship to groupware, e-mail, Internet Relay Chat (IRC), and listservs. CSSNs are examined in terms of social-network theory—where the size, structure, and composition of virtual communities and workgroups are applied to the types of communication that affect telework, domestic work, and the larger networked organization.

* Reprinted with permission from the *Annual Review of Sociology*, Vol. 22, © 1996, by Annual Reviews http://www.AnnualReviews.org.

COMPUTER-SUPPORTED SOCIAL NETWORKS

When computer networks link people as well as machines, they become social networks, which we call computer-supported social networks (CSSNs). Three forms of CSSNs are rapidly developing, each with its own desires and research agendas. Members of virtual community want to link globally with kindred souls for companionship, information, and social support from their homes and workstations. White-collar workers want computer-supported cooperative work (CSCW), unencumbered by spatial distance, while organizations see benefits in coordinating complex work structures and reducing managerial costs and travel time. Some workers want to telework from their homes, combining employment with domestic chores and Arcadian retreats; management foresees reduced building and real estate costs, and higher productivity.

We examine here the extent to which people work and find community on CSSNs. Is it possible to sustain productive or supportive relationships online with network members who may never meet in-person? What will the composition and structure of CSSNs be like, with their weaker constraints of distance and time, their easy connectivity, and limited social presence? What are the implications of such changes for the societies within which they are proliferating?

These questions have captured the public's imagination. Pundits argue about whether we will have computer-supported utopias—"the most transforming technological event since the capture of fire" (Barlow 1995:40)—or dystopias—"this razzle-dazzle . . . disconnects us from each other" (Hightower, quoted in Fox 1995:12). The popular media is filled with accounts of life in cyberspace (e.g., Cybergal 1995), much like earlier travellers' tales of journeys into exotic unexplored lands. Public discourse is (a) Manichean, seeing CSSNs as either thoroughly good or evil; (b) breathlessly present-oriented, writing as if CSSNs had been invented yesterday and not in the 1970s; (c) parochial, assuming that life online has no connection to life off-line; and (d) unscholarly, ignoring research into CSSNs as well as a century's research into the nature of community, work, and social organization.

The Nets Spread

CSSNs began in the 1960s when the U.S. Defense Department's Advanced Projects Research Agency developed ARPANET to link large university computers and some of their users (Cerf 1993). The Electronic Information Exchange System, modeled after a government emergency communications network, started supporting computerized conferences of scientific researchers (including social network analysts) in the mid-1970s (Freeman 1986; Hiltz & Turoff 1993). Other systems were also proposed and partially implemented in this period.

Since the mid-1980s personal computers have become increasingly connected (through modems, local networks, etc) to central communication hosts. These hosts have become linked with each other through the worldwide "Internet" and the "World Wide Web" (encompassing information access as well as communications). Together with other interconnecting computer networks, the overall network has become known simply as "The Net," a "network of networks" (Craven & Wellman 1973) that weaves host computers (using high-capacity communication lines), each of which is at the center of its own local network. While the Net originally only encompassed nonprofit (principally university) computers, commercial users were allowed on in the early 1990s. Between October 1994 and January 1995, the number of Internet hosts grew by 26% (Treese 1995).

Other computer networks have grown concomitantly, while the cost of access has decreased. Those principally for leisure use range from community bulletin board systems (Marx & Virnoche 1995) to global, for-profit networks such as America Online that have developed commercial activity and the structured provision of information (e.g., airline guides, movie reviews). In late 1995, America Online had an estimated 4.5 million subscribers worldwide, CompuServe had 4 million, while Prodigy had 1.5 million (Lewis 1996). The development of World Wide Web services may displace such commercial systems. Local low-cost Internet service providers are proliferating, and Windows95 comes ready to connect to the Internet.

Competitive pressures have led these commercial systems to link with the Internet, making the Net even more widely interconnected. The Net has been growing, perhaps doubling its users annually. Its rapid growth and structure as a network of networks makes it difficult to count the number of users, for one must count both the computer systems directly connected to the Net and the users on each system. For example, estimates of recent Internet use in mid-1995 ranged between 27 million and 10 million adults (*Insight New Media* 1995; Lewis 1995). Besides exchanging private e-mail messages, Internet members participated (as of January 27, 1996) in 24,237 collective discussion groups (Southwick 1996). There is much scope for growth: In 1994 only 17% of the 2.2 million Canadian computer users logged onto the Net (Frank 1995). Moreover, users vary between those who rarely log on to those who are continuously connected. Given such uncertainties and the tendency of enthusiasts and marketers to forecast high levels of network membership, many estimates of the number of users are unreliable.

There is little published information about the demographic composition of Net users, although this should change as it develops as a commercial marketing milieu. There is general agreement that users are largely politically conservative white men, often single, English-speaking, residing in North America, and professionals, managers, or students (*Newsweek* 1995; Treese 1995). One survey of web users in Spring 1995 found that women comprised less than one fifth of their sample, although the proportion of women users had doubled in the past six months (Pitkow & Kehoe 1995). Two thirds of this sample had at least a university education, an "average" household income of U.S. $59,600, and three quarters lived in North America. By contrast, Algeria had 16 registered Internet users in July 1995 and Bulgaria had 639 (Danowitz et al. 1995). Trends suggest an increasing participation of women, non-English speakers, and people of lower socioeconomic status (Gupta et al. 1995; Kraut et al. 1995; On-line Research Group 1995). Nevertheless, French President Jacques Chirac (1995) has warned that if English continues to dominate the information highway, "our future generations will be economically and culturally marginalized.... To defend the influence of the French language is to defend the right to think, to communicate, to feel emotions and to pray in a different way."

Possibly more people participate in private organizational networks than on the Net, either using CSCW from offices or teleworking from homes. They use proprietary systems such as Lotus Notes or Internet tools adapted for use on private "intranets." In 1991 there were 8.9 million participants in Fortune 2000 companies (Electronic Mail Association 1992). In late 1995, there probably were still more users of private networks than of the Net, but there were no available estimates. There is also no published demographic information about private network participants, but presumably they are even more homogeneous than those on the Net. To protect organizational security, private networks often are not connected to the Net. However, pressure from professional employees to have access to colleagues and information elsewhere is leading many organizations to connect to the Net (Pickering & King 1995).

Types of Systems

Almost all CSSNs support a variety of text-based interactions with messages entered on keyboards and transmitted in lowest-common denominator ASCII code. Basic electronic mail (e-mail) is asynchronous communication from one person to another or from one person to a distribution list. When e-mail messages are forwarded, they concatenate into loosely bounded intergroup networks through which information diffuses rapidly. E-mail is bidirectional, so that recipients of messages can reply with equal ease. By contrast to these single-sender arrangements, "groupware" (Johnson-Lenz & Johnson-Lenz 1978) supports computerized conferencing that enables all members of a bounded social network to read all messages. Many private networks support computerized conferencing as does the Net through "list servers" (such as the Progressive Sociology Network) and leisure-time "Usenet newsgroups."

The online storage of most messages allows computer-mediated communication (CMC) to be asynchronous so that participants can be in different places and on different schedules. This gives people potentially more control over when they read and respond to messages. Moreover, the rapid transmission of large files between individuals and among groups increases the velocity of communication, supports collaborative work, and sustains strong and weak ties (Feldman 1987; Finholt & Sproull 1990; Eveland & Bikson 1988; Sproull & Kiesler 1991). Online storage and digital transmission also help intruders to read files and messages, although computerization does provide cryptographic means of protecting privacy (Weisband & Reinig 1995).

Far fewer people participate in synchronous "real-time" CSSNs, although improved technology should lead to their growth. The "chat lines" of commercial services and the Internet Relay Chat (IRC) system operate in real time, providing multithreaded conversations like cocktail parties (Bechar-Israeli 1995; Danet et al. 1996). As widespread Internet access and microcomputer multitasking develop, it is likely that many currently asynchronous users will see messages when they arrive, creating the potential for more widespread synchronic social exchanges. Multi-User Dungeons (MUDs) and kindred systems are a special play form of real-time computerized conferencing. Those who enter MUDs don pseudonymous persons and role play in quests, masquerades, and other forms of intense online communal interaction (Danet et al. 1995, 1996; Reid 1996; Smith 1996).

Current trends supplement text with graphics, animation, video, and sound, increasing social presence. However, this increases cost and requires good hardware and communication lines. Desktop and group videoconferencing is currently limited to research groups and large-screen corporate meeting rooms (Ishii 1992; Mantei et al. 1991; Buxton 1992; Moore 1997). Other experimental systems include video walls (in which large-screen videos link widely separated lounges to promote informal coffee-machine conversation), video hallways (Fish et al. 1993; Dourish & Bly 1992) that allow participants to check the availability of others at a glance, and agents or avatars that move, speak and search online (Maes 1995; Riecken 1994; Stephenson 1992). Hence, we focus in this chapter on the most widely used, text-based forms of CSSNs such as e-mail and computerized conferences. We look only at interpersonal communication. We do not cover impersonal broadcast e-mail (such as electronic newsletters), distance education, passively accessible sites (such as file transfer [FTP] and websites), and the exchange of data online (as in manufacturing processes or airline reservation systems).

Research into CSSNs has involved several disciplines—principally computer science, communication science, business administration, and psychology. There are annual CSCW conferences with published proceedings. Despite the inherently sociological nature of the matter, sociology is underrepresented, and gatekeepers are mostly members of other disciplines (Dillon 1995). Although mutually germane, studies of virtual community, CSCW, and telework generally have not informed each other.

COMMUNICATION ONLINE

Early research developed from "human-computer" analysis of single-person interfaces with computer systems to analyzing how small group communication is mediated by computer systems. Many of these studies examined how the limited "social presence" of CMC (as compared to in-person contact) affects interactions and group decision making. What are the effects of losing verbal nuances (e.g., voice tone, volume), nonverbal cues (e.g., gaze, body language) physical context (e.g., meeting sites, seating arrangements) and observable information about social characteristics (e.g., age, gender, race)? Research in this approach links the technical characteristics of CMC to task group outcomes such as increased participation, more egalitarian participation, more ideas offered, and less centralized leadership (Hiltz et al. 1986; Kiesler et al. 1984; Rice 1987; Adrianson & Hjelmquist 1991; Weisband et al. 1995). Limited social presence may also encourage people to communicate more freely and creatively than they do in person, at times "flaming" others by using extreme, aggressive language (Kiesler et al. 1984).

Although groups supported by CMC often produce higher quality ideas, reaching agreement can be a lengthy and more complex process as the greater number of ideas and the lack of status cues hinder group coordination (Hiltz et al. 1986; Kiesler & Sproull 1992; Valacich et al. 1993). However, status cues are not completely absent, as social information is conveyed though language use, e-mail address, and signatures such as "VP-Research" (Walther 1992). As messages are often visibly copied to others, they also indicate social network connections. Some participants prefer in-person contact to CMC for ambiguous, socially sensitive, and intellectually difficult interaction (Culnan & Markus 1987; Daft & Lengel 1986; Rice 1987; Fish et al. 1993; Jones 1995). However, CMC is also used to maintain social distance, document contentious issues, or when the message involves fear, dislike, awkwardness, or intimidation (Markus 1994a; Walther 1996).

Much CMC research has been individualistic and technologically deterministic, assuming a single person rationally choosing among media (Lea 1991). To go beyond this, some CMC analysts now consider how social relationships, organizational structures, and local norms affect the use of communication media (Finholt & Sproull 1990; Orlikowsi et al. 1995; Huber 1990; Markus 1990, 1994b; Sproull & Kiesler 1991; Lea et al. 1995; Orlikowski et al. 1996b; Zack & McKenney 1995). For example, people do not "choose" to use e-mail in many organizations: It is a condition of employment (Fulk & Boyd 1991). Even when e-mail use is voluntary, a critical mass of users affects the extent to which people use it (Markus 1990). Thus the laboratory basis of most CMC research sets limits for understanding CSSNs in natural settings. Sociological research needs to take into account the social characteristics of participants (e.g., gender, SES), their positional resources (CEO or mail-room clerk, broker or densely knit star), the interplay between ongoing online and off-line relationships, and their ongoing social relationships.

SUPPORT ONLINE

Information

Much of the communication on CSSNs involves the exchange of information. For example, in two weeks of March 1994 the 2,295 newsgroups in the top 16 Usenet newsgroup hierarchies received 817,638 messages (Kling 1996b). Online digital libraries are growing, along with search tools (Kling & Lamb 1996), although locating the right information is difficult in large organizations and communities. The nature of the medium supports a focus on information exchanges, as people can easily post a question or comment and receive information in return. Broadcasting queries through CSSNs increases the chances of finding information quickly and alters the distribution patters of information. It gives those working in small or distant sites better access to experienced, skilled people (Constant et al. 1996).

However, as anyone can contribute information to most newsgroups and distribution lists, the Net can be a repository of misleading information and bad advice, as some health care professionals have charged (Foderaro 1995). Such worries discount the fact that people have always given each other advice about their bodies, psyches, families, or computers (e.g., Wellman 1995; Kadushin 1987). The Net has just made the process more accessible and more visible to others, including experts whose claims to monopolies on advice are threatened (Abbott 1988).

The flow of information through CSSNs itself generates access to new information. Online information flows spill over unexpectedly through message forwarding, providing access to more people and new social circles, thus increasing the probability of finding those who can solve problems (Kraut & Attewell 1993). People often bump into new information or new sources of information unintentionally through "leaky...quasi social networlds" (Brent 1994:online). Information obtained serendipitously helps solve problems before they occur and helps keep people aware of organizational news. Weak online ties are bridges between diverse sources of information. In one large organization, those with more diverse ties obtained better online advice (Constant et al. 1996).

Social Support

If CSSNs were solely a means of information exchange, then they would mostly contain narrow, specialized relationships. However, information is only one of many social resources exchanged online. Despite the limited social presence of CMC, people find social support, companionship, and a sense of belonging through the normal course of CSSNs of work and community, even when they are composed of persons they hardly know (Rice & Love 1987; McCormick & McCormick 1992; Haythornthwaite et al. 1995; Walther 1996; Wellman & Gulia 1996). Although providing such types of support often does not require major investments of time, money, or energy, CSSN members have also mobilized goods, services, and long-term emotional support to help each other (e.g., Lewis 1994). Thus while most of the elderly users of the "SeniorNet" virtual community joined to gain access to information, their most popular online activity has been companionable chatting (Furlong 1989; see also Hiltz et al. 1986; Walther 1994; Rheingold 1993; Meyer 1989; Kraut et al. 1995). An informal support group sprang up inadvertently when the "Young Scientists' Network" aimed primarily at providing physicists with job hunting tips and news stories. Similarly, the "Systers" mailing list, originally designed for female computer scientists to exchange information, has become a forum for companionship and social support (Sproull & Faraj 1995). The members of a computer science laboratory frequently exchange emotional support by e-mail. Because much of their time is spent online, and many of their difficulties happen at their terminals, it is natural for them to discuss problems online (Haythornthwaite et al. 1995).

Some CSSNs are explicitly set up to be support groups that provide emotional aid, group membership, and information about medical treatment and other matters (Foderaro 1995; King 1994). One therapist who provides one-to-one counseling through a bulletin board reports that, while she has less social presence and cues than through in-person sessions, the greater anonymity of CMC allows her clients to reveal themselves more (Cullen 1995). For example, Peter and Trudy Johnson-Lenz (1990, 1994) have organized online groups for 20 years, working to build self-awareness, mutually supportive activities, social change, and a sense of collective well-being. Their software tools, such as passing around sacred "talking sticks," rearrange communication structures, vary exchange settings, mark group rhythms, and encourage lurkers to express themselves.

RELATIONSHIPS ONLINE

Specialized and Multiplex Ties

CSSNs contain both specialized and multiplex relationships. The structure of the Net encourages specialized relationships because it supports a market approach to finding social resources in virtual communities. With more ease than in almost all real life situations, people can shop for resources from the safety and comfort of their homes or offices, and with reduced search and travel time. The Usenet alone houses more than 3,500 newsgroups (Kling 1996b) to which anyone may subscribe, with diverse foci including politics (e.g., feminism), technical problems (e.g., SPSS), therapeutics (e.g., alcoholism), socializing (e.g., singles), and recreation (e.g., BMWs, sexual fantasies). Net members can browse through specialized channels on synchronous chat lines before deciding to join a discussion (Danet et al. 1996). Relationships in these virtual communities are often narrowly defined.

The narrow focus of newsgroups, distribution lists, and chat lines allows people to take risks in specialized relationships that may only exist in a single partial online community. Some CSSNs even allow people to be anonymous or use nicknames when they want to speak freely or try on different personas (Hiltz & Turoff 1993). However, the inclusion of e-mail addresses in most message headers provides the basis for more multiplex relationships to develop. In the absence of social and physical cues, people are able to get to know each other on the Net on the basis of their communication and decide later to broaden the relationship or move it off-line (Rheingold 1993). Thus more than half of the recovering addicts on electronic support groups also contact each other by phone or in-person (King 1994). Soon after an especially intense computerized conference, many "of the participants altered their business and vacation travel plans to include a face-to-face meeting with one another" (Hiltz & Turoff 1993:114).

Strong Ties

Can the medium support the message if the limited social presence of computer-mediated communication works against the maintenance of socially close, strong ties on CSSNs? Many online ties do meet most of the criteria for strong ties. They facilitate frequent, reciprocal, companionable, and often supportive contact, and the placelessness of CSSN interactions facilitates long-term contact without the loss of relationships that often accompanies residential mobility. Virtual communities are quite voluntary, while CSSN participation varies between voluntary and mandatory in CSCW and telework (Hiltz & Turoff 1993; Johnson-Lenz & Johnson-Lenz 1994; Rheingold 1993). Certainly many accounts report great involvement in online relationships. Community members came to regard each other as their closest friends even though they seldom or never met in-person (Hiltz & Turoff 1993). Net members tend to base their feelings of closeness on shared interests rather than on shared social characteristics such as gender and SES. That the siren call of CSSNs sometimes lures net members away from "real-life" argues for the potential strength of online relationships and networks.

Many computer-mediated communication ties are moderately strong "intimate secondary relationships" that are frequent and supportive but only operate in one specialized domain (Wireman 1984). Over time, some of these relationships become more personal and intimate. Perhaps the limited social presence and asynchronicity of CMC only slows the development of intimacy, with online interactions eventually developing to be as sociable and intimate as in-person ones (Walther 1995).

In part, concerns about whether online ties can be strong ties are wrongly specified. Although CSSNs do transcend time and space, not all ties are either totally online or off-line. Much online contact is between people who see each other in person and live locally. At work, computer scientists intermingle in-person and by e-mail communication. At some offices, employees chat privately by e-mail while they work silently side-by-side (Garton 1995; Labaton 1995). In such situations, conversations started on one medium continue on others. As with the telephone and the fax (Wellman & Tindall 1993), the lower social presence of CMC may be sufficient to maintain strong ties between persons who know each other well. For example, kinship networks use the Net to arrange weddings and out-of-town visits (Hiltz & Turoff 1993), while an American woman gave up her job and flew to Britain to marry a Net friend whom she had never met in person (Toronto News Radio 680, Sept. 3, 1995).

Weak Ties

There are low logistical and social costs to participating in CSSNs. People can participate within the comfort and safety of their own homes or offices, at any time, and at their own convenience. Limited social cues online encourage contact between weak ties. Very often, the only social characteristic that people learn about each other online is a Net address, which provides very little information. The egalitarian nature of the Net encourages responses to requests. It also generates a culture of its own, as when humorous stories sweep CSSNs, possibly fostering a revival of folk humor.

On the face of it, CSSNs should not support much reciprocity. Many online ties are between persons who have never met face-to-face, who are weakly tied, socially and physically distant, and not bound into densely knit work or community structures. Computerized conferences allow free-rider "lurkers" to read others' messages invisibly without contributing (Kollack & Smith 1996a).

Nevertheless, there is evidence of reciprocal supportiveness on CSSNs, even between people with weak ties (Hiltz et al. 1986; Walther 1994). Providing reciprocal support and information online is a means of increasing self-esteem, demonstrating technical expertise, earning respect and status, and responding to norms of mutual aid (e.g., Constant et al. 1994, 1996; Kraut & Attewell 1993; Kollock & Smith 1996b). In some organizations, employees are encouraged to help each other or to direct those in need to others who could help. Computerized conferences and public archives reinforce this supportiveness by making it visible to all coworkers and managers (Constant et al. 1995; Kraut & Attewell 1993; Kollock & Smith 1996b). Such processes also arise in densely knit virtual communities and are common among frequent contributors to computerized conferences. People having a strong attachment to an organization or electronic group will be more likely to participate and provide assistance to others. For example, computer hackers involved in illegal activities are reluctant to change their pseudonyms because the status they gain through online demonstrations of technical expertise accrues to that pseudonym (Meyer 1989).

Some commentators have warned about the consequences of making connections on CSSNs teeming with strangers whose biographies, social positions, and social networks are unknown (Stoll 1995). Nevertheless CSSN members tend to trust strangers, much as people gave rides to hitchhikers in the flower child days of the 1960s. This willingness to engage with strangers online contrasts with in-person situations where bystanders are often reluctant to intervene and help strangers (Latané & Darley 1976). Yet bystanders are more apt to intervene when they are the only ones around and they can withdraw easily in case of trouble. Analogously, online requests for aid are read by people alone at their screens. Even if the request is to a newsgroup and not by personal e-mail, as far as the recipient of the request knows, s/he is the only one who could provide aid. At the same time, online intervention will be observed by entire groups and will be positively rewarded by them. It is this visibility that may foster the kindness of strangers. Just as physical proximity provides the opportunity for observing face-to-face interaction, CSSNs provide social exemplars to large numbers of passive observers as well as to active participants. Individual acts can aggregate to sustain a large community because each act is seen by the entire group and perpetuates a norm of mutual aid (Rheingold 1993; Barlow 1995; Lewis 1994).

Stressful Ties

Most research into antisocial behavior online has studied uninhibited remarks, hostile flaming, nonconforming behavior, and group polarization (Hiltz et al. 1978; Kiesler et al. 1985; Siegal et al. 1986; Sproull & Kiesler 1991; Lea et al. 1992; Walther et al. 1994). The limited social presence of computer-mediated communication encourages the misinterpretation of remarks, and the asynchronous nature of most conversations hinders the immediate repair of damages, stressing and even disrupting relationships. There are numerous anecdotes about antisocial behavior online. Hackers disseminate viruses, entrepreneurs "spam" (flood) the Net with unwanted advertisements, stalkers harass participants online, and scoundrels take on misleading roles such as men posing online as women to seduce others electronically (Cybergal 1995; Slouka 1995).

SOCIAL NETWORKS ONLINE

In what kinds of social networks are online relationships embedded? Because they operate somewhat differently, we separately discuss virtual community and computer-supported work groups. For both community and work, we consider the composition of computer-supported social networks— the nature of the participants in them, and the structure of CSSNs—the network pattern of relationships and hierachies of power.

Size and Composition

Virtual Community

Although contemporary people in the western world may know 1,000 others, they actively maintain only about 20 community ties (Kochen 1989). Easy access to distribution lists and computerized conferences should enable participants to maintain more ties, including more strong ties. Communication also comes unsolicited through distribution lists, newsgroups, and forwarded messages from friends. These provide indirect contact between previously disconnected people, allowing them to establish direct contact. Newsgroups and distribution lists also provide permeable, shifting sets of members, with more intense relationships continued by private e-mail. The resulting relaxation of constraints on the size and proximity of one's personal community can increase the diversity of people encountered (Lea & Spears 1995). Thus the Net facilitates forming new connections between people and virtual communities.

The relative lack of social presence online fosters relationships with Net members who have more diverse social characteristics than are normally encountered in person. It also gives participants more control over the timing and content of their self-disclosures (Walther 1995). This allows relationships to develop on the basis of shared interests rather than to be stunted at the onset by differences in social status (Coate 1994; Hiltz & Turoff 1993; Jones 1995; Kollock & Smith 1996a). This is a technologically supported continuation of a long-term shift to communities organized by shared interests rather than by shared neighborhoods or kinship groups (Fischer 1975; Wellman 1979, 1994). When their shared interests are important to them, those involved in the same virtual community may have more in common than those who live in the same building or block (Rheingold 1993). Indeed, people have strong commitments to their online groups when they perceive them to be long-lasting (Walther 1994). There is a danger, though, that virtual communities may develop homogeneous interests (Lea & Spears 1992). Furthermore, the similarity of social characteristics of most current Net participants also fosters cultural homogeneity.

This emphasis on shared interests rather than social characteristics can be empowering for members of lower-status and disenfranchised social categories (Male 1996). Yet although social characteristics have become less apparent on CSSNs, they still affect interactions. Women often receive special attention from males (Shade 1994; Herring 1993; O'Brien 1996). In part, this is a function of the high ratio of men to women online. "Reveal your gender on the Net and you're toast" claims one (fictional) female participant (Coupland 1995:334).

Cooperative Work

The evidence is mixed about whether CSSNs reduce the use of other communication media, add to the total amount of communication, or boost the use of other communication media (Garton & Wellman 1995). One study found that work groups using CMC have a higher level of communication than those that do not (Bikson & Eveland 1990), while another found that heavy CMC use reduces face-to-face and telephone communication (Finholt et al. 1990).

People can greatly extend the number and diversity of their social contacts when they become members of computerized conferences or broadcast information to other CSSN members. In one large, physically dispersed organization, four fifths of the e-mail messages were from electronic groups and not individuals. More than half of these messages were from unknown people, different buildings, or people external to their department or chain of command (Finholt & Sproull 1990; Kiesler & Sproull 1988). In another study, an online work team formed more subcommittees than did an off-line team and was better able to involve its members in its activities (Bikson & Eveland 1990). Where the organizational climate fosters open communication, the lack of status cues fosters connections across hierarchical or other forms of status barriers (Sproull & Kiesler 1991; Eveland & Bikson 1988).

Structure

Virtual Community

The architecture of the Net may nourish two contradictory trends for the structure of virtual communities. First, the Net fosters membership in multiple, partial communities. People often belong to several computerized conferences, and they can easily send out messages to separate personal distribution lists for different kinds of conversations. Moreover, they can vary in their involvements in different communities, participating actively in some and occasionally in others. Second, the ease of responding to entire groups and forwarding messages to others foster the folding in of online networks into broader communities (Marx & Virnoche 1995). Moreover, MUDs and similar role-playing environments resemble village-link structures if they capture their members' attention.

The proliferation of CSSNs may produce a trend counter to the contemporary privatization of community. People in the western world are spending less time in public places waiting for friends to wander by, and where they can introduce them to other friends (Wellman 1992; *Economist* 1995). Community has moved indoors to private homes from its former semi-public, accessible milieus such as cafés, parks, and pubs. This dispersion and privatization means that people must actively contact community members to remain in touch instead of visiting a café and waiting for acquaintances to drop by. By contrast, computerized conferences support connections with large numbers of people, providing possibilities for reversing the trend to less public contact. Because all members of newsgroups and discussion groups can read all messages—just as in a café conversation—groups of people can talk to each other casually and get to know the friends of their friends. "The keyboard is my café," William Mitchell enthuses (1995:7). Moreover, each participant's personal community of ties connects specialized, partial communities, providing cross-cutting links between otherwise disconnected groups.

Work Groups

There has not been much research into how widespread use of CSSNs affect broad organizational structures of management and control. Research has focused more narrowly on CSSNs themselves. For example, organizational CSSNs are maintained by system administrators who may support management goals by monitoring online activities and devising procedures that affect social outcomes. Some administrators promote the "appropriate" use of the CSSN and admonish those who use it for recreational or noncompany purposes (Chiu 1995; Orilowski et al. 1995). Managers fear that CSSNs will threaten control by accelerating the flow of (mis)information, including rumors, complaints, jokes, and subversive communications (Finholt & Sproull 1990). For example, management closed an employee "Gripenet" when group discussions challenged long-standing corporate practices (Emmett 1982). Even when organizations support informal electronic groups, managers often view them with distrust (Perin 1991). When women in a large corporation established a computerized conference to discuss careers, management monitored the messages because they feared it would lead to demands for unionization and affirmative action (Zuboff 1988).

Nevertheless, CSSNs support a variety of agendas, not only those sanctioned by the organization. For example, striking Israeli university professors used both private and group messages to coordinate their nationwide strike (Pliskin & Romm 1994). Less confrontationally, managers and staff use discussion groups to cross status and power boundaries by exchanging information about shared leisure interests. In one decentralized corporation, more than half of those surveyed use e-mail a least occasionally to keep in touch, take work breaks, and take part in games and other entertaining activities (Steinfield 1985). Such groups are larger, more dispersed, and more spontaneous than the distribution lists which the organization requires employees to be on, and their exchanges emphasize fun rather than displays of competence (Finholt & Sproull 1990). Such informal messaging may reduce work stress (Steinfield 1985), integrate new or peripheral employees (Eveland & Bikson 1988; Rice & Steinfield 1994; Steinfield 1985), and increase organizational commitment (Huff et al. 1989; Kaye 1992; Sproull & Kiesler 1991).

Much "groupware" has been written to support the social networks of densely knit and tightly bounded work groups in which people work closely with a focused set of colleagues. For example, videoconferencing systems enable spatially dispersed coworkers to confer instantly (Moore 1997), while co-writing systems support joint authorship (Sharples 1993). Yet both the Internet and within-organization intranets are also well-suited to support work relationships in sparsely knit, loosely bounded organizations whose members switch frequently and routinely among the people with whom they are dealing throughout the day, as they move between projects or need different resources (Fulk & DeSanctis 1995; Kling & Jewett 1994; Koppel et al. 1988; Weick 1976; Wellamn 1996). In such organizations, work outcomes depend more on the ability of people and groups to bridge cognitive distances than on having people and other resources located in the same place (Mowshowitz 1994). This relatively autonomous mode of work is often found among professionals, scholars, or academics who have to make multiple, often unexpected, contacts with colleagues within and outside their own organizations (Abbott 1988; Burt 1992; Hinds & Kiesler 1995; Star 1993; Walsh & Bayama 1996).

From an organizational perspective, dispersed work teams require social as well as technical support (Wellman et al. 1994; Garton 1995). Studies of collaboration among scientific communities suggest that an initial period of physical proximity is necessary to build trust and to come to consensus on the focus of proposed projects (Carley & Wendt 1991). Such collaborations may need different forms of CMC support at different points in a project. For example, work groups tightly focused on a single project need different types of CSCW support than do individuals switching among multiple tasks and relationships (Mantei & Wellman 1995).

Shifting boundaries characterize networked virtual organizations, not only within the organizations but between them. Interorganizational CSSNs can help an organization in negotiations between buyers and sellers and in coordinating joint projects. They also help managers and professionals maintain a large network of potentially useful contacts, stockpiling network capital for the time when they need to obtain information externally. These interorganizational networks also help employees to maintain a sense of connection with former colleagues and can provide support during job changes and other stressful events. CSSNs blur organizational boundaries, supporting "invisible colleges" of dispersed professionals. (Constant et al. 1994, 1996; Hesse et al. 1993; Hiltz & Turoff 1993; Kling 1996; Meyer 1989; Carley 1990; Kaufer & Carley 1993; Huff et al. 1989; Kaye 1992; Rice & Steinfield 1994; Walsh & Bayama 1996). They can knit scientific researchers into "highly cohesive and highly cooperative research groups, ... geographically dispersed yet coordinated" (Carley & Wendt 1991:407). However, there is less use of CSSNs in disciplines such as chemistry where practitioners want to protect unwanted commercial use of their knowledge (Walsh & Bayama 1996).

TELEWORK ONLINE

Implementation

To date, most developments in organizational CSCW have been to improve connections between existing workplaces. However, CSSNs provide opportunities for developing relatively new forms of work organization. Thus, telework (aka "telecommuting") is a special case of CSCW in which CMCs link organizations to employees working principally either at home or at remote work centers (Fritz et al. 1994). Most writing about telework has been programmatic, forecasting, or descriptive, assuming that the technology of telework will determine its social organization (e.g., Hesse & Grantham 1991; Helms & Marom 1992; Grey et al. 1993). Yet teleworking's growth has been driven by new market conditions that are promoting organizational restructuring, reducing employees, eliminating offices, and giving more flexibility to remaining employees (Salaff & Dimitrova 1995a, b). Although teleworkers now comprise a tiny fraction of the workforce (DiMartino & Wirth 1990), their growing number includes many salespeople, managers, professionals, and support personnel. Entire offices of data entry clerks and telephone services have moved to home or other remote offices (Kugelmass 1995).

Research is moving from technological determinism to studying the interplay between telework and work organization. Several analysts have shown managerial inertia and organizational lethargy to be barriers to telework. Many employees favor telework to gain more work autonomy or to accommodate family, but many managers feel their power threatened (Kraut 1988, 1989; Olson 1988; Huws et al. 1990; Grantham & Paul 1994; Tippin 1994). Although there have been concerns that the careers of teleworking managers and professionals would suffer because of less visibility in organizations, this has not yet been the case (Tolbert & Simons 1994). Despite the proliferation of telework and great public interest in the subject, there has not been much systematic research into what teleworkers actually do, their connections with their main offices, their links with coworkers (peers, subordinates, and supervisors), and the implications of their physical isolation for their careers within organizations or for labor solidarity.

Communication

Teleworkers do not communicate more frequently online with coworkers or supervisors than do similarly occupied nonteleworkers (Kinsman 1987), although teleworkers do have less postal and in-person contact (see also Olszewski & Mokhtarian 1994). However, teleworking leads to more structured and formalized communication with supervisors and, to a lesser extent, with coworkers. This may be due as much to physical separation from the organizational office as to the use of CMC (Olson 1988; Heilmann 1988; Huws et al. 1990; Olson & Primps 1984).

There has been contradictory evidence about how teleworking affects informal communication among coworkers. One study notes that personal conversations among teleworking programmers have decreased and their informal relationships have deteriorated (Heilmann 1988). Another study finds that the restructuring of work accompanying the shift to telework among pink-collar workers curtails informal communication (Soares 1992). By contrast, university employees, both white- and pink-collar, who work at home have more informal contact with other employees (McClintock 1981). At the same time, teleworkers can increase autonomy by being slow to respond to online messages (Wellman et al. 1994). The nature of informal communications by teleworkers appears to depend on the employees' social status, their previous relationships, and the support of the organization. For example, British Telecom reports (1994) that pink-collar teleworkers complain less about isolation than about the slowness of help in fixing computers and the lack of news about main office events (see also Shirley 1988).

Telework may only be a continuation of existing task independence and work flows already driven by messages and forms on computer screens (Dimitrova et al. 1994). This may explain why some studies find that professional teleworkers maintain work-related networks, but pink-collar clerical workers become more isolated (Durrenberger et al. 1996). New workforce hierarchies that emerge from teleworking segregate those who lack informal contacts, while those that have them benefit richly (Steinle 1988). In this way, CSSNs may further bifurcate the workforce.

Work Organization

Most research on the impact of telework addresses workplace issues such as the control and autonomy of teleworkers, flexibility of work schedules, job redesign, remote supervision, and productivity. Although much post-Fordist hype suggests that teleworking will liberate workers (e.g., Toffler 1980), research supports the neo-Fordist conclusion that managers retain high-level control of planning and resources but decentralize the execution of decisions and tasks. Companies that implement teleworking to cut costs often tighten control. This strategy is most effective with abundant pink-collar labor, typically women with children. The more severe the employees' personal constraints (e.g., child-care, disabilities) and the less the demand for their skills, the more likely they are to experience tighter control (Olson 1987). Thus management has increasing control of clerks who become teleworkers, while professionals have gained more autonomy (Olson & Primps 1984; Simons 1994; Soares 1992).

Thus the divergent impact of telework on control and job design follows the logic of the dual nature of labor markets, with company strategy determining the outcome (Steinle 1988; Huws et al. 1990). Where a company seeks to retain scarce skills by reducing personal constraints, teleworking provides more discretion over work arrangements. Professionals often obtain greater autonomy, flexibility, skills, and job involvement, but they may have more uncertainties about their careers and incomes (Olson 1987; Simons 1994; Bailyn 1989).

Telework, Domestic Work, and Gender

Telework is part of changing relationships between the realms of work and nonwork: a high proportion of women working, more part-time and flextime work, and the bifurcation of workers into the information-skilled and -deskilled (Hodson & Parker 1988; Olson 1988; Steinle 1988). Women and men often experience telework differently, although the evidence is somewhat contradictory.

Telework reinforces the gendered division of household labor because women teleworkers do more family care and household work. Women are more likely to report high stress over the conflict of work and family demands, and the lack of leisure time (Olson & Primps 1984; Christensen 1988). Women say they are satisfied with teleworking, possibly because blending work and family space may ease role strain between family and work, and it may improve family relations (Falconer 1993; Higgins et al. 1992; Duxbury 1995). Thus, female teleworking clerks are more family oriented than are their office counterparts (French 1988; DuBrin 1991).

Yet fusing domestic and work settings can be disruptive and can embed women more deeply in the household (Ahrentzen 1990; Calabrese 1994; Heck et al. 1995). Women doing paid work at home spend a similar amount of time on domestic work regardless of their job status, number and ages of their children, part-time or full-time employment, or the structure of their household (Ahrentzen 1990). Although teleworking women may benefit from flexibility in their "double load," managers and researchers alike claim that doing paid work at home is not a good way to provide early childcare (Christensen 1988). Teleworkers are almost as likely to use paid childcare, and indeed most have higher childcare expenses than do office workers (Falconer 1993). Yet mothers with older children are better able to work while their children are in school, to greet them after school, and to be available in emergencies.

Fathers who telework report better relationships with their children than do comparable nonteleworkers. They have more leisure time and less stress than before they began teleworking, and they play more with their children (Olson & Primps 1984). Yet gender dynamics are different. Men see teleworking as a privilege because they want more autonomy, and they get more interaction with their families as a bonus. Women see teleworking as a compromise because family responsibilities limit their employment opportunities, and they want flexible scheduling (Olson 1987; Gerson & Kraut 1988).

GLOBAL NETWORKS AND LITTLE BOXES

Despite their limited social presence, CSSNs successfully maintain strong, supportive ties with work and community as well as increase the number and diversity of weak ties. They are especially suited to maintaining intermediate-strength ties between people who cannot see each other frequently. Online relationships are based more on shared interests and less on shared social characteristics. Although many relationships function off-line as well as online, CSSNs are developing norms and structures of their own. The are not just pale imitations of "real life." The Net is the Net.

Organizational boundaries are becoming more permeable just as community boundaries already have. The combination of high involvement in CSSNs, powerful search engines, and the linking of organizational networks to the Net enables many workers to connect with relevant others elsewhere, wherever they are and whomever they work for. If organizations grow toward their information and communication sources (Stinchcombe 1990), CSSNs should affect changes in organizational structures.

Social networks are simultaneously becoming more global and more local as worldwide connectivity and domestic matters intersect. Global connectivity de-emphasizes the importance of locality for work and community; online relationships may be more stimulating than suburban neighborhoods and alienated offices. Even more than before, on the information highway each person is at the center of a unique personal community and work group.

The domestic environment around the workstation is becoming a vital home base for neo–Silas Marners sitting in front of their screens day and night. Nests are becoming well feathered. Telework exaggerates both trends. Although it provides long-distance connections for workers, it also moves them home, providing a basis for the revival of neighborhood life. Just as before the Industrial Revolution, home and workplace are being integrated, although gender roles have not been renegotiated.

The privatization of relationships affects community, organizational, and coworker solidarity. Virtual communities are accelerating the ways in which people operate at the centers of partial, personal communities, switching rapidly and frequently between groups of ties. Whether working at home or at an office workstation, many workers have an enhanced ability to move between relationships. At the same time, their more individualistic behavior means the weakening of the solidarity that comes from working in large groups.

Such phenomena give sociologists wonderful opportunities. A Bellcore vice president says that when "scientists talk about the evolution of the information infrastructure,...[we don't] talk about...the technology. We talk about ethics, law, policy and sociology.... It is a social invention" (Lucky 1995:205). Yet there has been little sociological study of computer-supported social networks. Research in this area engages with important intellectual questions and social issues at all scales, from dyadic to world system. It offers stimulating collaborations with other disciplines, industry, labor, and government. It provides opportunities to develop social systems and not just study them after the fact. As our computer science colleague William Buxton tells us, "the computer science is easy; the sociology is hard."

ACKNOWLEDGMENTS

More than 100 scholars responded to our online requests for germane work. We regret that we are unable to cite them all or to include relevant references to mainstream sociology. We thank Aaron Dantowitz, Paul Gregory, and Emmanuel Koku for help in gathering information, Beverly Wellman for editorial advice, and Ronald Baecker, William Buxton, and Marilyn Mantei for introducing us to computer science. Our work has been supported by the Social Science and Humanities Research Council of Canada, Bell Canada, the Centre for Information Technology Innovation, and the Information Technology Research Centre's Telepresence project.

LITERATURE CITED

Abbott A. 1988. *The System of Professions: An Essay on the Division of Expert Labor.* Chicago: Univ. Chicago Press

Adrianson L., Hjelmquist E. 1991. Group processes in face-to-face and computer-mediated communication. *Behav. Info. Tech.* 10(4):281–96

Ahrentzen S. B. 1990. Managing conflicts by managing boundaries: how professional homeworkers cope with multiple roles at home. *Environ. Behav.* 22(6):723–52

Bailyn L. 1989. Toward the perfect workplace. *Commun. ACM* 32(4):460–71

Barlow J. P. 1995. Is there a there in cyberspace? *Utne Reader*:50–56

Bechar-Israeli H. 1995. From ⟨Bonehead⟩ to ⟨cLonehEad⟩: nicknames, play and identity on Internet Relay Chat. *J. Computer-Mediated Commun.* 1(2):online URL: http//www.usc.edu/dept/annenberg/vol1/issue2

Bikson T., Eveland J. D. 1990. The interplay of work group structures and computer support. See Galegher et al. 1990, pp. 245–90

Brent D. A. 1994. Information technology and the breakdown of "places" of knowledge. *EJournal* 4(4):Online

British Telecommunications. 1994. Teleworking: BT's Inverness. London: Br. Telecommun. 16 pp.

Burt R. 1992. *Structural Holes.* Chicago: Univ. Chicago Press

Buxton W. 1992. *Telepresence: integrating shared task and person spaces.* Pres. Graphics Interface '92 Conference, Vancouver

Calabrese A. 1994. Home-based telework and the politics of private women and public man. In *Women and Technology*, ed. U. E. Gattiker, pp. 161–99. Berlin: Walter de Gruyter

Carley K. 1990. Structural constraints on communication: the diffusion of the homomorphic signal analysis technique through scientific fields. *J. Math. Soc.* 15(3–4):207–46

Carley K., Wendt K. 1991. Electronic mail and scientific communication. *Knowledge* 12(4):406–40

Cerf V. 1993. How the Internet came to be. In *The Online User's Encyclopedia*, ed. Bernard Aboba, pp. 527–35. Boston: Addison-Wesley

Chirac J. 1995. Speech to La Fancophonie summit. (Transl. and reported by John Stackhouse), *Toronto Globe and Mail*, Dec. 4, 1995, pp. A1, A10

Chiu Y. 1995. E-mail gives rise to the e-wail: a blizzard of personal chat raises worries about office productivity. *Washington Post* (August 18): D1, D8

Christensen K., ed. 1988. *The New Era of Home Based Work.* Boulder, CO: Westview, 213 pp.

Coate J. 1994. *Cyberspace innkeeping: building online community.* Online paper: tex@sfgate.com

Constant D., Kiesler S. B., Sproull L. S. 1994. What's mine is ours, or is it? A study of attitudes about information sharing. *Info. Sys. Res.* 5(4):400–21

Constant D., Sproull L. S., Kiesler S. B. 1996. The kindness of strangers: the usefulness of electronic weak ties for technical advice. *Organ. Sci.* 7(2): In press

Coupland, Douglas. 1995. *Microserfs.* New York: HarperCollins

Craven P., Wellman B. S. 1973. The network city. *Soc. Inquiry* 43:57–88

Cullen D. L. 1995. Psychotherapy in cyberspace. *Clinician* 26(2):1, 6–7

Culnan M. J., Markus M. L. 1987. Information technologies. In *Handbook of Organizational Communication*, ed. F. M. Jablin, L. L. Putnam, K. H. Roberts, L. W. Porter, pp. 420–43. Newbury Park, CA: Sage

Cybergal. 1995. The year of living dangerously. *Toronto Life-Fashion* 1995:104–9

Daft R., Lengel R. 1986. Organizational information requirements, media richness and structural design. *Manage. Sci.* 32:554–71

Danet B., Rudenberg L., Rosenbaum-Tamari Y. 1996. Hmmm... Where's all that smoke coming from? Writing, play and performance on Internet Relay Chat. In *Network and Netplay*, ed. S. Rafaeli, F. Sudweeks, M. McLaughlin. Cambridge, MA: MIT Press. In press

Danet B., Wachenhauser T., Bechar-Israeli C., Cividalli A., Rosenblum-Tamari Y. 1995. Curtain time 20:00 GMT: Experiments in virtual theater on Internet relay chat. *J. Computer-Mediated Commun.* 1(2):online URL: http//www.usc.edu/dept/annenberg/vol1/issue2

Danowitz A. K., Nassef Y., Goodman S. E. 1995. Cyberspace across the Sahara: computing in North Africa. *Commun. ACM* 38(12):23–8

Dillon T. 1995. Mapping the discourse of HCI researchers with citation analysis. *Sigchi Bull.* 27(4):56–62

Di Martino V., Wirth L. 1990. Telework: a new way of working and living. *Int. Labour Rev.* 129(5):529–54

Dimitrova D., Garton L., Salaff J., Wellman B. 1994. *Strategic connectivity: communications and control.* Pres. Sunbelt Soc. Networks Conf., New Orleans

Dourish P., Bly S. 1992. Portholes: supporting awareness in a distributed work group. In *Proc. CHI '92*, ed. P. Bauersfeld, J. Bennett, G. Lynch, pp. 541–47. NY: ACM Press

DuBrin A. J. 1991. Comparison of the job satisfaction and productivity of telecommuters versus in-house employees. *Psychol. Rep.* 68:1223–34

Dürrenberger G., Jaegerand C., Bieri L., Dahinden U. 1996. Telework and vocational contact. *Technol. Stud.* In press

Duxbury L., Higgins C. 1995. *Summary Report of Telework. Pilot Product Number 750008XPE, Statistics Canada.* 57 pp.

The Economist. 1995. Mais où sont les cafés d'antan. *The Economist* June 10, p. 50

Electronic Mail Association. 1992. *Electronic Mail Market Research Results.* Arlington, VA.

Emmett R. 1982. VNET or GRIPENET. *Datamation* 4:48–58

Eveland J. D., Bikson T. K. 1988. Work group structures and computer support. *ACM Trans Office Info. Sys.* 6:354–79

Falconer K. F. 1993. *Space, gender, and work in the context of technological change: telecommuting women.* Ph.D. thesis. Univ. Kentucky, Lexington. 202 pp.

Feld S. 1982. Social structural determinants of similarity among associates. *Am. Sociol. Rev.* 47:797–801

Feldman M. S. 1987. Electronic mail and weak ties in organizations. *Office Tech. People* 3:83–101

Finholt T., Sproull L. 1990. Electronic groups at work. *Organ. Sci.* 1(1):41–64

Finholt T., Sproull L., Kiesler S. 1990. Communication and performance in ad hoc task groups. See Galegher et al. 1990, pp. 291–325

Fischer C. 1975. Toward a subcultural theory of urbanism. *Am. J. Sociol.* 80:1319–41

Fish R., Kraut R., Root R., Rice R. 1993. Video as a technology for informal communication. *Commun. ACM* 36(1):48–61

Foderaro L. 1995. Seekers of self-help finding it online. *New York Times*, March 23

Fox R. 1995. Newstrack. *Commun. ACM* 38(8):11–12

Frank J. 1995. Preparing for the information highway: information technology in Canadian households. *Can. Soc. Trends* Autumn:2–7

Freeman L. 1986. The impact of computer based communication on the social structure of an emerging scientific speciality. *Soc. Networks* 6:201–21

French K. J. F. 1988. *Job satisfactions and family satisfactions of in home workers compared with out of home workers.* Ph.D. thesis. Univ. Calif., Berkeley

Fritz M. E., Higa K., Narasimhan S. 1994. Telework: exploring the borderless office. In Proc. *27th Ann. Hawaii Int. Conf. on Sys. Sci.*, ed. J. F. Nunamaker, R. H. Sprague Jr., IV:149–58. Washington, DC: IEEE Press. 971 pp.

Fulk J., Boyd B. 1991. Emerging theories of communication in organizations. *J. Manage.* 17(2):407–46

Fulk J., DeSanctis G. 1995. Electronic communication and changing organizational forms. *Organ. Sci.* 6(4):337–349

Fulk J., Steinfield C. W. 1990. *Organizations and Communication Technology.* Newbury Park, CA: Sage

Furlong M. S. 1989. An electronic community for older adults: the SeniorNet network. *J. Commun.* 39(3):145–153

Galegher J., Kraut R., Egido C. eds. 1990. *Intellectual Teamwork.* Hillsdale, NJ: Erlbaum

Garton L. 1995. *An Empirical Analysis of Desktop Videoconferencing and Other Media in a Spatially Distributed Work Group.* Laval, Que: Ctr. for Inform. Technol. Innovation

Garton L., Wellman B. 1995. Social impacts of electronic mail in organizations: a review of the research literature. *Commun. Yearbk.* 18:434–53

Gerson J., Kraut R. 1988. Clerical work at home or in the office? See Christensen 1988, pp. 49–64

Grantham C. E., Paul E. D. 1994. *The greening of organizational change: a case study.* Work. Pap. Inst. Study of Distributed Work. Oakland, CA. 26 pp.

Grey M., Hodson N., Gordon G. 1993. *Teleworking Explained.* Toronto: Wiley. 289 pp.

Gupta S., Pitkow J., Recker M. 1995. *Consumer Survey of WWW Users.* Website: http://www.wmich.edu/sgupta/hermes.html

Haythornthwaite C., Wellman B., Mantei M. 1995. Work relationships and media use. *Group Decisions & Negotiations* 4(3):193–211

Heck R., Owen A., Rowe B. eds. 1995. *Home-Based Employment and Family Life.* Westport, CT: Auburn House

Heilmann W. 1988. The organizational development of teleprogramming. See Korte et al. 1988, pp. 39–61

Helms R., Marom R. 1992. *Telecommuting: A Corporate Primer: IBM Tech. Rep. No. TR-74.098.* Toronto: IBM

Herring S. C. 1993. Gender and democracy in computer-mediated communication. *Elect. J. Commun.* 3(2):Online/unpaginated. (Available through Comserve at vm.its.rpi.edu)

Hesse B. W., Grantham C. E. 1991. *Electronically distributed work communities.* Work. Pap. Ctr. for Res. on Tech., Am. Inst. for Res. 33 pp.

Hesse B. W., Sproull L. S., Kiesler S. B., Walsh J. P. 1993. Returns to science computer networks in oceanography. *Commun. ACM* 36(8):90–101

Higgins C., Duxbury L., Lee C. 1992. *Balancing work and family: a study of Canadian private sector employees.* Work. Pap. Sch. Bus. Admin, Univ. Western Ontario. 107 pp.

Hiltz S. R., Johnson K., Agle G. 1978. *Replicating Bales Problem Solving Experiments on a Computerized Conference.* Computerized Conferencing and Communications Ctr. New Jersey Inst. Technol.

Hiltz S. R., Johnson K., Turoff M. 1986. Experiments in group decision making: communication process and outcome in face-to-face versus computerized conferences. *Hum. Commun. Res.* 13(2):225–52

Hiltz S. R., Turoff M. 1993. *The Network Nation.* Cambridge. MA: MIT Press

Hinds P., Kiesler S. 1995. Communication across boundaries: work, structure, and use of communication technologies in a large organization. *Organ. Sci.* 6(4):373–393

Hodson R., Parker R. 1988. Work in high-technology settings: a review of the empirical literature. *Res. Soc. Work* 4:1–29

Huber G. P. 1990. A theory of the effects of advanced information technologies on organizational design, intelligence, and decision making. See Fulk & Steinfield 1990, pp. 237–74

Huff C., Sproull L. S., Kiesler S. B. 1989. Computer communication and organizational commitment: tracing the relationship in a city government. *J. Appl. Soc. Psych.* 19:1371–91

Huws U. 1988. Remote possibilities: some difficulties in the analysis and quantification of telework in the UK. See Korte et al. 1988, pp. 61–76

Huws U., Korte W. B., Robinson S. 1990. *Telework: Towards the Elusive Office.* Chichester, England: Wiley. 273 pp.

Insight New Media. 1995. *Internet facts: antihype for the information age.* Work. Pap. December

Ishii H. 1992. ClearBoard: A seamless medium for shared drawing and conversation with eye contact. In *Proc. ACM Conf. on Human Factors in Comp. Sys. CHI '92,* 525–32. NY: ACM Press. 714 pp.

Johnson-Lenz P., Johnson-Lenz T. 1978. On facilitating networks for social change. *Connections* 1:5–11

Johnson-Lenz P., Johnson-Lenz T. 1990. Islands of safety for unlocking human potential. *Awakening Technol.* 3:1–6

Johnson-Lenz P., Johnson-Lenz T. 1994. Groupware for a small planet. In *Groupware in the 21st Century,* ed. P. Lloyd, pp. 269–85. Westport, CT: Praeger

Jones S. G. 1995. Understanding community in the information age. In *CyberSociety: Computer-Mediated Communciation and Community,* ed. S. G. Jones, pp. 10–35. Thousand Oaks, CA: Sage

Kadushin C., Lerer N., Tumelty S., Reichler J. 1987. *"With a little help from my friends"*: *Who helps whom with computers?* Work. Pap. Ctr. Soc. Res., City Univ. of New York. 54 pp.

Kaufer D., Carley K. 1993. *Communication at a Distance: The Influence of Print on Sociocultural Organization and Change.* Hillsdale, NJ: Erlbaum. 474 pp.

Kaye A. R. 1992. Computer conferencing and mass distance education. In *Empowering Networks*, ed. M. Waggoner, Englewood Cliffs, NJ: Educational Technology

Kiesler S. B., Siegal J., McGuire T. W. 1984. Social psychological aspects of computer-mediated communication. *Am. Psychol.* 39(10):1123–34

Kiesler S. B., Sproull L. S. 1988. *Technological and Social Change in Organizational Communication Environments.* Pittsburgh: Carnegie Mellon Univ. Press

Kiesler S. B., Sproull L. S. 1992. Group decision making and communication technology. *Org. Behav. Hum. Decision Proc.* 52:96–123

Kiesler S. B., Sproull L. S., Eccles J. S. 1985. Pool halls, chips, and war games: women in the culture of computing. *Psychol. Women Q.* 9:451–62

King S. 1994. Analysis of electronic support groups for recovering addicts. *Interpersonal Comp. Tech.* 2(3):47–56

Kinsman F. 1987. *The Telecommuters.* Chichester, UK: Wiley. 234 pp.

Kling R. 1996. Synergies and competition between life in cyberspace and face-to-face communities. *Soc. Sci. Comp. Rev.* 14(1):50–54

Kling R. 1996a. *Computerization and Controversy.* San Diego: Academic Press. 2nd ed. In press

Kling R. 1996b. Social relationships in electronic forums: Hangouts, salons, workplaces and communities. See Kling 1996a

Kling R., Jewett T. 1994. The social design of worklife with computers and networks: an open natural systems perspective. *Adv. Computers* 39:239–293

Kling R., Lamb R. 1996. Analyzing visions of electronic publishing and digital libraries. In *Scholarly Publishing: The Electronic Frontier*, eds. G. B. Newby, R. Peek. Cambridge MA: MIT Press. In press

Kochen M. 1989. *The Small World.* Norwood, NJ: Ablex

Kollock P., Smith M. A. 1996a. *Communities in Cyberspace.* Berkeley: Univ. Calif. Press

Kollock P., Smith M. A. 1996b. Managing the virtual commons: cooperation and conflict in computer communities. In *Computer-Mediated Communication*, ed. S. Herring. Amsterdam: John Benjamins. In press

Koppel R., Appelbaum E., Albin P. 1988. Implications of workplace information technology: control, organization of work and the occupational structure. *Res. Soc. Work* 4:125–152

Korte W. B., Robinson S., Steinle W. J. 1988. *Telework: Present Situation and Future Development of a New Form of Work Organization.* Bonn: Elsevier Science

Kraut R. E. 1988. Homework: What is it and who does it? See Christensen 1988, pp. 30–48

Kraut R. E. 1989. Telecommuting: the trade-offs of home work. *J. Commun.* 39(3):19–47

Kraut R. E., Attewell P. 1993. *Electronic mail and organizational knowledge.* Work. Pap. Carnegie Mellon Univ.

Kraut R. E., Scherlis W., Mukhopadhyay T., Manning J., Kiesler S. 1995. HomeNet: A field trial of residential Internet services. HomeNet 1(2):1–8

Kugelmass J. 1995. Telecommuting: *A Manager's Guide to Flexible Work Arrangements.* New York: Lexington. 226 pp.

Labaton, S. 1995. Clinton papers' index in Foster office vanished after suicide, aide says. *New York Times*, August 2

Latané B., Darley J. 1976. *Help in a Crisis: Bystander Response to an Emergency.* Morristown, NJ: General Learning

Lea M. 1991. Rationalist assumptions in cross-media comparisons of computer-mediated communication. *Behav. Info. Tech.* 10(2):153–172

Lea M., O'Shea T., Fung P. 1995. Constructing the networked organization. *Organ. Sci.* 6(4):462–78

Lea M., O'Shea T., Fung P., Spears R. 1992. 'Flaming' in computer-mediated communication. In *Contexts of Computer-Mediated Communication*, ed. M. Lea, pp. 89–112. New York: Harvester Wheatsheaf

Lea M., Spears R. 1992. Paralanguage and social perception in computer-mediated communication. *J. Org. Comp.* 2(3–4):321–41

Lea M., Spears R. 1995. Love at first byte? Building personal relationships over computer networks. In *Understudied Relationships*, eds. J. T. Wood, S. Duck, pp. 197–233. Thousand Oaks, CA: Sage

Lewis P. H. 1994. Strangers, not their computers, build a network in time of grief. *New York Times*, 8 March: A1, D2

Lewis P. 1995. Report of high internet use is challenged. *New York Times* (December 13)

Lewis P. 1996. Prodigy said to be in role of a silent son. *New York Times* (January 16).

Lucky R. 1995. What technology alone cannot do. *Sci. Am.* 273(3):204–5

Maes P. 1995. Artificial life meets entertainment: lifelike autonomous agents. *Commun. ACM* 38(11):108–114

Mantei M. M., Baecker R., Sellen A., Buxton W., Milligan T., Wellman B. S. 1991. Experiences in the use of a media space. In *CHI '91 Conf. Proc.*, eds. S. P. Roberson, G. M. Olson, J. S. Olson, pp. 203–208. Reading, MA: Addison-Wesley. 511 pp.

Mantei M. M., Wellman B. S. 1995. *From groupware to netware.* Work. Pap. Ctr Urban & Commun. Stud., Univ. Toronto

Markus M. L. 1990. Toward a "critical mass" theory of interactive media. See Fulk & Steinfield 1990, pp. 194–218

Markus M. L. 1994a. Finding a happy medium: explaining the negative impacts of electronic communication on social life at work. *ACM Trans. Info. Sys.* 12(2):119–149

Markus M. L. 1994b. Electronic mail as the medium of managerial choice. *Organ. Sci.* 5:502–27

Marx G., Virnoche M. 1995. *Only connect': E.M. Forster in an age of computerization: a case study of the establishment of a community network.* Pres. Am. Sociol. Assoc., Washington, DC

McClintock C. C. 1981. *Working Alone Together: Managing Telecommuting.* Pres. at Natl. Telecommun. Conf., Houston

McCormick N., McCormick J. 1992. Computer friends and foes: content of undergraduates' electronic mail. *Computers in Hum. Behav.* 8:379–405

McKinney E. 1995. New data on the size of the Internet and the matrix. Online URL: http://www.tic.com, October

Mele C. 1996. Access to cyberspace and the empowerment of disadvantaged communities. See Kollock & Smith 1996

Meyer G. R. 1989. *The Social Organization of the Computer Underground.* Master's thesis. N. Ill. Univ.

Mitchell W. 1995. *City of Bits: Space, Time and the Infobahn.* Cambridge, MA: MIT Press

Moore G. 1997. Sharing faces, places and spaces: the Ontario Telepresence Project. In *Video-Mediated Communication,* eds. K. Finn, A. Sellen, S. Wilbur. Mahwah, NJ: Lawrence Erlbaum. Forthcoming

Mowshowitz A. 1994. Virtual organization: a vision of management in the information age. *Info. Soc.* 10:267–88

Newsweek. 1995. Cyberspace tilts right. Jan. 27:30

O'Brien J. 1996. Gender on (the) line: an erasable institution? See Kollock & Smith 1996

Olson M. H. 1987. Telework: Practical experience and future prospects. In *Technology and the Transformation of White-Collar Work,* ed. R. Kraut, pp. 135–55. Hillsdale, NJ: Erlbaum

Olson M. H. 1988. Organizational barriers to telework. See Korte et al. 1988, pp. 77–100

Olson M. H., Primps S. B. 1984. Working at home with computers: work and nonwork issues. *J. Soc. Iss.* 40(3):97–112

Olszewski P., Mokhtarian P. 1994. Telecommuting frequency and impacts for state of California employees. *Tech. Forecasting Soc. Change* 45:275–86

Online Research Group. 1995. *Defining the Internet Opportunity 1994–1995.* Sebastopol, CA: O'Reilly

Orlikowski W. J., Yates J., Okamura K., Fujimoto M. 1995. Shaping electronic communication: the metastructuring of technology in the context of use. *Organ. Sci.* 6(4):423–44

Perin P. 1991. Les usages privés du téléphone. *Commun. & Stratégies* (2):157–62

Pickering J. M., King J. L. 1995. Hardwiring weak ties: interorganizational computer-mediated communication, occupational communities, and organizational change. *Organ. Sci.* 6(4):479–86

Pitkow J., Kehoe C. 1995. *Third WWW User Survey: Executive Summary.* Online. Internet: WWW http://www.cc.gatech.edu/gvu/usersurveys/survey/or/1995, Graphic, Visualizaton and Usability Center, Georgia Inst. Technol.

Pliskin N., Romm C. T. 1994. *Empowerment effects of electronic group Communication: a case study.* Work. Pap. Dep. Manage., Faculty Commerce, Univ. Wollongong

Reid R. 1996. Hierarchy and power: social control in cyberspace. See Kollock & Smith 1996

Rheingold H. 1993. *The Virtual Community.* Reading. MA: Addison-Wesley. 325 pp.

Rice R. 1987. Computer-mediated communication and organizational innovation. *J. Commun.* 37(4):65–95

Rice R., Love G. 1987. Electronic emotion: socioemotional content in a computer-mediated communication network. *Commun. Res.* 14(1):85–108

Rice R., Steinfeld C. 1994. Experiences with new forms of organizational communication via electronic mail and voice messaging. In *Telematics and Work*. eds. J. E. Andriessen, R. Roe, pp. 109–137. E. Sussex, UK: Lea

Riecken D. ed. 1994. Intelligent agents. *Commun. ACM* 37(7):18–146

Salaff J., Dimitrova D. 1995a. *Teleworking: a review of studies of this international business application of telecommunications. Work. Pap*. Toronto, Ctr for Urban Community Stud., Univ. Toronto

Salaff J., Dimitrova D. 1995b. *Teleworking: a review of studies of this international business application of telecommunications*. Pres. Conf. Global Business in Transition: Prospects for the 21st Century, Hong Kong

Shade L. R. 1994. Is sisterhood virtual?: Women on the electronic frontier. Trans. Royal Society Canada VI 5:131–42

Sharples M., ed. 1993. *Computer Supported Collaborative Writing*. London: Springer-Verlag

Shirley S. 1988. Telework in the UK. See Korte et al. 1988, pp. 23–33

Siegel J., Dubrovsky V., Kiesler S., McGuire T. W. 1986. Group processes in computer-mediated communication. *Org. Behav. Hum. Decision Proc.* 37:157–87

Simons T. 1994. *Expanding the boundaries of employment: professional work at home*. Ph.D. thesis. Cornell Univ. 215 pp.

Slouka M. 1995. *War of the Worlds: Cyberspace and the High-Tech Assault on Reality*. New York: Basic Books. 185 pp.

Smith A. D. 1996. Problems of conflict management in virtual communities. See Kollock & Smith 1996

Soares A. S. 1992. Telework and communication in data processing centres in Brazil. In *Technology-Mediated Communication*, ed. U. E. Gattiker, pp. 117–145. Berlin: Walter de Gruyter

Southwick S. 1996. Liszt: *Searchable Directory of E-Mail Discussion Groups*. http://www.liszt.com. BlueMarble Inform. Serv.

Sproull L. S., Faraj S. 1995. Atheism, sex and databases. In *Public Access to the Internet*, eds. B. Kahin, J. Keller, 62–81. Cambridge, MA: MIT Press

Sproull L. S., Kiesler S. B. 1991. *Connections: New Ways of Working in the Networked Organization*. Boston, MA: MIT Press. 205 pp.

Star S. L. 1993. Cooperation without consensus in scientific problem solving: dynamics of closure in open systems. In *CSCW: Cooperation or Conflict?*, ed. S. Easterbrook, pp. 93–106. Berlin: Springer-Verlag

Steinfield C. 1985. Dimensions of electronic mail use in an organizational setting. *Org. Behav. Hum. Dec. Proc.* 37:157–87

Steinle W. J. 1988. Telework. See Korte et al. 1988, pp. 7–19

Stephenson N. 1992. *Snow Crash*. New York: Bantam

Stinchcombe A. L. 1990. *Information and Organizations*. Berkeley: Univ. Calif. Press. 391 pp.

Stoll C. 1995. *Silicon Snake Oil: Second Thoughts on the Information Highway*. New York: Doubleday. 247 pp.

Tippin D. 1994. *Control processes in distant work situations: the case of satellite offices*. Presented at Can. Sociol. & Anthro. Assoc., Calgary

Toffler A. 1980. *The Third Wave*. New York: Morrow

Tolbert P. S., Simons T. 1994. *The impact of working at home on career outcomes of professional employees*. Work. Pap. 94-04: School of Industrial and Labor Relations, Ctr. for Adv. Human Resource Studies, Cornell Univ. 21 pp.

Treese W. 1995. *The Internet Index Number 6*. Online: treese@openmarket.com

Valacich J. S., Paranka D., George J. F., Nunamker J. F. Jr. 1993. Communication concurrency and the new media. *Commun. Res.* 20:249–76

Walsh J. P., Bayama T. 1996. Computer networks and scientific work. *Soc. Stud. Sci.* 26(4): In press

Walther J. B. 1992. Interpersonal effects incomputer-mediated interaction: a relational perspective. *Commun. Res.* 19(1):52–90

Walther J. B. 1994. Anticipated ongoing interaction versus channel effects on relational communication in computer-mediated interaction. *Hum. Commun. Res.* 20(4):473–501

Walther J. B. 1995. Relational aspects of computer-mediated communication. *Organ. Sci.* 6(2):186–203

Walther J. B. 1996. Computer-mediated communication: impersonal, interpersonal and hyperpersonal interaction. *Commun. Res.* 23(1):3–43

Walther J. B., Anderson J. F., Park D. W. 1994. Interpersonal effects in computer-mediated interaction: a meta-analysis of social and anti-social communication. *Commun. Res.* 21(4):460–87

Weick K. 1976. Educational organizations as loosely coupled systems. *Admin. Sci. Q.* 21:1–19

Weisband S., Reinig B. 1995. Managing user perceptions of email privacy. *Commun. ACM* 38(12):40–47

Weisband S. P., Schneider S. K., Connolly T. 1995. Computer-mediated communication and social information: status salience and status difference. *Acad. Manage. J.* 38(4):1124–51

Wellman B. S. 1979. The community question. *Am. J. Sociol.* 84:1201–31

Wellman B. S. 1992. Men in networks: private communities, domestic friendships. In *Men's Friendships*, ed. P. Nardi, 74–114. Newbury Park, CA: Sage

Wellman B. S. 1994. I was a teenage network analyst: the route from the Bronx to the information highway. *Connections* 17(2):28–45

Wellman B. S. 1995. Lay referral networks: using conventional medicine and alternative therapies for low back pain. *Soc. Health Care* 12:213–23

Wellman B. S. 1996. An electronic group is virtually a social network. In *Research Milestones on the Information Highway*, ed. S. Kiesler. Hillsdale, NJ: Lawrence Erlbaum. In press

Wellman B. S., Gulia M. 1996. Net surfers don't ride alone: virtual communities as communities. In *Communities in Cyberspace*, eds. P. Kollock, M. Smith. Berkeley: Univ. Calif. Press

Wellman B. S., Salaff J., Dimitrova D., Garton L. 1994. *The virtual reality of virtual organizations*. Pres. at Am. Sociol. Assoc., Los Angeles

Wellman B. S., Tindall D. 1993. Reach out and touch some bodies: how social networks connect telephone networks. *Progress Commun.* Sci. 12:63–93

Wireman P. 1984. *Urban Neighborhoods, Networks and Families.* Lexington, MA: Lexington Books

Zack M. H., McKenney J. L. 1995. Social context and interaction in ongoing computer-supported management groups. *Organ. Sci.* 6(4):394–422

Zuboff S. 1988. *In the Age of the Smart Machine.* New York: Basic Books

12

Anatomy of a Flame: Conflict and Community Building on the Internet*

Vivian Franco, Hsiao-Yun Hu,
Bruce V. Lewenstein, Roberta Piirto,
Russ Underwood, Noni Korf Vidal

The authors break down the barriers of electronic communities to expose their most basic element, communication. Like Wellman et al., the authors discuss the significance of computer-mediated communication (CMC) and its association with the behavioral issue of flaming. Flaming, which occurs when community members have a breakdown in communication or understanding, results in hostile, aggressive, and threatening language that is exchanged through email or real-time discussion. While flaming has the ability to cause great personal distress and anguish, it is not an entirely disruptive community force. It has the ability to bring to light hidden issues that need to be handled in a constructive and collaborative manner by the community at large. By examining the anatomy of a flame, we are provided with a glimpse of the phases and trends that affect the complex interactions that develop through a shared or common community language. This is explored through a case analysis that presents the make-up of a flame from a real-world normative viewpoint. Additionally, the authors explain that flames are commonly affected by our natural male/female or passive/aggressive personalities as well as the nonverbal cues that are inherent within CMC and social networks.

The authors are with the Departments of Communication and Science & Technology Studies. Cornell University, 321 Kennedy Hall, Ithaca, NY 14850. Authors are listed alphabetically. This article is the product of a course in qualitative research methods taught by Bruce V. Lewenstein, to whom correspondence should be addressed
* © 1995 IEEE. Reprinted with permission from *IEEE Technology and Society Magazine* (Summer 1995): 12–21.

209

Although some social theorists have predicted that widespread computer-mediated communication will produce utopian communities in cyberspace, the presence of "flames" and other activities often perceived as hostile to communal standards raises questions about whether and how such communities might come to exist. Here we examine the anatomy and progress of a particular "flame" that occurred in a listserv (unmoderated mailing list group) devoted specifically to the development of online communities ("Free-nets"). Contrary to existing literature that treats "flames" as undesirable, we suggest that a "flame" can help communities identify common values.

NEW TELECOMMUNICATIONS AGE

In the 1970s, the rising ascendancy of computerized telecommunications led many social theorists to proclaim the dawning of a new age. The age was variously called the post-industrial society,[2,30] the information revolution,[18] the communications age or mediacracy,[24] the electronics revolution,[8] and the information economy.[25] With the increasing number of computers hooked to networks, the coming social changes became more firmly dependent on technology, in the eyes of many social theorists. This computer-driven society was called the network nation,[12] the republic of technology society,[4] the micro revolution,[19,20] the third wave,[29] the computer state,[5] and the information age.[7] All of these authors were arguing that society was experiencing a technological revolution on a global scale. Many commented on possible implications for societal organization and control of the rapid changes in mass media and telecommunications technologies. In many of these scenarios the future was seen to be more egalitarian and more decentralized. The shape of a society, these pundits claimed, is determined by the types of technology it adopts.

This technological determinist view was echoed in the subsequent push for a "National Information Infrastructure"[22] and an "information highway."[10] The implication, which was sometimes explicitly stated and sometimes only implied, was that if we build it, wonderful things will happen. The technology was considered an end in itself.

A technological determinist vein also permeates the academic literature that focuses more narrowly on the nature of computer-mediated communication (CMC). This literature characterizes CMC as a social,[16] more impersonal,[17] deindividuating,[15] and ruder and more uninhibited medium than face-to-face communication.[26] All of these studies were done in organizations or university settings and used either workers who had just been introduced to e-mail systems or student subjects who were not necessarily computer users.

IMPORTANCE OF CONTEXT

Research that imposes an artificial social context for communication, however, may have little relevance to CMC that occurs within established electronic groups. Although much experimental psychological research assumes that results can be extended beyond the specific context in which they are produced, the complexity of CMC is still sufficiently unexplored that we don't know the circumstances in which one set of results can be extended to another context. In this case, research relying on artificial social contexts tends to consider all CMC (electronic mail, conferences, bulletin boards) as one environment with a common character, fails to factor in individual differences, and assumes that social relations (or the lack thereof) have no effect on the way people evaluate communication. This view has several obvious shortcomings. It fails to account for the social factors that influence all communication, both via computer and face-to-face, both online and offline. It fails to conceptualize communication as a process; people who rate one communication experience with an unknown person as unsatisfying might change their perceptions as their knowledge of the system and their expectations about their co-communicants change and develop with subsequent contact. In other words, the users (or factors related to the users), rather than the computer, may cause negative evaluations of CMC.

Early communication theorists grappled with the question of technological determinism versus social context and developed an "individual differences" perspective to resolve the tension.[14] This perspective holds that the mass media have limited ability to manipulate and mold an audience, because different individuals respond differently to the same message (and technology). To the extent that this is so, effects can be traced to attributes within the members of the audience themselves. On the other hand, the early theorists also noted that the same individual responds differently to different messages. To the extent that this is so, the effects can be traced to message or technological differences. This view assumes that the individual develops attitudes, values, and beliefs based on unique personal experiences. In other words, the reactions of individuals are to some extent determined by past experiences. Another view attributes differences in how receivers perceive messages and technology to the broad social categories in which people fall.[21] Those of the same age, sex, wealth, and education are more likely to react in similar ways.

These theories are important for the purposes of this study because they emphasize the user-oriented attributes that need to be considered in analyzing the success or failure of the process of communication. Communication occurs when the message sent equals the message received; but this simple equation is not sufficient. Miscommunication can occur at any point in the process. Once a message is sent, the receiver must attend to it adequately and comprehend it in some manner that is roughly in line with the sender's meaning.[34]

"Second-guessing" theory suggests that evaluations of messages (and therefore comprehension) will be closely linked to the receiver's evaluation of the sender.[11] This theory holds that people believe messages are biased, so they constantly "second-guess" the sender's intentions to try to get a truer version of the communication. Whether a message comes from acquaintances, coworkers, government officials, or friends, people constantly sift through the information they have about sources to try to evaluate the message and correct for distortions.

This theory has large implications for CMC research. CMC relies completely on the verbal, textual channel (except for a very few experimental situations in which visual or audio material is added to the channel). People who communicate through computers get none of the nonverbal or paralinguistic cues and feedback that enhance meaning and help to soften the often harsh effects of words alone. Often the age, sex, or social status of co-communicants is unknown. Second-guessing theory suggests that people communicating through their computer screens might place greater emphasis on all the other information they have about their co-communicants. Some of this information will come from the text itself, including writing style, word style, word choice, and any clues about the author's identity. Other information might come from the communication context—the nature of the electronic environment in which the communication occurs.

Both individual differences and social categories appear to affect user perceptions of online communication. This study analyzes the community consequences of a "flame"—a lengthy, often personally insulting debate in an electronic community. In this study, the flame was caused by a gender-biased comment and the subsequent concerns raised by members of the electronic community. As Tannen[28] and others have suggested, men and women have different ways of using language to express themselves. Women often take a more inclusive, less direct, "relate" approach, designed to avoid confrontation, while men often speak bluntly and seek confrontation (a "debate" style). Online, people who normally use a "debate" style of communication mix with people who prefer the "relate" style of communication,[13] usually with no easy way to discern these style differences until after a conflict occurs. How might this affect the communication process?

These research traditions suggest to us that, in CMC, technology does not erase or reduce the interpersonal and social factors that affect all communication. The personalities and social categories of the communicators, the social networks they belong to, and the context in which the communication occurs are all crucial elements in electronic communication, as they are in other types of communication. Further, elements of computerized communication may make people rely even more on interpersonal and social factors in their attempts to avoid miscommunication.

LISTSERVS, COMMUNITIES, AND FLAMES

Miscommunication happens both online and off. Online communication is like a conversation in text; because the full extent of the conversation is captured in the words (unlike offline conversations, where gestures and other nonverbal cues are part of the conversation), the record of the conversation provides a rich environment in which to study communication failures. This study looks at one extended incident of miscommunication and how it affected the process of community building on a newly formed "listserv" on the Internet, "the global computer metanetwork."[33] Technically, a listserv is an automated mailing list, in which messages sent to the listserv are redistributed to all list subscribers. A listserv may be moderated, meaning that a moderator approves (and sometimes has the power to edit) messages before they are posted to the list; in the case studied in this article, however, the list was unmoderated—all messages went directly to all subscribers. Messages are sent asynchronously, so there can be a long gap between the time the message is sent and when it is received, depending on how often the receiver checks his or her e-mail. Conceptually, a listserv is a community of people with at least a nominal interest in a common topic.

The listserv is also a communication environment. As in any environment, the organizing principle of the list and the system operators' guidelines convey cues about the types of messages that are acceptable.[1,23] The listserv analyzed in this study was called "Communet," an unmoderated list organized to bring together people who were interested in the principle of community computing, sometimes called "Free-nets." The list had only existed for a month or two at the time of the flame under study. One of the founding members of the list was Tom Grundner, president of the National Public Telecomputing Network, and founder of the Cleveland Free-net. The basic premise of NPTN is that all people have a right to access the Internet and that computer network resources should be as readily available to the public as are the materials in the public library system. The people on the Communet listserv shared some interest in these principles. The list provided a valuable setting for our study on electronic communities because it was a group that by its organizing principle was self-reflexive about the process of creating community.

The miscommunication in this case was a group of electronic messages, which together constituted a "flame." To flame is "to speak rapidly or incessantly on an uninteresting topic or with a patently ridiculous attitude."[27] The term "flaming" was coined by the computer hacker community and has become a well-documented effect of electronic communication.[13,26] Flaming is usually characterized as noise, indicative of the uninhibited behavior CMC encourages. It is characterized as an inherently negative effect of computerized communication.

Although flames are usually taken to inhibit the growth of online communities, some anecdotal evidence suggests that flaming can help an electronic community define its common values, and encourage people either to bond more closely or to leave the community, after evaluating the congruence between the group's values or interests and their own. Flaming has been termed a "rite of passage" that helps define any new electronic group.

The flame in this study occurred on Communet shortly after the listserv was started in early 1993. We were interested in how the flame affected the participants' impressions of the Communet community. We were also interested in whether there was a sense of community on the list. A sense of community can be loosely defined as a shared sense of purpose and a commitment to continued communication. We were also interested in determining the interpersonal and social factors that would cause a flame to have an effect on members' impressions of community.

CASE AND METHODS

At 18:00 on Tuesday, March 29, 1993, in response to a request for information regarding Free-nets. Tom Grundner wrote,

> "...and for our better customers, we can send a 15 minute videotape on community computing—suitable for showing to potential funders, recalcitrant computer center managers, wives (who are wondering what the hell you are up to now), and other informationally challenged individuals."

The first public response to Grundner's message, posted shortly before 9:00 the following morning by a woman, noted in a mildly humorous manner his reference to wives as "informationally challenged," and added that "the video is also great for husbands who are wondering what the hell you're up to now." Another response was sent to Grundner by private e-mail from "Mabel,"* who chastised him more strongly, noting that his use of sexist language "is just [the] kind of attitude that alienates women from computers and information technology."

Apparently believing that Mabel had posted her message publicly to the entire listserv, Grundner responded publicly, expressing his belief that "this medium [online communication] holds out perhaps the greatest hope we will see in our lifetime for communication which transcends racial, sexual, and economic barriers" as long as "professional victim-mongers" are not allowed "to screw it up." He ended by exhorting Mabel to stop blaming someone else, "get off your butt, and get more than three women to the next meeting of your group."

Over the next several days, a series of messages ensued regarding Grundner's messages and the responses to them. To define the flame, we selected from the hundreds of messages posted to the Communet listserv between the end of March and the beginning of April those most relevant to the original Grundner/Mabel exchange. To be included, messages had to refer either to other messages contained in the flame or address issues discussed by messages in the flame, such as gender equity and community in online systems. Fifty-eight messages were selected, beginning with Grundner's original message regarding wives "and other informationally challenged individuals," and ending around noon on Saturday, April 3, as a new flame on free speech was building steam.

We then conducted a two-part analysis. First, we did a content analysis of the messages in the flame. Then we sent a survey to a sample of the people then registered as subscribers to the Communet listserv.

For the content analysis, each message was assigned a brief label according to its focus ("sexism," "building community," etc.). Then each was coded according to valence on a five-point scale, with five being "unifying" and one "divisive." Unifying messages were characterized by inclusive "we" references, agreement with previous contributors, and overt references to solutions and creating com-

---

* All names except Grundner's have been changed

munity. Divisive messages included name-calling, presuming to "speak for" the group against an idea or individual, or otherwise belittling someone or something. The time each message was posted to the listserv, its length (number of lines), and the name supplied by its author were also noted. In addition, the "importance" of each message was assessed by recording the number of times other writers referred to it.

Finally, when necessary, messages were coded as "system errors." For example, Grundner believed Mabel had posted her response to him publicly, when in fact the message had been sent to him privately. Based on this misunderstanding, Grundner flamed her publicly. In another example, one writer failed to post a response he had written to another of Grundner's comments until over a day after composing the message. However, system errors were rare.

Two individuals, working independently, coded each message. Intercoder reliability, while not formally checked, was strong, even with regard to the most "subjective" category of valence; when disagreements arose, they were differences of degree (how unifying or how divisive) rather than of kind.

Finally, the flame was charted according to the three dimensions of time, valence, and importance in order to give a fuller sense of the "shape" or structure of the exchange.

For the survey, we sent questionnaires by electronic mail to 75 subscribers to the Communet listserv about a month after the flame. We chose these individuals because they had posted messages to the listserv during the time of the flame. Our message was brief, to help ensure a greater return rate, and asked relatively open-ended questions.

We received 53 responses, 3 of which were refusals to participate, for a 67% response rate. More than 50% of the responses came within 24 hours of our mailing, more than 80% within 72 hours. We did not do any follow-up for the nonrespondents. Headers were removed from messages to preserve anonymity.

All 75 of the questionnaires were personally addressed, first and last name, to give a higher return rate. The names of the individuals were taken either directly from their posted messages, or by cross-checking their addresses against their names as found in the subscriber list obtained from the Communet listserv.

A brief thank-you was sent out as a group mailing to a list of all respondents. To keep respondents unaware of the names of the other members who had responded to our query, the thank-you was sent to a member of our own research group, with a "blind carbon copy" to the list of respondents. We mention this process because it generated a question from one of the respondents who wondered how it could be that a message addressed to the sender could have arrived in his mailbox. While the problem does not seem to be a big one, it did call attention to itself. We used the mail program Eudora; other programs may have their own idiosyncrasies that should be carefully studied to avoid compromising the anonymity of the respondents.

Several respondents seemed to misunderstand our questionnaire and believed that we were asking for their response *only if* they had written on the topic of gender bias. Their responses might have been more helpful had they understood that we were interested in their opinions regardless of the topic that they posted to the list.

PHASES AND TRENDS

Grundner's second message, his response to Mabel, was viewed by many other writers as a personal attack, and it received more responses than almost any other message in the exchange. Following Grundner's flame against Mabel, Thomas Nolan expressed his concern about the personal tone of Grundner's response. Grundner defended himself by arguing that Mabel had called his motives "into question." In her first public message regarding Grundner's comments, Mabel replied that her own motives had been questioned and that indeed Grundner had made unfair assumptions about her by labeling her a "victim-monger."

Following this initial phase, which introduced the three major contributors to the ongoing discussion (Grundner, Mabel, and Nolan), other subscribers to the Communet listserv began voicing their opinions on the subject of Grundner's comments, flames generally, the listserv community, and issues of gender online. This second phase began around noon on March 30, and lasted about a day. Most of the messages posted during this phase addressed either Grundner's first message, which generally was regarded as sexist, or his second message, which generally was interpreted as hostile.

The third and final phase of the flame began about 10:30 on April 1, when Grundner posted a conciliatory message, which fundamentally changed the tenor of the debate. In it, he proposed "a new thread," asking people to "post specific suggestions as to how to encourage women (and other minorities) to use this technology, or how to reduce barriers to their using it." He also called for volunteers to serve as "official recorders" of the suggestions presented. The third most referred-to-message in the exchange, Grundner's appeal for solutions met with almost universal support. Subsequent messages contained suggestions concerning ways to increase access to online services among minorities and women, and even Mabel and Nolan responded positively, volunteering to be recorders. One correspondent reflected the mood of the listserv population with regard to Grundner when she wrote, "I am willing to forgive your oversites [sic]. . . . It's a good move on your part."

Interspersed with the positive, community-oriented messages that characterized the third phase of the flame were several more divisive messages focusing on the issue of free speech. The first specific reference to free speech occurred toward the end of the second phase, when Dave Dorsey flamed another correspondent who had hinted that the online community must "set standards that maintain human dignity in our interactions." According to Dorsey, this "just screams Net Police." Dorsey's words seemed to spark a string of relatively negative messages that contrasted strongly with the solution responses appearing on the list at about the same time. Eventually, this "spin-off" debate, which clearly originated within the first exchange, evolved into a separate flame, with its own distinct cast of contributors, as well as its own, somewhat uglier tone.

Our most interesting finding concerned the "shape" or changing valence of the flame (Fig. 12.1). After the relatively divisive tone of the messages contained in the first phase of the flame, messages gradually took on a more unifying tone. Indeed, following initial comments condemning sexism and sexist language, contributors seemed to tire of negativity and began directly addressing the issue of community. A sample of comments from this transitional second phase follows:

- "Cooperation and good will is what netting is all about.... Racism, sexism, etc.... has no place in the net."
- "I thought we were all interested in working together here to build something good."

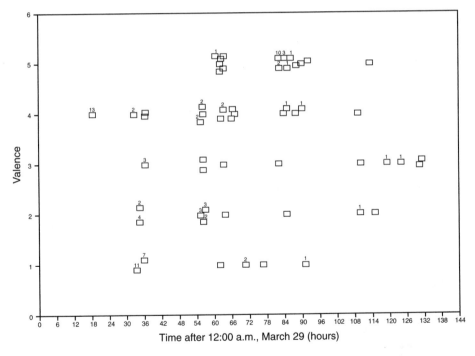

FIGURE 12.1 Schematic Map of Time and Valence of the Gender Flame. Higher valence numbers indicate more unifying messages, numbers above individual messages indicate subsequent citations to that message. Notice the more divisive nature of earlier heavily cited messages (especially those around 36 hours), compared to the more unifying nature of later heavily cited messages (especially those around 80–90 hours). A second flame, on free speech issues, begins to develop at 71 hours with a message having a valence of 1; it subsequently appears to move toward more unifying messages

- "This list is in danger of putting a big chip on its shoulder whenever this guy [Grundner] writes in. . . . Let's get on with the Business of Making Community Networks!"

Significantly, perhaps, the last message posted before Grundner's appeal for solutions was an imaginative and self-reflective satire of the Communet community's response to the flame, implicit in which were the assumptions that (1) such a community now existed and (2) that the flame had in some way served to illustrate or even define the ways in which community members related to one another.

The overall trend of the flame was from negative to positive, divisive to unifying, as members of the listserv moved from criticism to discussion and finally to community problem solving.

As mentioned above, the seeds of a second flame on free speech appeared to "spin-off" from a side discussion that concerned the issue of flame management. This second flame, to the extent that it appears in Fig. 12.1, seems to follow a similar pattern, moving from initially divisive messages to relatively more unifying ones.

Contrary to Grundner's early and rather optimistic assertion that "this medium holds out perhaps [our] greatest hope ... for communication which transcends racial, sexual, and economic barriers," it seems clear that two factors, personality and prestige, did significantly affect the dynamics of the first flame. Four of Grundner's five contributions to the exchange were widely cited, but only two other writers received a significant number of references: Mabel, Grundner's foil (her first, private message appears only to the extent that Grundner quotes it in his response), and Nolan, who can be said to have earned a sort of prestige by being flamed himself by Grundner early in the exchange. Other messages, some long and clearly well thought-out, were cited hardly at all. One respondent posted four messages that we read as relevant to the flame, but received not one citation from another member of the community. It is also clear that, as the central figure in the exchange, Grundner's views altered the terms of the discussion. His call for solutions, especially, prompted a small flood of suggestions and volunteerism. It seems doubtful that such a call to arms from any other member of the listserv could have generated such a strong and immediate response.

This analysis suggested to us that a flame, rather than simply being noise, might play a positive role in creating a sense of community in an online system by encouraging the active and candid participation of a range of people with diverse personalities, opinions, and beliefs.

To explore the idea that a flame could contribute to the development of a community, we looked for statements in the survey responses that expressed positive, negative, or neutral opinions about the idea of community. We found no clear trends; responses ranged from very positive to very negative, spread evenly between the extremes (see Fig. 12.2).

Some individuals decided to unsubscribe as a result of the flame, while others said that "I am still subscribing to Communet, and enjoying it thor-

POSITIVE	NEGATIVE
* I am still subscribing/enjoying it thoroughly	* I unsubscribed/signed off
* Strong sense that "I am in the right place at the right time"	* Stupid and time wasting posturing
* It was a good experience for me and the list	* I don't have time for those things
* I learned a great deal	* I got irritated at the volume of the flame mail/I was somewhat annoyed by the level of fire
* The discussion was helpful	* I erased/deleted it
	* I was a little worried that the controversy would inhibit growth of electronic community

NEUTRAL
* "Been there, done that" feeling
* Mild reaction/I smiled at it
* I was not affected
* I didn't notice it/I don't remember

FIGURE 12.2 Reactions to the Flame

oughly." Among those who decided to unsubscribe, some said they left "partly because of the flame...and its fallout," while others said "I signed off the list because it got generally too chatty and conversational. There was too much negative energy and not enough constructive, inspirational suggestion for how to establish vibrant, essential community networks." In between were those who said they were not affected by the flame at all: "The discussion did not affect my perception of the o-l c [on-line community] because I viewed the flame/counter-flame situation as an aspect of the medium of teletype e-mail—not as a reflection of any person or group in the community."

Some individuals were not affected by this particular flame, but by other flames that followed: "My perception of the online community of Communet has not changed significantly due to this one discussion. It has, however, changed significantly as a result of other and cumulative discussions since that time." One correspondent, in particular, became vitriolic in the weeks after the Grundner/Mabel flame: "All in all, though, I have been MUCH MORE PUT OFF by the remarks of [the offending person] to this list....I may eventually desubscribe because this person creates an unpleasant virtual environment."

Regarding the flame itself, some individuals thought it was useful, while others considered it a waste of time, or annoying. Some people could not remember the flame at all. Those who found the flame helpful sometimes commented specifically on its community-building character: "I think it was a good experience, both for me and for the Communet list," wrote one. "I read all the arguments, and I learned a great deal," wrote another. A third said that "The exchange provided me with a strong sense that I am in the right place at the right time."

Among those upset by the flame, the predominant feeling was of time wasted. "It was stupid and time wasting posturing," wrote one person, while another said that "Personally, I got irritated at the volume of flame mail and almost discontinued my membership to the list." The irritation seemed to be directed at the list itself, not the individuals: "I was somewhat annoyed by the level of the fire," wrote one, while another said that "I quickly lost my original hope that some valuable dialogue might occur on this list."

A few people were not irritated but frightened. "Since the listserv was just starting I was a little worried that the controversy would inhibit the growth of a fairly tight electronic community," wrote one person. Another was even more explicit about the hostility unleashed by the flame: "The entire incident has scared me to death."

But many responses, which we classified as neutral, might more valuably be called complex. "I smiled, perhaps ruefully, at the entire flame war. As an English teacher, I have always reminded myself and my students of the great differences between speech and writing," wrote one person. Another wrote: "You asked how I reacted. Answer: Mildly. Here's why....I perceived it as an error that he used picturesque language that others decided to go after." Perhaps the most representative answer in the neutral group read: "The exchanges didn't affect my perception of the Communet community except to give me that 'been there, done that' feeling so common on the net."

Many of the complex responses revealed mixed or changing feelings. "My own reaction was somewhat mixed," wrote one person. "The list has NOT evolved in the way I expected, and because of that I'm much more interested in what it is up to." Another person said "My own perceptions changed as a result of the dialogues. It also felt good to still be able to change ⟨grin⟩." Most of those who said they changed position moved from a negative attitude to a more positive position: "If the exchange changed anything in my mind, it would (believe it or not) be for the better."

Finally, some of the responses showed a clear ability to ignore or forget the interactions that occur online. "With an over-busy schedule and an overflowing e-mail mailbox, I deleted virtually all of the messages on the topic after they began to repeat themselves after the first day, believing that I had seen the direction of the debate and the fact that it was generating lots of heat but little light," wrote one person. Another recalled, "As the flame war progressed, I responded as I normally do: I ignored it. I posted items to the list about other issues." And others simply blocked out their memories: "I'm sorry. I didn't notice the discussion," wrote one, while another said "I honestly cannot recall what I posted to the list any more—even what you say by way of context rings no bells at all. Sorry."

One recurring theme, regardless of the attitude toward the flame, dealt with the technology itself. Many people noted that, in an online community, flames are inevitable. Implicitly challenging the technological determinism argument, they suggested that individuals had to take responsibility for their own remarks: the author of a message has to decide either to flame or to apologize, they said. Although we had noted that vagaries in the system, especially regarding whether "replies" went to the list or to the original message poster, affected the discourse, none of the respondents made a point of this or ascribed problems to any inherent quality of the technology. There seemed to be a general consensus that it was the user's responsibility to properly use the technology and that though the speed and anonymity of the system certainly created a different context for communication, people will continue to make human mistakes.

COMMUNITY BUILDING

On the central issue of community building, the survey responses suggest that the general attitudes toward the Communet listserv were both good and bad. Some respondents considered the Communet community "a group of dedicated people with a common goal" or described interactions on Communet as "intelligent and reasoned, frequently witty." These people also viewed any electronic forum benignly, saying these forums "reach a more diverse audience than most other discussion forums and so a wider range of opinions will be presented." However, quite a few people unsubscribed from Communet because they believed the discussion had become too chatty and was not constructive.

On the specific issue of the role of the flame in building community, the responses also varied (see Fig. 12.3). Some people felt that the stress helped bond the group together, with the flame evoking a social consciousness among the group. "Communet managed to go through the stresses of a flame war intact, and has perhaps become even more bonded by the stresses...," wrote one person. "In my experience, shared stress frequently bonds groups of people." After the flame worked itself out, according to this perspective, the Communet listserv became a more human and real group. Those who objected to the flame felt that the discussion was irrelevant, sapping energy from the group and inhibiting the growth of the community. They described the flames as a "shouting match."

Given the complex mix of responses to the flame and the question of community-building, perhaps the most interesting responses were those that pointed to the reflexive thinking that occurred in list participants. (The ability of computers to generate reflexive thought has been noticed by many researchers, most notably Sherry Turkle.)[32] "The exchanges reaffirmed my belief in the general level of social consciousness of Internet list participants," wrote one person, "and my sense that this group, in particular, will have a strong impact in the shaping of future community networks. The exchange provided me with a strong sense that 'I am in the right place at the right time.'" Another person wrote that "the

POSITIVE	NEGATIVE
* Stress bonds	* Scaps energy/Inhibits grouth
* Consciousness-raising	* Irrelevant/More cautious
* Thing worked itself out	* Things go wrong easily/Group frustration
* More human	* Shouting match
* Realness of life	

FIGURE 12.3 Community Building

discussion allowed me to once again see how it is a struggle to begin to adopt new ways of thinking and new ways of writing." Not everyone appreciated the opportunity for reflexive thought: the flame and related discussion was "largely irrelevant to the more crucial issues facing networkers. Networkers...seem to prefer the kind of dialogue you mention precisely because they will not be called upon to significantly change their attitudes and values about such matters." But the predominant feeling was that the exchange would become a part of the community's shared culture: "I bet we're permanently affected by it—more cautious, I think."

For many respondents, debates and disagreements are simply a part of life, and online they take the form of flames. "People who had seemed caustic in early postings, came back seeming quite rational in other postings," wrote one person. "It was educative, and it made the discussion group seem more dynamic and 'real.'" Overall, the effect was to help participants understand what issues were important. "I started getting an idea of how participants on the list really feel about gender issues, and that made the whole group seem more human," wrote one person. Another said that "people share a genuine interest and involvement in a common interest. Indeed, that was one of the fascinating things about communet—how it emerged as a community over a weekend! So some real sharing does take place which I think may make it a more comfortable habitat for women especially, but also for men."

COMPLEX INTERACTIONS

Clearly, an analysis of one flame on one listserv cannot claim great power in describing the world of computer-mediated communication. But the particular nature of this flame, in an online community specifically devoted to building communities, suggests that it provides a useful window into understanding the complex interactions of personal reactions and social structures that give meaning to online communication. This study suggests that, while flames are clearly divisive and can cause people great distress, and some people may leave an online community if they perceive flames to be a part of the culture of that community, the flame is not entirely a destructive force. As with any source of tension, a flame can highlight specific issues in a community, forcing members of the community to deal with the issues. If the community finds a constructive way to deal with the divisiveness—as it did in this case, when the community responded to Grundner's appeal for solutions—then the flame can contribute to strengthening the community's structure and values.

REFERENCES

1. A. Baum and S. Valins. *Architecture and Social Behavior*. Hillsdale, NJ: Erlbaum, 1977.

2. D. Bell. *The Coming of Post-industrial Society: A Veniure in Social Forecasting.* New York: Basic Books, 1973.

3. D. Bell. "The social framework of the information society." in *The Computer Age: A Twenty-Year View.* Michael L. Denouzos and Joel Moses, eds. Cambridge. MA: M.I.T. Press, 1979.

4. D. J. Boorwin. *The Republic of Technology: Reflections on Our Future Community.* New York: Harper & Row, 1958.

5. D. Burnham. *The Rise of the Computer State.* New York: Random House, 1983.

6. M. L. Denouzos and J. Moses, eds. *The Computer Age: A Twenty-Year View.* Cambridge, MA: M.I.T. Press, 1979.

7. W. P. Dizard, Jr., *The Coming Information Age: An Overview of Technology. Economics, and Politics.* New York: Longman, 1982.

8. L. B. Evans. "Impact of the electronics revolution on industrial process control." *Science,* vol. 195. pp. 1146–1151, Mar. 18. 1977.

9. Finholt and L. S. Sproull. "Electronic groups at war." *Org. Sci.* vol. 1, no. 1, pp. 41–63, 1990.

10. A. Gore. "Infrastructure for the global village." *Sci. Amer.* pp. 150–153, Sept. 1991.

11. D. E. Hewes and M. L. Graham. "Second guessing theory: Review and extension." in *Commun. Yearbook.* J. A. Anderson, ed., vol. 12, pp. 212–247, 1989.

12. R. S. Hilu and M. Turoff. *The Network Nation: Human Communication Via Computer.* Reading. MA: Addison, Wesley, 1978.

13. Hoai-An Truong, B. Williams, J. Clark, and A. Couey. "Gender issues in online communications," presented at Bay Area Women in Commun, Computers, Freedom and Privacy Conf., San Francisco, CA, Mar.–Apr. 1993.

14. C. I. Hovland and L. Janis, Eds., *Personality and Persuasibility.* New Haven. CT: Yale Univ. Press, 1959.

15. L. M. Jessup, T. Connolly, and D. A. Tansik. "Toward a theory of automated group work: The deindividuating effects of anonymity." *Small Group Res.,* vol. 21, no. 3, pp. 333–348, 1990.

16. S. Kiesler, J. Siegel, and T. W. McGuire. "Social psychological aspects of computer-mediated communication." *Amer. Psychol.,* vol. 39, no. 10, pp, 1123–1134, 1984.

17. S. Kielser, D. Zubrow, A. M. Moses, and V. Geller. "Affect in computer-modiated communication: An experiment in terminal-to-terminal discussion," *Human-Computer Interaction,* vol. 1, pp. 77–104, 1984.

18. D. M. Lamberton, ed. "The information revolution." *Annuls Amer. Acad. Polit. Soc. Sci.,* vol. 412, Philadelphia, PA: Amer. Acad. Political and Social Sci., 1974.

19. P. Large. *The Micro Revolution.* London: Fontana, 1980.

20. P. Laurie. *The Micro Revolution: Living with Computers.* New York: Universe, 1981.

21. P. F. Lazarsfeld. "Communication research," in *Current Trends in Social Psychology.* W. Dennis et al., eds. Pittsburgh, PA: Univ. Pittsburgh Press, 1949, pp. 218–273.

22. A. Metmud and F. D. Fisher. *Towards a National Information Infrastructure: Implications for Selected Social Sectors and Education.* New York: New York Univ. Center for Educational Technology and Economic Productivity, 1991.

23. G. Oldham and N. Rotchford. "Relationships between office characteristics and employee reactions: A study of the physical environment." *Admin. Sci. Quart.*, vol. 2S, pp. 542–556, 1983.

24. K. P. Phillips. *Mediacracy: American Parties and Politics in the Communications Age.* Garden City, NJ: Doubleday, 1975.

25. M. U. Porat. *The Information Economy: Definition and Measurement.* Washington, DC: Office of Telecommunications. U.S. Department of Commerce, 1977.

26. L. Sproull and S. Kiesler. "Reducing social context cues: Electronic mail in organizational communication" *Manag. Sci.*, vol. 32, no. 11, pp. 1492–1511, 1986.

27. G. Steele. D. Woods, R. Finkel, M. Crispin, R. Stallman, and G. Goodfellow. *The Hacker's Dictionary.* New York: Harper & Row, 1983.

28. D. Tannen. *You Just Dan't Understand.* New York: Ballantine, 1990.

29. A. Toffler. *The Third Wave.* New York: Bantam Books, 1990.

30. A. Toursnine. *The Past-Industrial Society.* New York: Random House, 1971.

31. H. Trice and J. Beyer. "Studying organizational cultures through tires and ceremonials." *Acad. Manag. J.*, vol. 4, pp. 653–669, 1984.

32. S. Turkle. *The Second Self: Computers and the Human Spirit.* New York: Simon and Schuster, 1984.

33. R. Wright. "The new democrat from cyberspace." *New Republic.* pp. 18–27, May 24, 1993.

34. P. Yarbrough. "Communication theory and nutrition education research." *J. Nutrition Ed.*, vol. 13, no. 1, pp. s16–s27, 1981.

Making Large-Scale Information Resources Serve Communities of Practice*

Catherine C. Marshall, Frank M. Shipman III, and Raymond J. McCall

As communities of practice begin to store their collective knowledge in large-scale libraries, databases, or electronic memories, an important issue arises. How do communities "know what they know"? More importantly, "how do members learn about, access, and utilize what others have contributed to this collective knowledge store?" What Marshall, Shipman, and McCall term *community memory*—the open-ended set of collective knowledge and shared understandings developed and maintained by a community—becomes the key to unlocking the processes, intellectual capability, and evolutionary lifecycle of "what a community knows." The authors see community memories as having three distinct stages: seeding, evolutionary growth, and reseeding. Each of these stages becomes an interpretation of the daily activities and collective experiences of each member. However, as communities grow, the ability to identify and catalogue what is stored in community memory becomes overwhelming. Similarly, vibrancy—which requires continued maintenance to weed out growing inconsistencies and redundant contributions—becomes juxtapositioned with the need to remain connected to large-scale external resources, such as networked repositories or the Internet. These concepts are additionally addressed through viewing the community as an information agency. As the authors state: "Perhaps the central point about obtaining information within communities of practice is that informed people are frequently the best source of information. This function of a community as an information agency—as mediator of retrieval—is in fact one of the primary reasons for its existence."

* Reprinted from *Journal of Management Information System*, Vol. 11, No. 4 (1995): 65–86, with permission from M. E. Sharpe, Inc. Publisher, Armank, NY 10504.

CATHERINE C. MARSHALL *is an Associate Research Scientist in the Department of Computer Science at Texas A&M University. From 1988 to 1994, she was a member of the research staff at Xerox Palo Alto Research Center. She has been principal investigator on a series of projects to investigate analytic work practices and collaborative hypermedia, including Aquanet and its successor, VIKI: she was also a participant in the NoteCards hypertext project. Her research interests include spatial hypertext, computer-supported cooperative work, digital libraries, knowledge representation, and argumentation. She is Vice-Chair of SIGLINK, the ACM's special interest group for hypermedia.*

FRANK M. SHIPMAN III, *is an Assistant Research Scientist in the Department of Computer Science at Texas A&M University. He has been pursuing research in the areas of hypermedia, computer-supported cooperative work, and intelligent user interfaces since 1987. His doctoral work at the University of Colorado and subsequent work at Xerox PARC and Texas A&M has investigated combining informal and formal representations in interfaces and methods for supporting incremental formalization. Dr. Shipman has aided in the design and development of a number of collaborative hypermedia systems including the Virtual Notebook System, the Hyper-Object Substrate, and VIKI.*

RAYMOND MCCALL *is Associate Professor of Environmental Design and member of the Institute of Cognitive Science at the University of Colorado, Boulder. He has studied design argumentation and worked on the creation of argumentative hypertext systems since the mid-1970s. His current research is on the creation of hypermedia-based design environments providing integrated support for argumentation, graphical construction of solutions, knowledge-based computation, and multimedia information access. He received a Ph.D. in architecture from the University of California, Berkeley, in 1978.*

INTRODUCTION

In principle, digital libraries and large-scale information bases will provide physically distributed electronic communities access to a broad spectrum of archival materials, including those that we currently find in public, community, and work group repositories. But how will these communities bring ever-increasing electronic resources to bear on their work? How will people use digital libraries in their day-to-day activities? How will they apply these emerging collections to information-intensive intellectual tasks—research, design, education, analysis—work that requires information to be gathered, understood, and communicated to others? To make this wealth of online resources truly useful to emerging electronic communities, we must forge a link between the distributed repositories and the practices of information workers who will use them.

Community memories will form this vital link between large-scale collections and information-intensive work. Just as a digital library will provide a general structure and means of access to a collection of materials, a community memory will enable this library to serve the actual day-to-day needs of community members. It culls and indexes the library, evaluating and interpreting its contents according to those needs. In fact, the creation, maintenance, and use of this memory as a shared resource largely defines the community and constitutes the central vehicle for communication among community members. By augmenting members' abilities to perform tasks, use of community memory may provide the central motivation for membership in a community.

Community Memory and Electronic Communities

When people work together—whether they are designing a product, or creating training materials from video-based documentation, or writing a coherent analysis of a complex situation in the world—they require, and put effort into constructing and maintaining, shared understanding of what they are doing: the task, the pertinent body of material, preliminary findings, progress, and methods. We refer to the open-ended set of collective knowledge and shared understandings developed and maintained by the group as *community memory*.

Electronic communities are different from physical communities. They are ephemeral, forming and reforming according to interests, particular tasks, or issues. A person may be a member of many electronic communities, shifting his or her virtual presence from one locus of activity to another with ease. Our experience with electronic communities has drawn us to investigate ways of supporting these communities in the same medium in which they have formed.

Figure 13.1 illustrates our conceptualization of community memory in a distributed electronic community. Materials are drawn from many repositories, some archival, some transient (like wire service stories, electronic mail, and listserv contributions), and, through discourse and interaction, combined with artifacts relating to the task at hand to form the shared understandings that are community memory. Shared understandings in turn become the basis for communication and further work. Thus, community memory may include discourse, collected materials, answers to frequently asked questions, evaluations of these materials ("This is an important article") or sources ("This news group has

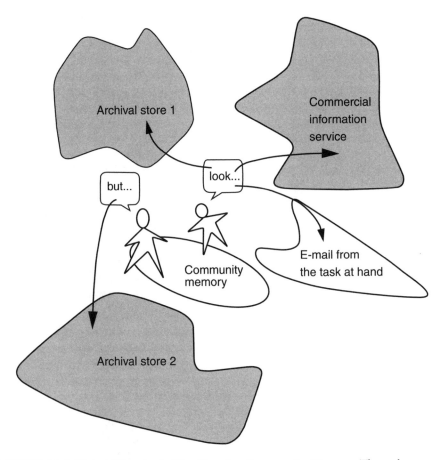

FIGURE 13.1 Digital Libraries in Use, Forming Community Memory. Through continuing discourse within a community, the materials in distributed digital library collections first become useful for performing the task at hand, then are recorded and made available for reuse through an evolving community memory

valuable information; this other one is a waste of time"), as well as marginalia and annotations, alternative organizations of materials, filters, and well-tuned queries.

Electronic Community Memory at Work: Early Examples

We can already see community memory at work in online communities on the Internet. Beyond providing access to distributed computing resources and remote information, the Internet has proven to be a particularly effective vehicle for human-human communication. It is the means by which electronic communities form and transient collections of materials grow in association with a task or topic. These collaborations, and their associated community memory, have the capacity to greatly extend the reach of the individual.

Augmenting the intellectual capacity of the individual through support for collaborative construction of knowledge is not a new idea; Engelbart saw such a potential with Augment.[5] Currently, this phenomenon is an important side effect of having the infrastructure in place to provide communities with extensive digital resources and improved connectivity.[25]

For example, in recent years researchers at different sites have met using this infrastructure as a means of organizing their conferences; they have discussed individual papers, the program, and decisions about conference content while referring to a set of submissions, and implicitly, to the body of literature in the field. In effect, through their conversations, they have formed a shared understanding about the current state of the field. In other cases, a topic (rather than a task) helps maintain a community: for example, high-energy physicists exchange preprints through the World Wide Web as a way of shortening the review and publication cycle.

NSF Collaboratory projects have acknowledged the feasibility of distributed communities in information-rich domains collaborating online. Schatz's account of the worm community discusses one such experience, including the characteristics of an online community that make it amenable to this approach, and the kinds of formal and informal artifacts that the worm community found it valuable to collect, organize, and annotate.[24]

A Spectrum of Resources

Physical collections exist to serve communities of many different sizes—from a few to thousands of members—and for every variation along this range, a community memory can and often does exist. Even individuals frequently have their own external memories in the form of highlighting and annotations scribbled on the pages of the books and articles in their personal collections. A group might collect a variety of formal materials such as specifications and informal materials such as e-mail and meeting notes to build up a project notebook. Patent attorneys working for a large company might enhance their understanding of documents retrieved from a formal intellectual property database with informal videotaped interviews with inventors. Network-wide community interactions over collections might result in something like World Wide Web home pages, where individual members of the community increase the value of existing materials by creating their own links to "useful resources" or "favorite starting places." Notice that in each of these cases, community memory acts not only as a filter, but more importantly as a *superstructure* to the more general information resource.

Prospective developers of digital libraries are planning to include community memory-like facilities to make tomorrow's electronic resources better serve the distributed communities that use them in their work.[9] Proposed digital library functions include: guided tours and automatically recorded reader paths; the ability to self-publish and move material in and out of the library at will; sharing of annotations; and voting schemes (as illustrated, for example, by Goldberg et al.'s Tapestry system).[10] Digital media and improved network connectivity make it much easier to collect these superstructural elements that rest on top of large-scale information resources.

Community memory introduces an important difference between the underlying information resources and the superstructure we discuss. While both physical and electronic information resources rely on the existence of fixed roles such as publishers, librarians, readers, and writers,[22] this kind of external memory generally implies far more fluid roles. At any given moment, a member of a community may act as contributor of information to the community memory, as recipient of information from it, or as interpreter of information in it. In the following sections, we take each of these roles as a separate vantage point and examine the issues and challenges each role raises.

Challenges

We thus find community memory to be a linchpin to the effective performance of intellectual work. But our thirty or so years of collective experience developing and deploying systems to support the elicitation and reuse of community memory, augmented by reflections on our own experiences with network-wide collaborations, have shown us that there are significant barriers to realizing a fully articulated, well-organized, usable electronic community memory.

Building useful and usable memories for distributed communities presents fundamental challenges.[2,32] Although it appears to be easy for a group to amass the kinds of materials that are part of a community memory—for example, electronic mail, culled, annotated library materials, "war stories" about how prototypical problems were solved in past situations, software that embodies a particular way of processing digital library information, or videotapes documenting design meetings—how to put these materials to productive use over time is still problematic.

Community memories need to be seeded, maintained, and generalized; they need to reflect the evolution of shared understanding. Members of the community must be mutually aware of each other's contributions, and the contributions must be mutually intelligible. Effective community memories cannot exist in isolation either from the tasks at hand or from the information resources to which they refer. Finally, and most crucially, they have to be useful to the members of the community: they must contribute directly to the work activities.

COMMUNITY MEMORY: ISSUES OF CONTRIBUTING, OBTAINING, AND USING INTERPRETIVE INFORMATION

We are looking at community memory as a shared interpretive layer on top of sifted subcollections that refer to materials taken from both within and outside digital libraries. To provide technological support for community memory, we must examine the situations from which it arises, and the challenges associated with our collective set of experiences designing systems to support community memory.

How do people use community memory as a resource for performing intellectual work? First, they find the materials they need for their work (many times by consulting colleagues, assistants, librarians, experts, and other human resources); they read or otherwise apprehend portions of materials they've gathered; finally, they modify these materials to suit the purposes at hand, where modification may include synthesis of diverse sources, paraphrasing, quoting outright, or using the gathered information as a starting point. Thus, to perform information-intensive intellectual work, a member of a community will contribute as well as extract.

We take each of these roles as a separate vantage point, and examine the issues and challenges raised by each. Because the materials must be in place before they may be used, we first take the contributor's perspective. Once these materials exist as a community-maintained electronic resource, we can begin to examine how people locate the relevant portions. Finally, we take a reader's view—how the materials may be understood outside a prescribed, predefined structure. We ground our discussion in smaller-scale experiences with hypermedia systems, since hypermedia is a good representational medium for creating community memory. We use these experiences to make informed speculations about how the issues revealed by these systems in use scale to tomorrow's much more extensive electronic resources.

Creating and Sustaining Community Memory: A Contributor's Perspective

Although it is easy to amass materials for community memory, it is difficult to provide the incentive to add the requisite organization that will make the shared resource useful to others.[4,7,20] In general, this difficulty is intrinsic to certain types of groupware: contributors' efforts may far outweigh the benefits they derive from the work.[12] Many existing efforts to provide group memory or support long-term community-wide discussion have found that without an individual's single-minded devotion to starting them, keeping them going, and maintaining them, the information space slowly dies and becomes irrelevant, even to its originators. It is difficult to ensure real, continuing participation as well as the casual browsing we might encounter today on the web.

The difficulties of acquiring community memory are exacerbated by both technological and social factors. First, contributors often do not derive benefits commensurate with the amount of effort they expend: there is a large gap between the collected materials they've used in their work (their files, for example) and materials that have been organized so that others may profitably use them. Not only does the structure of these materials arise over time and in conjunction with particular tasks, but any additional structure brings with it a considerable amount of overhead.[28] Second, as a changing, evolving form, community memory requires continuing thoughtful maintenance to weed out growing inconsistencies and redundant contributions. Finally, community memory arises out of tasks that take place in a distributed, heterogeneous environment, one that involves paper as well as digital media (see, for example, the description of analytic work in),[14] multiple authoring tools, and many different collections of source material, retrieved from a multiplicity of information services, each with its own formats, access methods, and protocols; this blend of materials, media, and technology presents significant obstacles to the construction of a side-product like community memory.

Internal Sources for Community Memory: Emergence of Structure through Incremental Formalization

Through our work with representational hypermedia tools such as Aquanet, VIKI, and HOS, we have shown that the groupware cost/benefit paradox may be amenable to solutions such as methods to support the gradual emergence and evolution of structure and techniques to support incremental formalization.[17,18,29] These tools and techniques emphasize low-cost means of adding the kinds of structure that may organize information from a digital library into a community memory.

Aquanet[16] is a good example of a group tool that suffered from the cost/benefit paradox inherent in community memory systems. One of Aquanet's principle roles was to act as a collaborative front-end for the exploratory manipulation and organization of large collections of documents relevant to a specific task; in particular, we had hoped people would work together to create large, tightly interlinked structures of argumentation and evidence in the course of performing long-term analyses. These structures would encourage people to develop multiple interpretations of large collections of always-changing, possibly conflicting materials, and would form a shared interpretive layer over institutional databases and commercial information services.

Aquanet provided specific support for users to create and manipulate complex graphical knowledge structures in the form of a schema editor for defining structured types of information objects and an infinite two-and-a-half-dimensional information space in which to create and manipulate instances of these types. In our original conception of the knowledge-structuring task, users would define graphical representations of the elements in their problem domain and specify (and constrain) all the ways in which these elements could be interconnected. They would then apply and change these structuring schemes or abstractions over the course of their tasks. Thus, Aquanet was intended to provide a flexible way for people to record the abstractions they use to interpret information, to reflect and critique their analytic frameworks, and to explicitly negotiate about how information is structured (all crucial elements to a successful community memory).

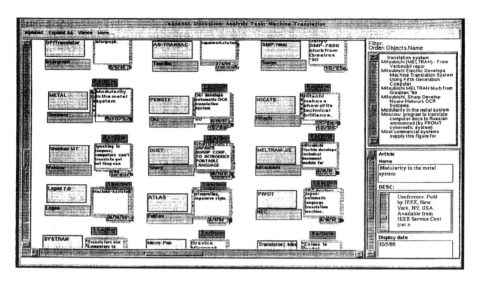

FIGURE 13.2 A Portion of Shared Space Created in Aquanet. Each graphical object represents underlying information, some of it drawn from universally available repositories, some referring to paper information sources, and the rest, interpretive information and extracted notes added by users

Figure 13.2 shows a portion of a shared information space that was created in Aquanet, one constructed during the course of an evaluation of foreign-language translation software and analysis of the field of machine translation. Each distinct visual symbol in the figure refers to an article from the trade press, notes about a software package, contact information for a company, or a label for other elements. Thus, schematic abstractions in this application included Systems, Institutions, Labels, and Articles (among others not captured in this framing of the space). But notice that the structural interconnections are absent from the picture; users relied on proximity and visual/spatial patterns in the layout to convey interrelationships. Much of the structure we would expect to be defined and created in the information has been left largely implicit.

If we consider Figure 13.2 as an example of superstructure, built on top of a large-scale information resource (in this case, primarily articles from a commercial information provider), the contents of the instances of Article types are the external material, drawn from the information provider's database. The other types of information objects (the notes about Systems and Institutions, and the Labels for the graphical layout) and the distinctive appearance of the Article type can all be thought of as part of the community memory.

This application of the Aquanet system illustrates a crucial point about anticipating a high degree of structure from contributors to a community memory. People find the definition, refinement, and use of sophisticated domain descriptions difficult, and insufficiently rewarding for the return. Instead, they will create a locally useful amount of structure—in the application shown in Figure 13.2, it was useful to be able to distinguish source articles from notes, and to create parallel types of notes on each different kind of system—and omit more formal definition of domain structure.

Thus, our experiences showed us that informal (and in this case, visual/ spatial) representations are crucial to coaxing out partially formed, emerging interpretations. One of Aquanet's strengths was the ability it gave people to express unexpected interpretations that were less than fully formed, in terms of visual appearance or position in the shared space. Extralinguistic means of expression proved to be vital, allowing categories to be created without labels and relationships between documents to be expressed visually; for example, sets could be created by putting references to particular documents close together, overlapping in the space. The kinesthetic process of "trying things out" (as one might do shuffling into papers in piles across every horizontal surface in one's office) was not eliminated because a person was using a computer instead of manipulable paper objects in the world.

How can we apply these lessons to develop a system to support a more informal, emergent facility for contributing to a community memory?

Out of our experiences with Aquanet, we designed VIKI, a tool to support emergent, dynamic, exploratory interpretation.[18] VIKI supports the ad hoc use of a visual symbol language so people can see and express structure as it becomes apparent to them. In contrast with Aquanet, developing this language is well integrated with the task at hand. Because interpretation—along with the concomitant act of organizing materials—is opportunistic, users are not confined to a particular working style; they may work from gathered subcollections from an existing information resource to develop structure, they can work schematically (the mode Aquanet enforced), or they may leave structure and meaning largely implicit. VIKI complements the ability to develop abstractions and reflect on and critique interpretive frameworks with the flexibility offered by ad hoc, visually salient representations. We see support for emergent structure as a partial solution to the cost/benefit paradox inherent in computer support for community memory.

Figure 13.3 shows a small portion of a shared space created by a group of contributors in VIKI. The space acts as a community memory for the group by providing a place to collect, structure, and annotate materials that pertain to the group's research activities. It includes internally authored materials describing individual projects (a portion of this is visible in the figure), intellectual property documents such as Invention Proposals and patent filings connected with the projects, and papers and short articles about competing products and projects drawn from a commercial information provider's databases.

In the portion of the subspace that is visible in Figure 13.3, the structures that people have built are notably similar to those shown in our Aquanet example—visually salient, regular, but not wholly conforming to a pattern, a mixture of typed and untyped entities. The distinct structures in the figure are, in fact, labeled lists of projects. VIKI includes facilities for recognizing, using,

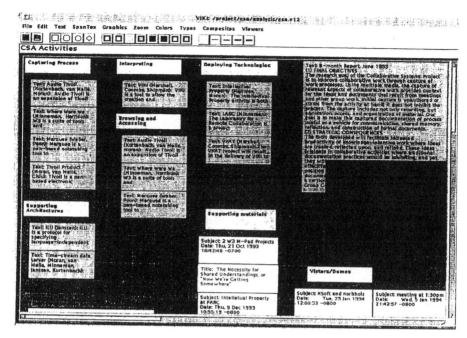

FIGURE 13.3 A Subspace of a Larger Community Memory Created in VIKI. As in Figure 13.2, each graphical object represents underlying information. Much of the structure in this diagram is implicit in the visual properties and spatial layout of the constituent objects

and declaring this kind of implicit structure. Visual structure is built up and becomes the basis for sharing knowledge. By using heuristics for automated recognition of the same kind of structure that humans perceive in a spatial layout, we can support the gradual (and, from the user's point of view, cost-effective) emergence of structure.

Since it has become clear from our experiences that people within a small working community are capable of sharing implicitly structured material, and that, given the opportunity, they have difficulty making such structure explicit, why are these structured representations and the mechanisms to help people use them even necessary?

As we discuss later, structure helps keep community memories intelligible to the members of a broader community by giving them the means to understand how the contributions of others fit into the community memory. But more importantly, formal structure is also computationally tractable, raising the possibility of computer support for a community's activities. With the Hyper-Object Substrate (HOS), we have investigated the process of incremental formalization to support the emergence of structure. To this end, HOS integrates hypermedia and knowledge-based representations. Hypermedia eliminates many of the cognitive costs of formalization that inhibit user input. Integration with a formal knowledge representation reduces the burden of formalization by allowing it to be distributed and making it demand-driven.[29]

To further lower the cost of formalizing information, HOS actively supports incremental formalization with mechanisms to recognize emergent structure implicit in the community memory and suggest formalizations based on this structure (a content-based analog to VIKI's visual/spatial structure perception). Experience with the use of HOS indicates some success and a greater potential for investigation of both methods for producing and interfaces to suggesting possible formalizations.

Life Cycle of Community Memory: Seeding, Evolutionary Growth, and Reseeding

We have observed three major types of processes—and stages—in the life cycle of community memories: seeding, evolutionary growth, and reseeding.[8] Seeding is the creation of the initial body of information in community memory. When this initial set of information reaches a certain size and level of relevance to the community, it starts to grow and evolve spontaneously as the result of additions made by its users (as has happened in the World Wide Web). Seeding ends with the start of this evolutionary growth. After this growth proceeds for some time, the memory starts to become less and less useful; as a consequence, both use and growth may diminish. This happens for a number of reasons, such as growing disorder in the memory and the "needle in the haystack" problem— that is, the increasing difficulty of finding useful information in the growing information collection. At this point, the community memory must be revised— that is, reseeded. Its contents must be organized, winnowed, prioritized, and generalized. The methods for locating things in memory may themselves need to be altered. If this reseeding is done successfully, the system can start another stage of evolutionary growth, after which it will in turn need to be reseeded if it is to continue to serve its users.

We have repeatedly experienced this threefold process in our attempts to build community memories, for example, with large issue-based information systems (IBIS) structures.[21] Very few IBIS for groups have gotten started without the dedication of a single person or small core group of people who were willing to create the seed—that is, the initial set of issues, positions, and arguments. We have found that attempting to get the IBIS users themselves to invent—out of the blue—relevant issues, answers, and arguments is a frustrating and generally unproductive experience for all concerned. Once there is some argumentative discussion for users to react to, the situation changes dramatically. It is easy to get people to react to what others have said, and the difficulty changes from trying to elicit information to trying to keep up with the information elicited. In our experience, this change makes it quite clear when the evolutionary growth stage of an IBIS has begun.

We found that as an issue base grows, its maintenance becomes increasingly difficult and prone to error, growth leads to increasing disorder in the issue base.

We also found that it became increasingly difficult to locate relevant information. These two problems have devastating synergies. For example, a given issue would often be raised and stored repeatedly, typically with slightly different wording. These redundancies were very difficult to detect, in part because of the difference in wording. Thus, group discussion became fragmented into parallel discussions. As time went on the fragmentations grew in number and even compounded themselves—with branches of the fragmented discussions in turn becoming fragmented. As a result, the IBIS increasingly ceased to function as a vehicle for group communication. To restore it to functionality, it was necessary to reseed the IBIS through a comprehensive edit of the issue base.

We have also observed this threefold process in the creation and development of a number of large software systems, such as Symbolic's Genera, UNIX, and the X-Windows system. In such systems, after the creation of the initial versions of the systems (seeding), users developed ad hoc additions to system functionality and often shared these as a community (evolutionary growth). These additions were often winnowed, refined, combined, and included in later official versions of the software (reseeding), after which they entered another stage of ad hoc additions to functionality (evolutionary growth).

External Sources for Community Memory: Connections to Information Resources

Attempts to create community memory seem certain to fail if the memory is not connected to large-scale external sources of information, such as distributed, networked repositories, as well as to the communications facilities of other members of the community.[14,20]

The assumption implicit in the design of many computer-based tools is that communication is a separate process from the user's main task. An analysis of computer network designers showed how the logical map, a representation of the design which shows network device interconnections, acted as the central artifact around which most communication occurred.[23] In response, XNetwork, an environment for supporting network design, provides designers with an integrated view of the design and the discussions about the design in conjunction with methods for importing electronic mail and bulletin board discussions into the design space. Figure 13.4 illustrates how the discussion and the design can be created and viewed together in XNetwork. The need to integrate discussion and artifact signals a more general need to integrate source information and produced information.

Just as community memories must be connected with the means of communication about their content, so must they be connected with the universal collections from which they arise. For example, prototypes of the Virtual Notebook System (VNS)[11,27] used generic hypermedia to overcome the difficulty of integrating various sources of biomedical research information. The VNS was intended as an electronic analog to a researcher's notebook that could also act as a shared repository of information gathered from early digital libraries and

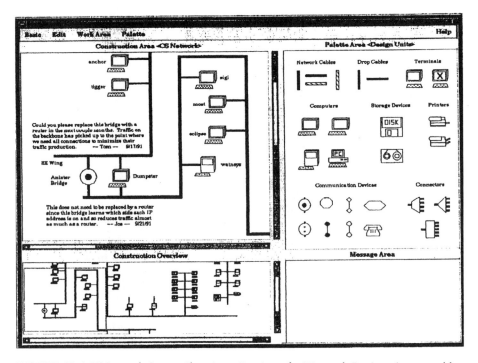

FIGURE 13.4 XNetwork Screen Showing a Portion of a Network Design, Annotated by a Discussion about an Issue that Arose during the Creation of the Design

other online sources. Such external information resources included the National Library of Medicine's Medline database containing bibliographic and abstract information on articles from medical journals. Users could connect to the Medline database through a graphical interface and could easily "paste" interesting information into their hypertext for later use.

Experience with these early prototypes of the VNS shows the difficulty of providing the needed connections to a variety of information sources and media. In addition to the Medline connection, researchers required that the VNS include interfaces to organizational information resources—such as to hospital and departmental information systems—as well as to their research information resources, such as genome and experimental data databases. As these examples show, the specific information resources used by a particular community can differ greatly in scope. The experimental databases were used by only one research group, the genome database was shared by a number of groups, and the hospital and departmental information systems were used by most of the staff within the institutions. Furthermore, as time goes on, information needs change, and the kinds of external resources that are available grow.

Thus, if we examine community memory from a contributor's viewpoint, we find that it is necessary to provide support for emergent structure, for maintaining both content and structure over the life cycle of the community memory, and for easily extending the reach of the community memory to include new external sources of content and artifacts for discussion. But supporting contributors is only part of the picture; once the materials have coalesced into a usable superstructure to universal information resources, how do other members of the community recover materials from (and through) the community memory? In the next section we assume the perspective of the person who is using this facility.

Obtaining Useful Information from Community Memory: A User's Perspective

It might at first seem that obtaining information from community memory is a classic information-retrieval problem and thus amenable to treatment by many existing information retrieval techniques. There are, however, decisive differences that are not addressed by existing retrieval techniques. One such difference is the nature of the information needs—the gaps in knowledge—of community members; another is the role of community in mediating retrieval. Addressing these requires new approaches.

"You Don't Know What You Don't Know": Mechanisms for Active Memory

Community members are often unaware that information they need is in community memory. In fact, they are often unaware that they need information of any kind. The principle is you don't know what you don't know. Since knowledge about knowledge is called metaknowledge, we might call this the principle of meta-ignorance. Because of it, users do not know when to pose queries to the memory, much less how to formulate such queries.

Active memory: Conventional information systems—those based on information retrieval principles—do not provide information unless queries are posed to them. Because they can only react to deliberate user requests, such systems do not enable community memory to fulfill its potential in informing the tasks of community members. Instead, what is needed is memory that actively suggests information to users on the basis of some sort of understanding of their information needs. To do this, memory must have active agents that "look over the shoulders" of community members as they work and spot potential needs for information, then alert users to the existence of information of potential use for their current tasks.

Such active memory systems will not rely solely or even primarily on content-based retrieval, as do systems that use information-retrieval techniques. They will instead index information by the tasks for which they are useful. We call this task-based indexing. This is not to say that content-based retrieval that responds to explicit queries will not play an important part in obtaining information from community memory. It will, but its role will be to supplement task-based retrieval.

The JANUS system supporting design uses the relationships between domain-oriented construction kits and domain-oriented issue bases to integrate argumentative information into the task of constructing solution forms.[7] JANUS employs knowledge-based critics that "look over the designer's shoulder" and critique partially constructed solutions, pointing out potential inadequacies and providing relevant rationales from a domain-oriented issue base.

Generalizing from JANUS's critics, XNetwork includes agents to support the recovery of relevant information from a community memory. Like JANUS's critics, XNetwork's agents volunteer information or take some action based on the user's current actions. XNetwork agents can be created by designers to act as proponents of certain information and opinions. As part of this creation, the designer can select among methods for informing potential recipients of the information; the agents can be more or less intrusive depending on the nature of the content. Agents thus act as surrogates for users, advertising the existence of important information. In this way the agents support communication among the members of a community.

Community as Information Agency

Perhaps the central point about obtaining information within communities of practice is that informed people are frequently the best source of information.[6] This function of community as information agency—as mediator of retrieval—is in fact one of the primary reasons for its existence. Supporting this function is thus decisive for the creation of successful electronic communities of practice.

Community memory can serve two crucial functions in helping people find information. First, it can serve as a cache for that information and evaluations of its worth, thus reducing the difficulty of search and increasing its effectiveness. Second, it can serve as a means for identifying community members who either know the information or can help in locating it. Community memory might, in fact, consist in large part of explicit records of the knowledge of the individuals in the community. This knowledge can be stored in a number of ways, perhaps the most basic of which is frequently asked questions (FAQs). In fact, an IBIS on recurring issues can be seen as nothing more than a souped-up FAQ collection.

As research on IBIS hypermedia has shown, the problem of retrieving issues is by no means merely a conventional information-retrieval problem. Above all, it requires more than retrieval by content or bibliographic reference. Retrieval of relevant information in complex question-based discussions is decisively aided by associative indexing—indexing by the relationships among questions.[20] For one thing, answering a query (question/issue) might be aided by the answers given to similar queries. The answer might also depend on the answers given to other queries. Such similarity and dependency relationships are also valuable information that can aid retrieval.

Most of the knowledge of community members is not and cannot be stored in community memory. Even so, a community memory can still be a decisive aid to retrieval of such knowledge if it can guide the question-asker to the community member who has the knowledge. There are at least two ways in which community memory can be of help in this situation. One is by storing the questions that its members want answered so that other members can become aware of these information needs. The other is by storing information about the types of knowledge possessed by its various members—who knows what types of things. Ackerman's Answer Garden system takes this approach.[1] Community members may themselves be the best guide for finding other knowledgeable community members.

Comprehension of Information from Community Memory: An Interpreter's Perspective

Once community members obtain information from memory, they attempt to use it for specific tasks. From the perspective of such an information user—an interpreter of the structure and contents of the community memory—there are two fundamental challenges. The first is to comprehend the information; the second is to apply it to the task at hand. For the former, a crucial issue is whether the representation of the information that seemed appropriate to the contributor is also appropriate for the user's current task. For the latter, the most crucial issue is whether the user will be able to reformulate and generalize the materials to apply them to the current situation.

Achieving a Shared Understanding: Enabling Metacommunication

Community memory critically rests on the idea that any one community member's contribution to such a shared resource is intelligible to other members of the community. But how do we ensure the intelligibility of material that results from a task that is not necessarily accessible in time (community memory is usually an asynchronous form of communication) or place (as we have seen, electronic communities are distributed groups)? Our past efforts have focused on two different tactics to make shared spaces mutually intelligible: metadiscussions within a space[13,16] to discuss the materials it contains, and shared representations that structure and organize the materials.[15,19,26] Yet the problem becomes much harder to solve as the community memory grows in size; rationale for the content and structure of the shared resource becomes opaque and inaccessible over time.

Realistically, some portion of emerging structure (and structure is continually emerging) will always be implicit. In systems to support collaborative intellectual work like NoteCards[31] and VIKI, the strategy to achieve mutual intelligibility has been to encourage contributors to explicitly record discussions about the work.

NoteCards is a hypertext-based information-organizing tool originally intended for individual use, but once a user community emerged, it became apparent that many tasks people were performing using the tool—writing papers, managing projects, collecting and analyzing information—were in fact group activities. As a result of this observation, NoteCards developers added facilities to support collaborative work.[13] Three of the more important facilities were: History Cards, tailored event-centered record keeping that could be annotated by collaborators; Guided Tours, a technique that allowed a presentation structure to be overlaid on a hypertext network; and TableTops, a means of contextualizing work by allowing a number of cards to be grouped as a visual composite.[33]

Each of these mechanisms involved a semi-automatic way of recording changes or state (for example, TableTops recorded which cards were together on the screen, including scrolling). What we learned is that these recordings of paths, process, or state need to be supplemented by human annotation.[16] This need for human annotation (or communication *about* a group information resource) has been confirmed by our experiences with subsequent systems. VIKI provided no explicit mechanisms for recording change history, so collaborators developed conventions (electronic Post-its) for communicating their changes to each other.

There is some perception that support for strong typing of materials will naturally bring about coherence; we have not found this to be the case. Aquanet relied on domain schemas to make contributions self-organizing and self-documenting, thereby rendering them intelligible to other group members; if one contributor creates, for example, a claim as part of an argument, the contribution's type (along with the role it plays in a community-defined structure) would allow other group members to interpret it. This strategy is based on two important assumptions: (1) people understand the meaning of the metaschematic description and use it in a uniform way, and (2) people fully use the schematic structures and leave little implicit. In practice, neither of these assumptions has been found to hold. Collaborators still found themselves discussing the abstractions and how they ought to be applied. They also left a great deal implicit (including why a particular element should occupy a specified position in the shared space), thereby introducing a great deal of ambiguity and inconsistency.

Structure recognition and incremental formalization techniques may be useful in finding implicit structure and making it available for discussion within a community of practice; the implicit structure does not need to be declared, only located. Specific support for conversations about recognizable implicit structures may help members of a community keep their own contributions to the shared resource intelligible.

Situatedness and Task Specificity: Representational Fluidity

The function of community memory is to inform the various information-intensive tasks that community members undertake. Since the information from memory can be represented in many alternative ways, we must ask which representation is appropriate. The most basic answer is that it depends on the nature of the tasks that communities of practice undertake.

The nature of community memory as a shared resource suggests that a given portion of the information might serve many different tasks. Thus, if we take use of community memory as reuse of information, we must consider two different types of reuse: reuse of the information itself (through generalization and reapplication) and reuse of the abstractions that structure this information. We look first at techniques for generalizing the materials themselves.

Generalization is a process in which details are removed and the resulting information is, in part, abstracted from its original context so that it may be applied to other situations. Generalizations are created with an expectation of future use. Different generalizations will be appropriate for different future situations. For example, in our experience with network design, the same design can be used as an example in situations with similar budgetary considerations and in situations using similar technology.[8] Providing fluid representations, where information can evolve in both structure and use, can facilitate such generalization. For example, XNetwork allowed designers to continually add and remove structure from the representation of the design and to make copies of the design available as more general examples within the community memory.

Since contributors cannot completely predict the situation of their audience, it is difficult to know how much background to provide to make their interpretations and knowledge useful at a later date.[1] There are at least two possible ways of addressing this problem. One is to record the context in which the contributions to memory were created. This is, however, limited because the contributors also cannot know which information about context is likely to be useful; and much of this information about context is likely to stay in the form of tacit background knowledge. The second way of the addressing the problem is to provide links from contributions to the contributors, so that users of information might communicate with contributors to elicit more information about this background (on a demand-driven basis).

We now turn our attention to the abstractions used to structure the materials—the metaschematic descriptions of domains of interest. One of the original motivations for providing this kind of abstraction is the ability to reapply it to interpret related materials. We found this kind of reuse may be difficult to support with tools that do not acknowledge the fluidity of abstraction, since the structures people define are based on an idealization of the task and of the materials and may not fit well with the contingencies of the actual situation.[28,30]

For example, in our experiences performing a long-term analysis task that involved assessing machine translation systems (see[17]), we found that the abstract types that highlighted certain technical aspects of the systems (like the approach they took to translation of natural language) were not entirely appropriate for a seemingly similar task of identifying candidate Spanish–English translation software for purchase. The new task required that aspects such as cost and hardware platform be made perspicuous, while the old task did not call for explicit structural representation of these characteristics. In general, fixed representations of domain structure tend to cause material that does not quite fit into the abstractions to get lost, to drop from sight. This problem with the application of abstractions would surely be amplified as a community memory grew and encompassed more materials and more related tasks.

We addressed this problem in our later work by assuming that representations are fluid, lightweight, and locally defined for the task. The appropriateness of different representation schemes for different tasks suggests that the "raw" information in community memory needs to be separable from the manner in which it is represented (as, for example, a *view* of the underlying materials rather than a property of the materials themselves). Representational variability will allow a given piece or collection of information to be generalized and reapplied, and the abstractions that structure it to be modified and reused.

CONCLUSIONS

Large-scale information resources, digital libraries and other significant and authoritative online repositories, are under development, ready to act as testbeds for communities of practice. Much of the research focus thus far has been on the technological basis for an infrastructure to provide storage and access to this wealth of materials. But we also must attend to the superstructure—community memory and similar forms of use-directed indexing, annotation, and informal augmentation—of these resources to make them serve the needs of people engaged in information-intensive intellectual work.

By taking different perspectives on this kind of superstructure, the perspective of a contributor, a user, and an interpreter of information, we can begin to realize the breadth of issues entailed by supporting communities who use large-scale information resources in their day-to-day activities. Just by looking at the World Wide Web,[3] which is itself a blend of repository and interpretive superstructure, we can see that these issues are close at hand.

Contributors add materials with little consistent representation of structure. They often have difficulty maintaining their contributions and ensuring the overall hygiene of the web, and they put effort into constructing new bridges to other online resources. Users are, as predicted, unaware of materials and other members of the community that can help them do their work; they must explore, probe, and become truly engaged in the web community's discourse before they can find their way around the extensive resources it offers. Finally, the reader's ability to comprehend and interpret web materials relies crucially on the contributor's adherence to emerging online document genres and structural conventions; knowledge of these genres and conventions on the part of both readers and authors is the surest way of being able to interpret the hypertext.

From our collective experiences we have identified different techniques that will support communities of practice in their use of these emerging large-scale information resources. First, taking a contributor's perspective, we pose structure recognition, incremental formalization, and representational flexibility to address the problems of evolving and, many times, implicit structure. Furthermore, we suggest that developers include superstructural support for the process of seeding, evolutionary growth, and reseeding to help address maintenance issues. Because distributed communities use distributed, heterogeneous resources, any community memory must provide ready connectivity and an open architecture.

As we have shown, information retrieval will not be sufficient to meet the needs of communities using large-scale information resources. A superstructure may also be used to support different methods for recovering information, such as techniques for active recovery of material from both the community memory and the underlying information bases and explicit support for community-mediated location. In effect, aspects of librarianship may be distributed among members of the community.

Finally, problems of comprehension, mutual intelligibility, and reuse of materials can be addressed by supporting human-annotated records of process, and by expecting fluid, highly situated representational forms.

By applying this collection of techniques, the emerging wealth of large-scale information resources can be put to work by groups and communities, and truly make a difference in the way we conduct our day-to-day lives.

REFERENCES

1. Ackerman, M. S. Augmenting the organizational memory: a field study of Answer Garden. In *Proceedings of ACM 1994 Conference on Computer Supported Cooperative Work*. Chapel Hill, NC: October 22–26, 1994, pp. 243–252.

2. Berlin, L., Jeffries, R., O'Day, V. L., Paepcke, A., and Wharton, C. Where did you put it? Issues in the design and use of a group memory. *Proceedings of InterCHI '93*. Amsterdam: April 24–29, 1993, pp. 23–30.

3. Berners-Lee, T., Cailliau, R., Luotonen, A., Nielsen, H. F., and Secret, A. The world-wide web. *Communications of the ACM, 37*, 8 (August 1994), 76–82.

4. Conklin, E. J., and Yakemovic, K. C. A process-oriented approach to design rationale. *Human Computer Interaction 6*, 3–4 (1991), 357–391.

5. Engelbart, D. Collaboration support provisions in AUGMENT. *Proceedings of the AFIPS Office Automation Conference*. Los Angeles: February 1984, pp. 51–58.

6. Ehrlich, K., and Cash, D. Turning information into knowledge: information finding as a collaborative activity. *Proceedings of Digital Libraries '94*. College Station, TX: June 19–21, 1994, pp. 119–125.

7. Fischer, G., Lemke, A., McCall, R., and Morch, A. Making argumentation serve design. *Human Computer Interaction 6*, 3–4 (1991), 393–419.

8. Fischer, G., McCall, R., Ostwald, J., Reeves, B., and Shipman, F. Seeding, evolutionary growth, and reseeding: supporting the incremental development of design environments. *Proceedings of CHI '94*. Boston: April 24–28, 1994, pp. 292–298.

9. Fox, E. A. *Source Book on Digital Libraries*. Version 1.0. Prepared for and sponsored by the National Science Foundation. Blacksburg, VA: Virginia Polytechnic Institute and State University, December 6, 1993.

10. Goldberg, D., Nichols, D., Oki, B. M., and Terry, D. Using collaborative filtering to weave an information tapestry. *Communications of the ACM, 35,* 12 (December 1992), 61–70.

11. Gorry, G. A., Burger, A., Chaney, J., Long, K., and Tausk, C. Computer support for biomedical research groups. *Proceedings of the Conference on Computer-Supported Cooperative Work.* Portland, OR: September 26–28, 1988, pp. 39–51.

12. Grudin, J. Why CSCW applications fail: problems in the design and evaluation of organizational interfaces. *Proceedings of the Conference on Computer-Supported Cooperative Work.* Portland, OR: September 26–28, 1988, pp. 85–93.

13. Irish, P. M., and Trigg, R. H. Supporting collaboration in hypermedia: issues and experiences. *Journal of the American Society for Information Science* (March 1989).

14. Levy, D. M., and Marshall, C. C. Going digital: a look at assumptions underlying digital libraries. *Communications of the ACM, 38,* 4 (April 1995), 77–84.

15. Marshall, C. C., Halasz, F. G., Rogers, R. A., and Janssen, W. Aquanet: a hypertext tool to hold your knowledge in place. *Proceedings of Hypertext '91.* San Antonio, TX: December 15–18, 1991, pp. 261–275.

16. Marshall, C. C., and Irish, P. M. Guided tours and on-line presentations: how authors make existing hypertext intelligible for readers. *Hypertext '89 Proceedings.* Pittsburgh: November 5–8, 1989, pp. 15–26.

17. Marshall, C. C., and Rogers, R. A. Two years before the mist: experiences with Aquanet. *Proceedings of European Conference on Hypertext (ECHT '92).* Milan: December 1992, pp. 53–62.

18. Marshall, C. C., Shipman, F. M., and Coombs, J. H. VIKI: spatial hypertext supporting emergent structure. *Proceedings of the European Conference on Hypermedia Technologies (ECHT '94).* Edinburgh: September 18–23, 1994, pp. 13–23.

19. McCall, R. *On the Structure and Use of Issue Systems in Design.* Doctoral dissertation, University of California, Berkeley, University Microfilms, 1979.

20. McCall, R., Bennett, P., d'Oronzio, P., Ostwald, J., Shipman, F., and Wallace, N. PHIDIAS: integrating CAD graphics into dynamic hypertext. *Proceedings of the European Conference on Hypertext (ECHT '90).* Paris: November 1990, pp. 152–165.

21. McCall, R., Schaab, B., and Schuler, W. An information station for the problem solver: system concepts. In C. Keren and L. Perlmutter (eds.), *Applications of Mini- and Microcomputers in Information, Documentation and Libraries.* New York: Elsevier, 1983.

22. McKnight, C., Meadows, J., Pullinger, D., and Rowland, F. ELVYN—publisher and library working towards the electronic distribution and use of journals. *Proceedings of Digital Libraries '94.* College Station, TX: June 19–21, 1994, pp. 6–11.

23. Reeves, B. N., and Shipman, F. M. Supporting communication between designers with artifact-centered evolving information spaces. *Proceedings of the Conference on Computer Supported Cooperative Work (CSCW '92).* Toronto: October 31–November 4, 1992, pp. 394–401.

24. Schatz, B. R. Building an electronic community system. *Journal of Management Information Systems, 8,* 3 (Winter 1991–92), 87–107.

25. Schuler, D. Community networks: building a new participatory medium. *Communications of the ACM, 37,* 1 (January 1994), 39–51.

26. Shipman, F. M. Supporting knowledge-base evolution with incremental formalization. Technical Report CU-CS–658–93, Department of Computer Science, University of Colorado, Boulder, 1993.

27. Shipman, F. M., Chaney, R. J., and Gorry, G. A. Distributed hypertext for collaborative research: the virtual notebook system. *Proceedings of Hypertext '89*. Pittsburgh: November 5–8, 1989, pp. 129–135.

28. Shipman, F. M., and Marshall, C. C. Formality considered harmful: experiences, emerging themes, and directions. Xerox PARC Technical Report ISTL-CSA–94–08–02, 1994.

29. Shipman, F. M., and McCall, R. Supporting knowledge-base evolution with incremental formalization. *Proceedings of CHI '94*. Boston: April 24–28, 1994, pp. 285–291.

30. Suchman, L. A. *Plans and Situated Actions: The Problem of Human-Machine Communication*. Cambridge: Cambridge University Press, 1987.

31. Suchman, L., Trigg, R., and Halasz, F. Supporting collaboration in NoteCards. In D. Marca and G. Bock (eds.), *Groupware: Software for Computer-Supported Cooperative Work*. Los Alamitos, CA: IEEE Computer Society Press, 1992, pp. 394–403.

32. Terveen, L., Selfridge, P. G., and Long, M. D. From "folklore" to "living design memory." *Proceedings of InterCHI '93*. Amsterdam: April 24–29, 1993, pp. 15–22.

33. Trigg, R. Guided tours and tabletops: tools for communicating in a hypertext environment. *ACM Transactions on Office Information Systems*, 6, 4 (October 1988), 398–414.

Index

Page numbers followed by *t* indicate a table.

Butterworth-Heinemann Business Books... for Transforming Business

Cultivating Common Ground: Releasing the Power of Relationships at Work,
   Daniel S. Hanson, 0-7506-9832-2

Flight of the Phoenix: Soaring to Success in the 21st Century,
   John Whiteside and Sandra Egli, 0-7506-9798-9

Getting Attention: Leading-Edge Lessons for Publicity and Marketing,
   Susan Kohl, 0-7506-7259-5

*Getting a Grip on Tomorrow: Your Guide to Survival and Success in the
   Changed World of Work,*
   Mike Johnson, 0-7506-9758-X

Innovation Strategy for the Knowledge Economy: The Ken Awakening,
   Debra M. Amidon, 0-7506-9841-1

Innovation through Intuition: The Hidden Intelligence,
   Sandra Weintraub, 0-7506-9937-X

The Intelligence Advantage: Organizing for Complexity,
   Michael D. McMaster, 0-7506-9792-X

Intuitive Imagery: A Resource at Work,
   John B. Pehrson and Susan E. Mehrtens, 0-7506-9805-5

The Knowledge Evolution: Expanding Organizational Intelligence,
   Verna Allee, 0-7506-9842-X

Large Scale Organizational Change: An Executive's Guide,
   Christopher Laszlo and Jean-Francois Laugel, 0-7506-7230-7

Leadership in a Challenging World: A Sacred Journey,
   Barbara Shipka, 0-7506-9750-4

Leading Consciously: A Pilgrimage Toward Self Mastery,
   Debashis Chatterjee, 0-7506-9864-0

Leading from the Heart: Choosing Courage over Fear in the Workplace,
   Kay Gilley, 0-7506-9835-7

Leading for a Change: How to Master the 5 Challenges Faced by Every Leader,
   Ralph Jacobson, 0-7506-7279-X

Learning to Read the Signs: Reclaiming Pragmatism in Business,
   F. Byron Nahser, 0-7506-9901-9

Leveraging People and Profit: The Hard Work of Soft Management,
   Bernard A. Nagle and Perry Pascarella, 0-7506-9961-2

Marketing Plans That Work: Targeting Growth and Profitability,
   Malcolm H. B. McDonald and Warren J. Keegan, 0-7506-9828-4

A Place to Shine: Emerging from the Shadows at Work,
  Daniel S. Hanson, 0-7506-9738-5

Power Partnering: A Strategy for Business Excellence in the 21st Century,
  Sean Gadman, 0-7506-9809-8

Putting Emotional Intelligence to Work: Successful Leadership is More Than IQ,
  David Ryback, 0-7506-9956-6

Resources for the Knowledge-Based Economy Series

  The Knowledge Economy,
    Dale Neef, 0-7506-9936-1

  Knowledge Management and Organizational Design,
    Paul S. Myers, 0-7506-9749-0

  Knowledge Management Tools,
    Rudy L. Ruggles, III, 0-7506-9849-7

  Knowledge in Organizations,
    Laurence Prusak, 0-7506-9718-0

  The Strategic Management of Intellectual Capital,
    David A. Klein, 0-7506-9850-0

  Knowledge, Groupware and the Internet,
    David Smith, 0-7506-7111-4

  Knowledge and Social Capital,
    Eric Lesser, 0-7506-7222-6

  Strategic Learning in a Knowledge Economy
    Robert Cross and Sam Israelit, 0-7506-7223-4

The Rhythm of Business: The Key to Building and Running Successful Companies,
  Jeffrey C. Shuman, 0-7506-9991-4

Setting the PACE® in Product Development: A Guide to Product And Cycle-time Excellence,
  Michael E. McGrath, 0-7506-9789-X

Time to Take Control: The Impact of Change on Corporate Computer Systems,
  Tony Johnson, 0-7506-9863-2

The Transformation of Management,
  Mike Davidson, 0-7506-9814-4

Unleashing Intellectual Capital,
  Charles Ehin, 0-7506-7246-3

What Is the Emperor Wearing? Truth-Telling in Business Relationships,
   Laurie Weiss, 0-7506-9872-1

Who We Could Be at Work, Revised Edition,
   Margaret A. Lulic, 0-7506-9739-3

Working From Your Core: Personal and Corporate Wisdom in a World of
   Change,
   Sharon Seivert, 0-7506-9931-0

To purchase any Butterworth-Heinemann title,
please visit your local bookstore or call 1-800-366-2665.